SOVIET STRATEGY–
SOVIET FOREIGN POLICY

To GITA,

for inserting belief into a cynic's heart

Soviet Strategy–
Soviet Foreign Policy

MILITARY CONSIDERATIONS AFFECTING SOVIET POLICY-MAKING

by

C. G. JACOBSEN, Ph.D.

Senior Research Fellow of the Russian Institute,
Columbia University, New York
Fellow of the School of International Affairs,
Carleton University, Ottawa

ROBERT MACLEHOSE & CO. LTD
The University Press   Glasgow

Sponsored by the Canadian Institute of International Affairs

This 1972 manuscript is based on 'Strategic Factors in Soviet Foreign Policy; Military Considerations affecting Soviet Policy-making', a Ph.D. thesis approved by the Senate of Glasgow University in 1971.
The manuscript was completed at the School of International Affairs, Carleton University, on 1 July, 1972.
The Queen's Printer, Ottawa, prepared a limited pre-publication edition of a draft version in April 1972, on order from Canada's Defence Research Board.

Printed in Great Britain by Robert MacLehose and Company Limited
The University Press, Glasgow

First printing 1972

ISBN 0 9502034 2 4

INTENT

(a) To present a historical analysis of the development by the USSR of the weapons, theories and concepts associated with true super-power status.
(b) To analyse military-Party relations, and the extent of military-Party integration, with a view to clarifying Soviet policy-makers' perceptions as to the utility and implications of the above.
(c) To present a synthesis which encourages a better understanding of present and future Soviet policy initiatives than has hitherto been possible.

Contents

Part III: General Purpose and Interventionary Forces;
Geopolitical Considerations

Part IV: Command Changes and Doctrinal Shifts

Part V: Chto Delat?

Acknowledgements

The following have rendered valuable assistance in the form of comments and ideas:

Professor Alec Nove, of the Institute of Soviet Studies, Glasgow;
Harriet Fast Scott and Colonel Scott, US Air Attache, Moscow;
Colonels B. Egge and K. Hope, (then) Senior Research Officers of Norway's Defence Research Establishment;
Dr. Brennan, Senior Research Officer, of the Hudson Institute, N.J., USA;
Research Officers J. Cable, D. Holloway and I. Smart of the Institute of Strategic Studies, London.

I am indebted to Hillel and Tanya Ticktin of the Institute of Soviet Studies, Glasgow, for their unwavering moral support, to Lesley Milne of Cambridge, for assistance in the preparation of the manuscript, and to Ruaidhri O'Donnell, of Dublin for concocting the index.

A collective thank you to all those other friends and colleagues who have given time and energy; a special thank you to my mother and father, who provided counsel and help when most needed.

All are due grateful thanks. But none are to blame for the chosen criteria, emphases and omissions – the final judgements were not theirs.

Finally: a thank you to the libraries and agencies of Washington, Glasgow, Edinburgh, London, Oslo and Moscow, which provided staff, time and effort, to secure material of interest.

Author's Note on sources, military debates, and third powers' status

The main difficulty related to the fact that much material of essence to the research was regarded as classified by the national authorities concerned. Two obfuscating factors exacerbated this difficulty. One relates to the authorities, and to the process of sifting and selection through which any classified material must pass before it reaches the decision-makers; conscious or unconscious discrimination en route from information gathering, to the delineation of alternative hypotheses, and to final decision-making, entails a (sometimes convenient) restricting of the data available, a restricting which may in itself prejudice the final option choice. The other obfuscating factor concerns 'convenient intelligence'. This is 'intelligence' and 'facts' released or leaked by the national authorities. This type of information all too often rests on politically-determined selection criteria; it always rests on some type of selection, from the already selected material available to the decision-makers. The resultant information is not necessarily wrong or misleading, but it would very often be different if the selection process from which it had emerged had been subject to different criteria.

This catholic caution relates also to Soviet military 'debates', and to the question as to whether contributions are 'genuine', or whether they merely reflect differing aspects of policy decisions already arrived at. The question is analysed more extensively in Chapter 2. But it is proper to indicate that the conclusion there arrived at encourages maximum caution lest one infer non-credible levels of antagonism from apparent debate discrepancies.

The debate analyses make it clear that an author's relative obscurity or prominence does not necessarily reflect on the importance of an article. Considerations such as relate to troop morale, the domestic economy, or international relations, often make relative or apparent obscurity a preferred forum for a text's dissemination. The more prominent the source, the more obviously the concerns of 'declaratory policy' intermingle with those of 'action policy'. For these reasons the debates are investigated primarily with a view to their illuminating or explaining of procurements and actions, – with a view to their relationship with ascertainable developments.

The data is available. The problem lies in acquiring sufficient knowledge to judge their comprehensiveness and their relative worth.

Some related factors, such as concern Chinese (or Japanese) capabilities and prospects, are not treated extensively. The reasons for this are inherent in the text, but may be synopsized as follows: Chinese nuclear warheads are neither sophisticated nor numerous; her missiles are first generational with regard to vulnerability, operational and in-flight control, and accuracy – they have a high rate of failure expectancy (degradation factors); she does not possess the technology either to build a protective ballistic missile defence complex, or to penetrate even a limited BMD deployed by an opponent. Her strategic technology is at the level reached by the US and the USSR twenty years ago. Today she is vulnerable to a take out first strike by either super-power. She is not capable of significantly penetrating the super-powers' defence of the 1970's.

This book analyses the process, completed by the USSR, but only very tentatively begun by China: the development of true super-power capabilities. China's super-power aura remains based on psychological factors. The last decade and a half of this century may justify a companion volume on China; it would not be justified today. Similar comments relate to 'Europe' and Japan – with self-imposed restraints providing an additional uncertainty factor in the case of Japan.

One should, perhaps, finally comment on the military-oriented fear and insecurity which prevailed in Moscow through much of the post-war period. Britain and France could remain satisfied with second rank status, protected as they were by US strategic might. Moscow could not in the long run be satisfied with a similar status, without abdicating her ideological aspirations, and without abdicating her role as leader and protector of the non-capitalist world. The balance was all too often seen as a zero-sum equation. This appeared to have changed by the late 1960's and early 1970's. And this change could entail that the aspect of fear will not be as central to China's possible development as it was to Moscow's. It might also entail less pressure on China to achieve true counter-balancing capabilities, in spite of the absence of a trusted protector. But the answers to these questions await later decades.

Foreword

A tentative Strategic Arms Limitation Talks (SALT) treaty was signed in Moscow in May of 1972.¹ Subsequently public concern tended to focus on the desirability of a follow-up treaty on Mutual and Balanced Force Reductions (MBFR) in Europe.

The SALT agreement was of scant military value, although it represented a psychologically vital first step towards a halting of the arms race and, ideally, disarmament. It accepted the inevitability that the superpowers would proceed with the deployment of some Ballistic Missile Defence (BMD) capability. However, it also exhibited the superpowers' concurrence that such capabilities should be restricted. It tacitly accepted that the qualitative improving of strategic offensive systems would continue apace, and that both sides would proceed with the introduction of Multiple Independently-targeted Re-entry Vehicles (MIRVs).² But it also confirmed the superpowers' acceptance of quantitative limitations. This acceptance entailed no sacrifice, since the United States had for some years been satisfied to leave the number of her missiles stable, and since the great Soviet quantitative increases of the late 1960's and early 1970's had shown definite signs of tapering off (see Chapter 4); both powers had already demonstrated their intent to pursue improvement through qualitative rather than quantitative steps. In military terms, the SALT agreement only confirmed existing development trends. But even if only non-essentials were banned, the agreement to ban anything at all did in itself entail at least a moral obligation to pursue future agreements of greater consequence.

1. The 'Treaty Between the United States of America and the Union of Soviet Socialist Republics on the Limitation of Anti-Ballistic Missile Systems' and the 'Interim Agreement Between the Union of Soviet Socialist Republics and the United States of America on Certain Measures with Respect to the Limitation of Strategic Offensive Arms' were both signed in Moscow on 26 May, 1972.

2. Presidential Special Advisor Henry Kissinger, in his Moscow Press Conference of 26 May, 1972, confirmed expectations that the USSR would also have mastered MIRV technology before the lapse of the 'Interim Agreement'.

MBFR appeared even more ephemeral. The desirability of MBFR was propagated by both East and West. Symbolic and limited first step agreements appeared possible as early as the mid-sixties. But both sides had always appeared strangely blind whenever the other made initiatives that actually looked substantive. Both sides showed a peculiar hesitancy in their approach to negotiations which both insisted they wanted.

Below are two discussion papers written for Carleton University's School of International Affairs in March of 1972.[3] The first one synthesizes some of the salient points of Chapter 4, and explains why a contemporary SALT agreement would have to take the form it took, two and a half months later. The second paper consists of a controversial, but hopefully thought-provoking, analysis of the approach to MBFR. It deals with the difference between action policy and declaratory policy. And it explores some psychological problem complexes that have considerable tangential implications for our thesis.

SALT

What are the prospects for agreement at the Strategic Arms Limitation Talks? What type of agreement might constitute real progress, as opposed to non-consequential agreements arrived at for political rather than strategic reasons?

The answers require a review of Ballistic Missile Defence (BMD) and Multiple Independently-targeted Re-entry Vehicles (MIRV) research and deployment developments.

There are three main factors which relate to BMD.

(1) The technology required for BMD exists. The problems lies in the BMD's cost-effectiveness, as measured by the so-called cost-exchange ratio. This is the ratio between the cost of the additional offensive force needed to offset a BMD deployed by another power, and the cost of the BMD needed to offset an opponent's increase in offensive force. In his 1967 and 1968 'posture statements' Secretary of Defence McNamara released figures which showed an inverse relationship between the aspirations of a BMD and its cost-effectiveness.

---

3. These were included as addenda to the limited pre-publication edition of this book which was prepared by the Queen's Printer in Ottawa in April, 1972, on order from Canada's Defence Research Board.

For a BMD restricting US fatalities from the otherwise expected 100–120 million down to 20–30 million, the cost-exchange ratio relating to a Soviet attempt to offset the BMD's effects through offensive increments would look as follows: one to four in favour of the offence to bring the expected fatality rate up to 40 million; one to two in favour of the offence to bring it up to 60 million; one to one to bring it up to 90 million. (The scenario was that of a Soviet second-strike, in response to a US first-strike). In other words, the Soviet offensive increases needed to up US fatalities to 40 million would cost only one-fourth of the US effort. But the Soviet offensive increases necessary to force a return to the previous status quo would incur greater costs than had the US BMD which had decreased the casualty expectations. The technology associated with BMD is new. One might therefore expect that advances in the coming years will improve the cost-exchange ratio in favour of defence.

A BMD intended to provide full protection against a superpower's strike potential is, and will probably remain, a practical impossibility. The technological difficulties would be immense, and the prohibitive cost would be beyond reach even to a superpower. But a limited BMD would suffice to eliminate the threat of accidents, and –

(2) It would eliminate the threat from smaller powers. A large number of nations now possess the technology required to build nuclear warheads and crude delivery systems. Cost is the only real deterrent to their building a Polaris, with ten missiles, and the theoretical capacity to destroy a superpower's ten largest cities. The capability would in a real sense give them superpower status and bargaining power. France and China considered this to be worth the cost; tomorrow India, Japan, Sweden, Israel, and others might make the same decision.

BMD technology, however, is not within the reach of these lesser powers. And their delivery systems are not sophisticated enough to penetrate even a limited BMD. By deploying a limited BMD the superpowers could reverse the dilution of their preeminence. They could remain militarily supreme, and militarily immune from all but each other.

(3) The third factor which had to be taken into account by the late 1960's was the fact of actual deployment. Both the superpowers were deploying limited BMDs and both publicly admitted that the development would not be reversed. The case for BMD had prevailed.

One ought, perhaps, to comment on the case of BMD opponents.

They feared the military's inclination to over-react and over-deploy, thus fuelling the vicious circle of the arms race. They feared that theoretical acceptance of BMD would inevitably lead to futile designs for a 'full' BMD, and give tragic encouragement to a new arms race round. They were confident that the crippling costs would produce even more unnecessary over-kill capabilities, without altering the basic balance. But the fears appear to have been over-pessimistic. The limited nature of the BMD deployment that has occurred indicates US and Soviet government appreciation of their critics' case. The governments appear to be aware of both the negative psychological factors and the prohibitive problems of technology and costs which relate to 'full' BMD concepts. They differ from their critics only in their appreciation of the political, and to a lesser extent technological and economic, advantages of a limited BMD.

MIRV involves two basic factors.

(1) The technology exists, and cost-effectiveness calculations are favourable. A MIRV with for example ten warheads, is considerably cheaper than ten individual inter-continental missiles. Not only does it obviate the need for the other nine booster rockets, it also obviates the need for their silos and launch facilities. This factor takes on even greater importance when related to the most secure element of super-power second-strike forces, the missile submarines. It drastically cuts the number of submarines needed to carry whatever striking-power is considered necessary.

As to technology, actual deployment in 1971 emphasized US mastery, and research and testing reports indicate that the USSR is not far behind.

(2) The second factor lies in the deployment, and in two peculiarities of MIRV. One is the fact that it can be tested secretly. The test release of only one of the warheads is sufficient. This means that a test's radar-print need not differ from that of an ordinary missile, and means that one cannot verify that testing is not taking place. The other peculiarity relates to its nature when deployed. Satelite pictures cannot differentiate between the cone of a MIRV and that of an ordinary missile. There is no way of verifying the number of warheads within the cone. For these reasons alone a sceptic must accept continued deployment to be inevitable. And in these matters one must be sceptical.

One must finally comment on the Pentagon's, and Secretary of Defence Laird's assertion, that the 'mirving' of the giant Soviet SS9 missiles might give the USSR the capability to inflict a take-out first-strike blow. Their motives appear to be primarily political. A fully 'mirved' SS9 force would in theory be capable of destroying all US land-based missiles. But it would probably be impossible in practice, because of one fact that is often overlooked. The geographical spread of the launch facilities and the geographical spread of the targets are of such a scale as to make co-ordinated impact an impossibility. Although theoretically and technologically feasible, the practical problems are insurmountable. There can be little doubt that a number of missiles would survive, to perform a second-strike role. Even if this fact was forgotten, however, there would still be the Polaris-Poseidon second-strike force. This is alone of sufficient force to deliver a devastating second-strike blow. And its practical immunity from attack is secure for the foreseeable future.

Real progress at SALT can therefore only mean one thing. It is utopian to expect either BMD or MIRV to be banned; if they were, deployment would continue in secret. But one can realistically expect limitations to be put on both.

The case for a limited BMD is clear, but one can expect assurances against unnecessary extensions which could only have negative implications. With regard to MIRV, the above factors entail that every superpower missile will sooner or later be 'mirved'. Because it is not possible to limit the percentage of missiles that is 'mirved', one must limit the number of missiles or boosters. And one must probably limit their size (a missile capable of carrying 50 warheads would obviously differ significantly from one capable of carrying 5). Realistic acceptance of these points could lead to agreements whereby the same basic balance remained, but unnecessary over-over-kill powers were dispensed with.

The superpowers will not disarm. Neither will they willingly allow themselves to become vulnerable to the forces of lesser powers. A limited BMD and a restricted all-MIRV offensive force would therefore constitute the necessary ingredients of any real progress. Even this may be unlikely, however. It may be that the most that can be expected of SALT are continuing meetings, and minor agreements intended to secure against any unnecessary race to procure over-over-kill capabilities. SALT may be more likely to develop into a forum for consultation and adjustment, than to lead to any dramatic treaty.

MUTUAL AND BALANCED FORCE REDUCTIONS (MBFR) AND
THE ROLE AND EFFECT OF AMERICAN FORCES IN EUROPE

MBFR is one of the most seriously discussed issues in East-West relations today. The leaders of both East and West have declared their strong and positive interest. If their statements are to be believed, real negotiations appear to be imminent. But the background to MBFR gives unusual encouragement to sceptics. The background invites the conclusion that nobody wants MBFR for the purported purpose of gradual disarmament. Unpublicized motives may, however, lead to negotiations, and to some measure of agreement. The background, these motives and their implications for the role and effect of American forces in Europe, will be surveyed below.

For more than two decades the Soviet Union and the Warsaw Pact have presented proposals for disarmament. These have been presented with added vigour since the mid-1960's. But they were always either ignored by the West or else dismissed as propaganda, and much too vague to warrant serious discussion. Because the proposals usually called for total disarmament, without delving into how it was to be achieved or what guarantees might be instituted against cheating, the Western reaction was understandable.

The West apparently feared that a Soviet propaganda victory could be the only result of negotiations which were bound to fail. The timid lack of response did, however, leave itself open to the interpretation that the West was not interested in disarmament. It certainly reflected a questionable lack of confidence in the propaganda facilities available to the West. By taking the offensive and presenting detailed counter-proposals, the West could surely have put the onus for any failure on the Soviet Union.

The situation appeared to change significantly between 1968 and 1971. Strategic arms were withdrawn from the equation and became a topic for US–Soviet negotiation: the first Strategic Arms Limitation Talks negotiating session convened in Helsinki in late 1969. US NATO allies were assured of consultation and consideration, and the USSR presumably made similar assurances to its own allies. But no other participant was allowed to attend the talks, and SALT remained basically a bilateral attempt to arrive at a mutually acceptable modus vivendi.

With regard to non-strategic arms, NATO in 1968 urged the initiation of talks on Mutual and Balanced Force Reductions. And it began a process of continuing consultation and discussion within the Alliance with a view to arriving at a common negotiating position. It stressed the complexity of issues involved. There were technical, as well as military and political, difficulties in arriving at equivalences: how did one assign relative worths to NATO and Warsaw Pact divisions and their equipment, and how did one relate these to varying mobilization and transportation potentials?

The Soviet Union at first merely reiterated its own sweeping proposals. Then, in 1971, Brezhnev ventured into the type of colourful language associated with Khrushchev. He alluded to the Western proposals and declared that if the West was really interested in the reality or meaning of Soviet proposals, it should stop looking at the bottle. If it wanted to sample the wine, it ought to go ahead and take a sip.

But he did not suggest a date, and the West did not appear eager to take the cork out of the bottle. NATO spokesmen suggested that Moscow and the Warsaw Pact had not yet had time to consider the complexities involved and would need more time to arrive at a common position. The first suggestion was based on dubious extrapolation. The second was at best a questionable estimate of the time needed by the USSR to secure the support of her allies.

The West did appoint the out-going NATO Secretary General, Brosio, as 'preliminary negotiator', and empowered him to go to Moscow, to 'explore opportunities'. But Moscow ignored the initiative; Brosio waited in vain for an invitation. This was no surprise, since Moscow has always viewed Brosio as a latter-day Dulles, less dangerous but equally odious. And the West must have known that Moscow could not accept Brosio as a sincere negotiator. Did the appointment therefore reflect a desire to cloak a preferred status quo with the appearance of flexibility and negotiating will?

It is tempting to relate the 1968 NATO proposal to the then growing sentiment in the US Congress in favour of decreasing US force levels in Europe. Was it a realization that these force levels would sooner or later be decreased anyway, if necessary unilaterally, and a desire to bargain while the chips were still available? Or was it, as implied above, based on the calculation that the movement for change would wither away in the face of apparent official support? And why did the USSR respond in 1971, just when it looked as if the US Congress might pass Senator Mansfield's motion to bring some of the troops back home? The Soviet response appeared to add decisive logic to President Nixon's plea that Congress refrain from undermining his bargaining position: Mansfield's motion was narrowly defeated.

President Nixon's support for a continuing undiluted American presence in Europe was and is presumably based on an appreciation of its political impact. European NATO allies in general, and Bonn in particular, still see this presence as their most secure guarantee that the United States will come to their aid if and when necessary. They still feel that the involvement of US blood in a conflict will entail the involvement of the full US might. Nixon presumably also appreciates the implication. The less confident the US allies become of US support, the more likely is a process of 'Findlandisation', and a gradual political and economic rapprochement with Moscow, to occur. The financial consequences could be as significant as the political. The position of American capital could be severely jeopardized.

Military considerations may be less important. NATO land forces are intended to stem the advance of an enemy offensive until the arrival of reserves from the United States. But NATO commanders appear to accept that Soviet forces could reach the English Channel in 24 hours. If current NATO force levels cannot hold the fort longer than that, and if the USSR has the capacity to attack with such forward dynamism, then one might question whether any fresh land reserve could conceivably arrive in time, or, if it did, whether it could achieve any success.

One might pose a complementary question. If current force levels are not sufficient and if they are allowed to remain insufficient, is that because the West considers the military threat today to be negligible? If so, is there any threat at all? If there is a threat, but of a political rather than military nature, ought one not to reallocate the military funds and to augment political counter forces, such as propaganda and counter-propaganda transmitters?

As regards Brezhnev's 1971 intervention, it invites the conclusion that the USSR does not want a US withdrawal of troops from Western Europe. This could logically be explained as follows: Moscow knows that European troop levels are irrelevant and that the threat, if there is a threat, comes from US strategic capabilities. But US troops in Europe provide the most easily identified symbolic representation of that threat. A withdrawal of this symbol might lull the USSR's allies. It might encourage a political and economic relaxation which would give opportunities for exploitation by subversive, nationalist, and anti-Soviet forces or agents.

It furthermore invites the conclusion that the USSR would not be interested in invading Western Europe. If she was, she would not have impeded the tendency towards US withdrawal. If she is not, one must ask why, and one tentative answer might start with George Orwell's memoirs from the Spanish Civil War, 'Homage to Catalonia'. His evidence indicates that the anti-Franco front would have won if the Moscow-oriented communists had not considered Trotskyists, left-Marxist, and Anarchists as even more inimical to their interests than the fascists. He describes the resultant internecine battles as primarily responsible for the defeat of the anti-Franco forces.

Or one might point to the abortive French revolution of 1968. Many members of the anti-Moscow Marxist–Trotskyist–Maoist–Anarchist 'groupuscules' which ignited and initially led the nation-wide movement remain convinced that it failed only because the French Communist Party refused to support it. They point to the fact that the Communist-controlled trade union never interrupted electricity and other supplies to the army. They are bitter that the French C.P. chose to view the situation as 'not ripe' for revolution and chose instead to negotiate with the establishment for mere wage, pensions, and like improvements.

If these allegations have validity, then it is true to say that Moscow prefers a truly capitalist regime to one led by left-wing factions which she distrusts and which she suspects might derail the 'historical process' which she considers as inevitable.

But these anti-Moscow Marxist-oriented factions are still thriving in Western Europe, and not only in France. In Britain, for example, they have during the last few years more than doubled their membership each year and now rival the established Communist Party. In view of the difficulties Moscow has had since the war in overcoming various types of anti-Soviet movements and agitation in East Europe, one is tempted to conclude that the last thing she would want, or could afford, is control over Western Europe today. And not because of Western Europe's 'fascist' groups, but because of some of her 'left-wing' movements! It is easier to ostracize and isolate an obvious opponent than one who can masquerade under your own banner (as Mao found out during the cultural revolution).

To return to MBFR, it appears that it may be gathering a momentum of its own and that limited negotiations and agreement may be expected. Limited, balanced force reductions are probably in the interest of both East and West. But the above analysis indicates that both East and West desire some continued force presence in the heart of Europe. And it indicates that both are motivated primarily by political and economic considerations and not by military considerations.

Introduction: Soviet Strategic Concepts

In what way, if any, does Soviet military doctrine differ from that of the West? Do Soviet strategic concepts merely mirror and follow those of the West, or are they developed independently, on the basis of purely Soviet realities and experiences? Later chapters provide analysis in depth, but a summary at this point may serve as a useful focus.

Soviet military doctrine clearly differed from the Western pattern in its early comprehensive acceptance of the implications of the nuclear age. Periodic Western speculation about its return to 'conventional-oriented' rather than 'nuclear-oriented' thinking has in every case proved to be mistaken. Soviet sources have been, and are, frank and unequivocal.[1] The introduction of nuclear arms was accepted as of quite a different scale of implication than, say, the introduction of planes or tanks.

Nuclear arms were seen to introduce a new era in the way that the introduction of gunpowder once did. The new era was one in which most previous concepts were irrelevant, and in which traditional military assumptions and techniques were obsolete, and unsuitable for all but the most limited of operations – such as against military pygmies (Czechoslovakia, 1968), or such as might be described as police operations (Ulster, after 1969, and possibly Czechoslovakia, 1968).

Soviet thinking reflected her awareness of the pitfalls of medium-scale conflicts such as the Vietnam war. The USSR was determined never to get involved in a like quagmire. A scantily opposed intervention protected by a nuclear umbrella was one thing, as was moral

1. See especially: Marshal I. Kh. Bagramian, Gen. S. P. Ivanov and others, *Istoria Voin i Voennovo Iskusstva*, Voenizdat, Moscow, 1970. See also N. N. Azovtsev, *V. I. Lenin i Sovetskaya Voennaya Nauka*, Voenizdat, Moscow, 1971; E. F. Sulimov, *Spravochnik Offitsera*, Voenizdat, Moscow, 1971; and Col. A. A. Siderenko, *Nastuplenie*, Voenizdat, Moscow, 1970. Of related interest: N. Y. Sushko and T. R. Kondratkov, *Metodologicheskye Problemi Teorii i Praktiki*, Voenizdat, Moscow, 1967.

and arms support for allies. But she was clearly prepared to use strategic or tactical nuclear armour in the event of a physical involvement of her own forces against enemy capabilities of consequence – for example, against China. Her ground forces were equipped with nuclear weaponry, and were trained to operate under nuclear conditions.[2] Soviet military doctrine also differed from that of the West in its explicit emphasis on the inter-dependence of military, economic and political considerations. There are purely military aspects. All branches of the Armed Forces are being trained to fulfil nuclear-oriented requirements. (The prime concerns relate to independent unit survival capabilities, and to the effecting of intra-Force and inter-Force operational flexibility.)[3] And they are all equipped with suitable material (the new naval destroyers, completely missile-oriented, and devoid of even a semblance of 'conventional' armour, are indicative).[4]

But there are also other aspects. Dispersed economic investments are sanctioned on strategic grounds even where concentration is economically optimal.[5] Civilians receive para-military training, oriented towards nuclear eventualities, and the combating of their effects.[6] And the conscious intertwining of functionally different societal concerns goes beyond the technical problems of planning and execution. There is a great stress on the psychological and moral foundation on which integration and homogeneity must rest[7] (see also Chapter 8).

2. A. A. Grechko, *Na Strazhe Mira i Stroitelstva Kommunisma*, Voenizdat, Moscow, 1971. Soviet strategists describe this book as being for the 1970's what Malinovsky's *Bditelnoe Stoyat na Strazhe Mira* was for the 1960's, namely the main authoritative guide to official thinking.

3. See e.g. *Krasnaya Zvezda*, 17 May, 1969; for evidence re the development trend see e.g. Col. Vorobev in *Krasnaya Zvezda*, 6 June, 1964; Col. Gen. Shtemenko in *Kommunist Vooruzhiennikh Sil*, No. 3, February, 1963; Col. Sidelnikov in *Krasnaya Zvezda*, 11 May, 1962; or Khrushchev's famous *Pravda* article of 15 January, 1960.

4. See e.g. Bundeswehr's *Soldat and Technik*, No. 11, 1969, p. 626, and same No. 10, 1970; article on 'Neue und Modernisierte Kriegschiff-typen der Sowjet-Flotte' (incl. survey on 'Kresta II').

5. Col. A. Lagovsky, '*Strategy and Economy* – A Sketch of their Mutual Interconnection and Influence', Voenizdat, Moscow, 1957: Officer specialists on military economy must be added not only to higher military staffs, but also to the planning organs and economical organs within the state administration; the military must today concern themselves also with non-military affairs; see also Marshal Grechko, Na Strazhe . . . , *op. cit*, (2·2).

6. A. Ivanov, I. Naumenko, M. Pavlov, '*Raketnoyadernoe Oruzhie i evo Porozhaioshchee Deistvie*', Voenizdat – Nauchno-Populyarnaya Biblioteka, Moscow, 1971. See also Chapter 8.

7. Efforts towards instilling a proper appreciation of the nation's defence forces at an early age are exemplified in the popular children's book '*Shiol po ulitse Soldat*', written by Sergei Barusdin (Isdatelstvo Detskaya Litteratura, Moscow, 1970). It had a first edition of 600,000 copies.

Soviet military development patterns did to a limited extent mirror those of the West. There was the development of an intercontinental delivery capability, and the adoption of concepts such as massive retaliation and deterrence. There was the consequent stress on the development of more secure and more powerful second-strike forces. And there was finally the apparent development of 'flexible response' and interventionary-type forces. Yet it might be argued that these developments reflected the obvious and logical choices of a nation that aspired to true super-power capabilities. If so, the copy-tag label becomes merely an irrelevant reflection of the fact that the US was the first to achieve super-power status.

Soviet development differed from that of the US in a number of significant areas. Her unwavering commitment to a strong land army capability[8] could be explained by her different geo-political location. Her relatively late development of global naval capabilities could be explained by priorities dictated by the same fact. Other differences are not so easily explained. She obviously regarded many of the more 'sophisticated' US theories, for example those pertaining to city-exchange and flexible response, as illogical or unrealistic.

She made no concession to the conventional-nuclear, and other 'stepping-stone', distinctions of McNamara's flexible response doctrine. She took it for granted that any major war would be nuclear. (This would not necessarily entail any US–Soviet strategic exchange; the following chapters indicate that any causal link between local wars, whether nuclear or not, and a strategic exchange, has been invalidated by the advent of mutually recognized second-strike capabilities.) She therefore proceeded with a more comprehensive nuclear-oriented conversion of her forces, non-strategic as well as strategic, than had the West.

But she not only effected a fuller integration of nuclear concepts and capabilities. As mentioned, she also proceeded to effect a greater degree of inter-force integration in general. Both theory and practice (exercises and manoeuvres) were oriented to this end, as were procurement patterns. Land, air and sea forces were complementary,

---

8. Note the following chapters' analysis of how this commitment not only persisted through Khrushchev's 'massive retaliation' period, but formed the explicit corollary to that strategic concept. Khrushchev strove to reduce Armed Forces personnel levels. This was not, however, to be synonymous with a lowering of capabilities. He consistently strove for an increase in non-strategic firepower and flexibility. His parallel commitments resulted in a more rapid stream-lining and nuclearization of the forces than would otherwise have been possible. Western commentaries which saw him as an opponent of land forces were superficial and misleading.

and never to be seen in isolation. Soviet conceptions of the nuclear era encouraged a qualitative conversion of her forces which by-passed the compromise conventional-nuclear stage.[9] By in a sense leap-frogging this stage in the development of US forces she effectively cut the time needed to achieve genuine counter-force capabilities. Her scorning of traditional large aircraft carriers is illustrative, as is the fact that the qualitative orientation of her Navy today does to a significant degree make up for her remaining quantitative inferiority.

A remarkably consistent pattern emerges. Most Western inferences of conflict between the strategic concepts of Khrushchev and those of post-Khrushchev Party leaders, or between those of the Party at any one time and those of the military, have proved to be misleading. The same can be said for most inferences of conflict with regard to priorities.[10] There must of course have been differences of emphasis. And there may at times have been conflict. The late 1960's hiatus in BMD deployment may in part have been due to a realization of the negative psychological implications of rapid and extensive deployment. If so, then it presumably occasioned some disagreement. Complete harmony on matters both of priority and timing would be near inconceivable. The point is that (a) The Soviet development patterns have been logical; and (b) The differences that did exist, if any, were not normally reflected in public debates. Apparent differences in public debates could usually be traced to motives not related to policy disagreement.

In conclusion, it might be said that the USSR had concentrated on developing, and had achieved military capacities which counter-balanced those of the US. Any prognosis of future trends would have to rest on a speculative extrapolation of historical and current data, and may therefore be left to the reader's discretion. But it should be noted that capabilities do not necessarily mirror intentions. The new power and sophistication of Soviet military might reflect a determination to achieve the security and policy choice flexibility reserved to true super-powers. It does not justify inferences of agressive designs, whether based on nationalism or ideology. The evidence of later

9. See I. A. Grudinen, *Dialektika i Sovremennoie Voennoe Delo*, Voenizdat, Moscow, 1971. This is reflected also in the fact that the Soviet Union had established a level of research and technological sophistication which was at least comparable to that of the US, and which in some cases surpassed that of the US. See Congressional testimony by Dr. John S. Foster Jr., as quoted by the *New York Times*, 18 February, 1972.

10. The now established facts of Khrushchev's efforts in favour of the non-strategic forces (see footnote 8), of his pre-Cuba up-grading of the Navy, and of his successors' acceptance of his basic premises (see following chapters), all constitute flat contradictions of the main stream of contemporary Western speculation.

chapters show that realism is not absent from Soviet policy delibera-
tion, and that it is in fact a very real adjunct to the new sophistication.
Neither nationalistic impulses nor ideological aspirations are permitted to obscure strategic realities. (See also the Foreword on
SALT and BMFR.)

The following chapters present detailed analyses of the Soviet
military 'debates', of Soviet strategic capabilities, of the strategic
hardware, and of the practical and psychological implications of
different weapon systems. But before proceeding to these analyses it
appears conceptually propitious to present a tentative period
delineation of the evolution of the Soviet Forces:

1945–53 was, as will be demonstrated in chapter one, a period
during which both Soviet strategic and Soviet non-strategic forces
were restricted to a continental environment. Effective Soviet strike
capabilities were confined to the Soviet home area and immediately
adjacent territory. She did have some intermediate range capability.
But she was not capable of striking effectively at the US home
area.

1954–57 saw increases in Soviet bomber range and capacity. But no
assured or confident long-range strike capability emerged; its
penetration prospects remained questionable. Although the limited
strike capability that did emerge puts these years in a limbo, it may
therefore be proper to view the period as basically an extension of that
of 1945–53. As far as capability confidence was concerned, Soviet
forces were still contained within the continental environment.

1958–61 was the period of initial long-range missile deployment.
1958 may justly be seen to signal the attainment by the strategic forces
of global capabilities and perspectives. But the capabilities related
primarily to first-strike calculations. The USSR had developed a
'force de frappe'; she had not yet attained real super-power status.

1962–66 finally saw the development of assured second-strike
forces. Efforts aimed at decreasing or eliminating missile vulnerability, and at rectifying first-generational qualitative deficiencies were
successful. Good strike survival, penetration and delivery prospects
were being acquired.

This period also saw the acceptance by land, air and naval forces of
global perspectives. Procurement developments and training patterns
were both being oriented towards such perspectives. Attention was

focused on the possible need to engage in conflict beyond the continental environment.

1967–72 (today) has seen the development by the USSR of true counter-force capabilities. The strategic second-strike forces were expanded until they offset those of the US. The USSR acquired sufficient surplus capacity to not only guarantee confidence, but to allow her to contemplate sophisticated city-preserving and like strategies. At the same time the conversion of her other forces continued apace. The 1970 Okean manoeuvre signalled the acquiring by the Navy of the physical wherewithall to back up her new global role and conceptions. The USSR had become a fully fledged super-power.

PART I: HISTORICAL BACKGROUND AND THE KHRUSHCHEV LEGACY

1

The 'Cold War' Period — Historical Strategic Balance Inequities

1945–1953: 'MIRROR MIRROR ON THE WALL . . . ?'

A number of western academics have in recent years reassessed the period in question.[1] In the process they have demonstrated that many previous analyses were too facile, too encumbered by ulterior motives, and hence too prone to black-white generalizations. Some of their data relate to our study, and will be presented below, together with further evidence of a similar nature.

This reassessment does not concern itself with the fact, or the morality, of the Soviet securing of hegemony over East Europe.[2] It concerns itself rather with the fear that Soviet actions had further aggressive implications, the fear which provided the *raison d'être* for the creation of NATO.

Adam B. Ulam's[3] presentation of the contradicting data serves as useful point of departure. He pointed out that the rapid contraction of the Soviet armed forces, from 11,365,000 men at the end of the war to 2,874,000 men by 1948, scarcely left more men than was needed for domestic and satellite 'garrison' duties.[4] The figure was certainly not compatible with any grandiose schemes of aggression. The demobilization may be partly explained by the pressures of domestic Soviet economic needs, of reconstruction and further industrialization. But this does not alter the implications of the demobilizations.

Ulam presented a number of Soviet statements and actions which cast doubt on the premises underlying the anti-Soviet convictions current among post-war US policy-makers; he then proceeded to refer to a book edited by A. G. Mileykovsky.[5] Mileykovsky asserted that the Marshal Plan had fuelled Soviet suspicions of US motives and designs, and that it had augmented the fear of capitalist encirclement. Moscow considered the plan's 'eventual aims' to be 'clearly military': 'The real purpose of the Marshall Plan was to create large standing armies that could threaten Russia while the Americans would back them up if necessary, with their naval strength and their atomic-armed Strategic Air Command.'[6]

The apparent generosity inherent in the Marshall Plan was dismissed as superficial. Moscow feared that the generosity merely mirrored a US calculation that 'it was cheaper to purchase British, French, German etc. soldiers than to equip American ones'. (This) 'explained why the Americans were not building a large standing army'. As a corollary to this interpretation: 'The US formula of 'containment' took on a much more sinister meaning: the doctrine of 'containment' (was seen to entail) such a building of "the positions of strength in the free world" as would allow a series of successful local wars against socialist states at the same time that one would be prepared for a major war'.[7]

Ulam accepted that this view was seriously held. He believed it constituted a natural ascribing to US policy of considerations underlying Soviet policy, 'i.e. avoiding a major conflict and at the same time justifying and inciting wars of "national liberation" '. There was therefore a real Soviet fear that Western Europe was being prepared to intervene in Eastern Europe.

Ulam synopsized his tenet as follows: 'The period is replete with historic ironies. America's monopoly of nuclear weapons lasted until the fall of 1949 and her economic preponderance in the world was never again so great. Yet for all this the vision of Soviet armies sweeping to the English Channel panicked some American policy-makers. For their part the Soviets appear to have been less alarmed by and responsive to American possession of the atom bomb than by the implications of that most non-aggressive initiative of US policy – the Marshall Plan.'[8]

Professor Ulam then went on to consider some Soviet initiatives which may have been too easily dismissed by the West. The proposals agreed upon at the 1950 Prague meeting of foreign ministers from the USSR and Eastern Europe,[9] and the Soviet Note of 10 March, 1952,[10] are illustrative.

The former proposed to forbid German militarization, but to allow for 'the creation of a unified, peace-loving democratic state'. An all-German Constituent Council, with equal representation for East and West Germany, was to prepare a constitution. And 'under certain conditions the German people could be directly asked to give their opinion on this proposal'. The 1952 Note was similar, but proceeded to express acceptance of rearmament by a unified Germany, provided that she pledge herself to neutrality.

Their timing suggests that the Prague proposals may have been sincere. They followed the Western decision to revise the Occupation Statute. This decision had furthermore been accompanied by indications that a West German force would be incorporated into NATO. Soviet apprehension must have been genuine. It may also have been strong. Other evidence at the time indicated a Soviet willingness to abandon East Germany if necessary.[11] If any credence is given to this evidence then the Soviet initiative must indeed have been genuine. Its ramifications were far preferable to that of the drastic, envisaged, alternative.

Timing is equally important for a consideration of the 1952 Note. It was preceded by the setting up of the European Defence Community, the granting of sovereignty to Bonn, and the definite agreement that the West German forces would join the Allies. The Korean War was waging, with General MacArthur advocating nuclear strikes against China. US Armed Forces were being very rapidly expanded, and 'roll back communism' advocates flourished in America. It would be surprising if concessions were not being considered in Moscow. A conflict at that time would have meant suicide for the USSR (see below).

The expansion of the US Armed Forces has been portrayed as follows: ' . . . after the war America demobilized. But only two years later, with Britain's withdrawal from Greece and the enunciation of the Truman Doctrine, the tide of military spending turned. . . . It surged during the Korean War, subsided briefly, and then continued to mount.'[12]

Among the 'roll back communism' advocates the most prominent was John Foster Dulles. His attitudes are representatively conveyed by the following quotes. In a 29 December, 1951 rebuttal to isolationist suggestions put forward by former President Hoover (in a 20 December broadcast) the then Republican adviser to the State Department began by highlighting the fear that a 'tide of communism' would 'roll on', with the US becoming 'encircled, isolated and finally engulfed'.

He played on the hysteria sprouted by the Korean War, and warned that some peoples 'are so inexperienced in the ways of self-government that it will be hard for them to preserve their independence in the face of the diabolically clever apparatus of Soviet communism. . . . But within the captive world there are grave internal weaknesses'. There was hope yet, however(!): 'War can be very unkind to rulers who are despots and who have systematically destroyed the individual initiatives of their peoples'. 'There is only one effective defence. That is the capacity to counter-attack. . . . The places of assembly (for the arsenal of retaliation) should be chosen not as places to defend but as places suitable for destroying the forces of aggression.'[13]

A year later, and now Secretary of State, Dulles stated that the US would not start a war, although she would prepare to defeat aggression. But he continued: 'To all those suffering under communist slavery . . . let us say this: "you can count on us" '.[14]

Such utterances and bellicosity were of course more than mirrored verbally by Soviet pronouncements. Among the best known are the harsh speeches by the Soviet delegates to the September 1947 founding of Cominform, Andrei Zhdanov and Georgi Malenkov. They saw the word as divided into hostile camps, the 'imperialist' and the 'peace-loving'. There could be no in-between; they considered those not explicitly allied with their cause to be enemies (Dulles' later inversion of this may be seen as one of history's little ironies). The 'peace-loving' would have to co-operate and organize defences against the 'imperialists'.[15]

But the propaganda mirror is false, and gives a misleading impression. Professor Ulam referred in passing to the American nuclear monopoly. Others have expanded on the same theme. One was Herman Kahn, who also pointed to the then decisive American monopoly of effective delivery capacity.[16] The monopoly was to last well into the 1950's. The US had the capacity to obliterate Soviet cities; the Soviet Union had no capacity to attack the American homeland. The constellation entailed a degree of Western impunity to engage in actions against Soviet controlled territory, with the US nuclear shield effectively deterring retaliation.

There were few overt acknowledgements of this total Soviet vulnerability. Yet Djilas reports that Stalin was intent on stopping the post-war Greek uprising because he knew that the Allies would not permit a Soviet breaking of their communication lines. (The uprising could not be sustained without outside support.)[17] Stalin accepted the fact that if the Allies would not permit it, then the Soviet Union had to concede. She could not afford to challenge the Allies directly.

The same realization may be seen as the logical premise behind the enforced development of the atomic and hydrogen bombs. The speed with which they were researched and developed in the face of domestic reconstruction demands indicate the priority assigned to the endeavour. And this priority unequivocally discredits assertions that the Soviet Union was unaware of the import of the US nuclear monopoly.

Soviet conceptions with regard to the motives under-pinning the Marshall Plan, together with the promulgation of the Truman Doctrine, increased US arms spending, and bellicose US anti-communist pronouncements (not least in conjunction with Korean events), all clearly combined to produce apprehension in Moscow. It is in this light that one should see J. V. Stalin's 1952 pronouncements, in which he pursued the need for 'peaceful co-existence' of a more comprehensive character than had previously been contemplated.[18] Now that Dulles had become Secretary of State in Washington, with MacArthur's sentiments (if not his person) continuing to attract adherents, the implications of Dulles' 'You can count on us' had to be seriously considered.

A further aspect, or curiosa, is worth mentioning. Following the removal of L. P. Beria, after Stalin's death, certain rumours about his foreign policy aspirations gained widespread currency in Eastern Europe. Tibor Meray presented this version: 'according to one report a secret Central Committee letter to satellite leaders accused Beria of having proposed, after the East German riots, to liquidate the East German regime in order to unify Germany in agreement with the Western powers'.[19]

The existence of the letter, not to mention Beria's intent, remains highly speculative. No conclusive evidence either way is available. The most plausible explanation may be that the leakage was inspired, in order to compromise Beria's reputation, and thus justify his removal. The leakage had the secondary effect of reinforcing East European fears of German revanchist potentials. It, therefore, encouraged their acceptance of Soviet tutelage.

What deserves recognition is the plausibility of an initiative such as was ascribed to Beria. It carried considerable logic as an alternative, on the basis both of immediate history (viz. the Prague proposals and the March 1952 Note) and of the international situation at the time.

B

Stalin feared that US extremists were attaining power, and that previous prognostications of US action-patterns might no longer be valid. There were all the more reasons for his heirs to fear the influence of these extremists in a situation of Soviet political disarray or uncertainty. The East German riots, and the lack of a definite and secure Soviet leadership hierarchy, encouraged fear of 'strike now while they are disorganized' advocates. It would be most surprising if concessions had not been considered, in conjuction with the need to 'buy time' until domestic and East European stabilization was secured.

But the prevailing view clearly saw a furtherance of Stalin's lower-key posture as sufficing to buy the time necessary for essential arms modernization and development. It is time to turn to the peculiarities of Soviet developments.

MALENKOV–KHRUSHCHEV

The years following the death of Stalin saw a stagnation of the post 1948, Cold War and Korean War-inspired growth of the Armed Forces. The maximum personnel strength of 5,763,000 men appears only to have been reached in 1955.[20] But the troop reductions initiated by the demobilization of 640,000 men in 1955[21] were foreshadowed by the military budget cuts of 2 per cent in 1953 and 8·9 per cent in 1954.

These budget cuts were based on Malenkov's championing of budgetary reallocations in favour of consumer goods priority, and on his efforts to ease international tensions.[22] His premise postulated that modern weapons of warfare entailed 'the destruction of world civilization', if war occurred; the logical consequence was a 'paralysing' of 'the law of the inevitability of war'.[23]

The doctrine that war had become impossible was the most notable doctrinal innovation of the Malenkov years. Emerging opposition (see below) soon forced him to restrict his vision of the consequences of war to orthodoxy's belief in the destruction of capitalism. But neither he nor his associates were ever to repudiate convincingly their belief in more all-embracing consequences (that is, the destruction of the USSR!).

Three interacting motives for his postulation of the doctrine may be envisaged. The first may be characterized as fear, fear arising from the credence which Moscow accorded to Dulles-type rhetoric, and reinforced by growing awareness of expanding US military might. The indications regarding Stalin's and Beria's attitude make this postulate likely. There was a realization that the United States was in too dangerous a mood for the Soviet Union to indulge in challenging postures, and that symbolic or otherwise concessions might have to be given. The realization was supported by the growing evidence (see above and following chapters) that, notwithstanding the recent testing of a Soviet hydrogen bomb, the USSR remained extremely strategically vulnerable and weak vis-à-vis the USA. Remaining sediments of international revolutionary ardour had to be encrusted in even greater caution than before.

Traditionalists would probably see the second motive underlying Malenkov's doctrine as based on a belief in the deterrence value of the European-hostage concept. Yet the apparent Soviet acceptance of this tenet, and the lack of any public acknowledgement of the USSR's vulnerability, and of her limited capabilities within an inter-continental context, should not be construed to mean that the deterrence was thought of as adequate or acceptable.

Two years later came public admissions or intimations of the real strategic relationship (see below). The main difference may be found in the USSR's later acquisition of some missile delivery capabilities. These entailed the promise of escape from the position of strategic inferiority. It is plausible to see the pre 1955 credence accorded to the European-hostage deterrence concept as politically and psycho-logically motivated. It would have been inopportune for Moscow to admit to profound vulnerability without being able to demonstrate a credible prospect for change in favour of security.

The increasingly messianic character of US anti-communism was clearly a supporting factor in nurturing the apparent Soviet accept-ance of the European-hostage deterrence concept. But, again, further consideration merely emphasizes the superficiality and tactical nature of the Soviet acceptance. Moscow could scarcely fail to appreciate that: the more fervent your convictions, and the greater the ultimate evil assigned to your opponent, the greater is the ultimate goal of his destruction, and the greater is the immediate suffering that can be tolerated in the furthering of that destruction. The greater the element of fear or distrust, the less could Moscow rely on its capabilities versus Europe deterring the USA.

The evidence presented above provides the rationale for fear or distrust. In conjunction with the effects of ideology and experience, it leads inexorably to the conclusion that the European-hostage concept never commanded conviction in Moscow. For ideological, political and psychological reasons, realities could not be broadcast to the public. But there must nevertheless have been acute awareness of the fact that a war would result in the destruction of only one super-power, the USSR, and of a Western Europe of increasingly minor significance as a power. Subsequent events and procurements indicate strongly that Moscow never really accepted the equation as being satisfactory.

The third factor that must be considered as a motive behind Malenkov's policies concerns the economy. The contradiction between military requirements and the need to buy time domestically entailed economic strains. The need for relaxation, and living standard increments (to alleviate the tense pace of Stalinist reconstruction and advance), was felt by some to be as great as that which related to the international situation. Malenkov certainly thought along these lines.[24]

One might, finally, suggest a fourth motive, that of pure humaneness recoiling from the horrors of war. But such purity as a prime action rationale is probably incompatible with emergence through any existing 'corridor' to political eminence in the East or in the West. The conclusion must therefore view a combination of the first and third factors as having been decisive. International relaxation and domestic economic advances were considered necessary, (the latter for political reasons at the time, and as a prerequisite to the creation of an infrastructure which might sustain necessary military procurements with less strain).

But opposition to Malenkov's doctrine, and to its consequences and implications, soon cropped up. For the first time there emerged what looked like purely military demands. Articles appeared which campaigned for the continued predominance of heavy industry, for continued international vigilance, and for greater attention to be paid to military preparedness prerogatives.[25]

The novelty of these demands, and the articles' eloquent neglect of Malenkov's consumer policies, may be seen to reflect on the novelty of the policies themselves. They may also have reflected the increased professional autonomy which was apparently delegated to the Military in late 1951. A 1951 decree is reputed to have highlighted the increasingly urgent need for military efficiency, and to have re-emphasized the principle of unified, one-man command.[26] (The intervening post-war years had witnessed the reintroduction of extensive political involvement in command procedures and duties.) One might interject that the purported decree fits into Stalin's preference for counterbalanced semi-competitive, and functionally different, 'conveyer belts' of power. But it may merely have related to the increasing international tensions.

The central point, however, is that the more open military opposition to the prevailing line was accompanied by, and probably received its main *raison d'être* from, evident opposition within the Party. This opposition obviously recognized the tenseness of the international situation. But it presumably judged it to be less precarious, and therefore less intimidating, than did Malenkov. The opposition furthermore took exception to Malenkov's view of the acuteness of the need for consumer reorientation. Doctrinal and Party-justifying considerations also encouraged a sceptical approach to Malenkov's doctrine.

In late 1954 Khrushchev gave a speech which strongly emphasized the place and role of heavy industry; and on December that year Pravda (representing the Khrushchev-led Party) and Izvestia (representing the Government and Malenkov) openly displayed the serious divergence of views.[27] Pravda supported, and was supported by, the articles in the military press. Izvestia persisted with the championing of Malenkov's consumer re-orientation program.

———

The Khrushchevite gaining of ascendency in early 1955[28] therefore entailed a semblance of victory also for the Armed Forces. This was further indicated by the promotions shortly thereafter, of two Generals to the rank of Marshals, of the war-hero Zhukov to the post of Minister of Defence, and of Marshal Bulganin (who although basically a political general, would presumably be aware of and possibly sympathetic to military requirements) to the post of 'Prime Minister'.[29]

The years of Zhukov prominence have been dealt with sufficiently elsewhere,[30] but a synopsis supplemented with some additional comments is appropriate.

While independence from Party control as such was never demanded, a number of military articles did demand the maximum possible degree of military professional autonomy. In September 1955 the purported 1951 decree was followed up. The role of the Party organs within the Armed Forces was limited to educational and political, as opposed to operational, concerns. The military seemed to shy away from the previous integration, to such an extent that it even affected party-military co-operation at the local levels.[31]

The military pursued efforts to increase the role of the professional commanders in the formulation of strategy and theory. These efforts were reflected in articles which exposed Stalin's military miscalculations, his dogmatic dismissal of the potential importance of strategic surprise, and his on occasion faulty dispositioning.[32] They were supplemented by intimations that political leaders in general might make mistakes if they engaged in strategic decision-making without paying attention to the professionals' advice: 'Political leaders must know the potentialities of strategy in order to set tasks – skilfully'.[33]

Such intimations, and the one-man command concept's corollary of a suppression of the old principles of criticism and self-criticism (according to which subordinates could criticize their commanders), obviously went against the grain of Khrushchev's inclinations. These may be synopsized as moving away from the 'conveyer-belts' of power practice, back to undiluted 'Leninist' Party dominance. Khrushchev favoured, albeit in a fashion primarily symbolic and not exempt from internal contradictions and vacillations, a lessening of disparities and a more egalitarian leadership. His introduction of Party Rules which at least in theory limited lengths of tenure and opportunities for patronage was indicative.[34]

There were a number of tactical reasons for Khrushchev's initial acquiescence with the military self-assertions. On the one hand the Party was not immune to divisive influences; supporters of Malenkov, as also he himself, remained prominent members. On the other hand the international situation remained strained, if not tense, and this psychologically bolstered the case of the military. The 1956 Hungarian crisis may for this reason have prolonged Khrushchev's tolerance.

A third reason may be found in the weakening of the security forces which presumably followed Beria's ousting. This would have militated against Party clamp-down conceptions. Zhukov's personality embodied a fourth reason. The combination of evident professional expertise and a vaunted war-hero reputation was in itself a deterrent under these conditions.

The alliance was also of political value. Khrushchev's praising of Zhukov, and the promotion of Zhukov to Praesidium candidate member,[35] secured Zhukov's possibly crucial help in the 1957 ousting of the 'anti-Party' group.

Zhukov's reward at the time was full Praesidium membership. This reflected his emergence as a wielder of ultimate power. Ironically, it also entailed his downfall. Within the setting of traditional Party antipathy towards potential rival power sources, his emergence could only lead to the crystallizing of a consensus in favour of his removal.

The first portent came in May of 1957, with a Central Committee instruction which reasserted the role and authority of political officers and organs within the Forces. The subsequent muting of efforts directed towards increased Party control reflected the summer events, and the political dictates which they generated. It was discarded in October. A more united and self-confident Khrushchev-led Party then utilized a Zhukov visit to Yugoslavia to arrange the publishing of a number of articles which reflected Khrushchev's views. By the end of the month Tass announced Zhukov's dismissal.

Yet this development did not precipitate a revoking of the professional autonomy that had been delegated to the military. Later events (see below) reinforce the impression that Khrushchev was attuned to and sympathetic to military requirements and their implications. The 1957 development was a reassertion of the bounds to the military professional autonomy, and it was a reflection on the inadmissability of Zhukov's 'Napoleonic' aura. It should not be interpreted as reflecting military-Party conflict beyond the bounds indicated above; most of the military demands had been limited to non-political concerns.

One of the military concerns which surfaced during this period is, however, of importance to our investigation, and demands some consideration at this stage. It dealt with the effects of nuclear weaponry, and with the potential role of strategic surprise.

The removal of the political restraints which had been imposed by Malenkov's doctrine was followed by articles which belittled the effects of nuclear weapons (in a way reminiscent of the Stalin era).[36] The articles were presumably inspired by a psychological need to bolster troop morale. Such a felt need would be a logical consequence of command awareness of strategic inferiority on an inadmissable scale.

These articles were then followed by superficially contradictory assertions, of the potential decisiveness of surprise attacks, and of the need for such sophisticated intelligence as would allow the USSR to react against hostile attack preparations.[37] The noting of the possible need for the Soviet Union to strike first indicated that she might otherwise be incapacitated. But the tenor of the first articles may not be as irreconcilable with that of the later articles as it first appears to be.

The discrepancy is explained if one views the latter articles as directed at policy-making Party levels. The fact that they were published, in spite of their incompatibility with the morale-raising endeavours, may then be seen to reflect on the acuteness of the military concern. This interpretation of acute concern is supported by the above-presented evidence ('political leaders must know the potentialities of strategy . . .'[38]), and it is supported by the intimations which that evidence contained, of the need for more professional strategic research facilities, and for new thinking.[39] Incoming progress reports of missile research would not have made the concern less acute. But they might have served to lessen inhibitions against acknowledging vulnerability.

Other areas of apparent friction, relating to specific aspects of strategy,[40] have been suggested by Western authors. But the evidence is scant. It is only with regard to the described aspects of more general military professional concern that one can safely ascertain the existence of friction. (See below and see Chapter 3, for cautions regarding the drawing of inferences from military debates.)

One must be careful about focusing on details of strategic friction within the Soviet hierarchies. One should also be careful about dismissing Soviet awareness of strategic constellations and thought processes. The lack, for example, of any explicit theoretical formulation of the deterrence-doctrine (until 1962[41]), did not entail lack of understanding.[42] It is more plausible to see it merely as reflecting the lack of the physical wherewithall, capacity, to allow for a credible well-elucidated deterrence posture. Public strategic debates at that time would have been incompatible with the described morale-upholding efforts. They would also have occasioned questions as to how much contradiction and undermining these efforts could sustain.

There can clearly be little doubt regarding military scepticism with respect to the practical value of the European-hostage deterrent. It is equally clear that this scepticism generated and stimulated the search for a deterrent of greater credibility, and for the securing of a maximum war-waging capability as insurance against its failure. The worries were most acute at the time of the Malenkov doctrine. But they were not dissipated by the advent of Khrushchev.

1957–1964 (See also Chapter 3)

The above referred to Khrushchev's attunement to military needs. This was indicated by his alliance with the military against Malenkov's relative degradation of heavy industry. It was also indicated by his early good relationship with the 'Stalingrad' generals, who he later promoted to Armed Forces leadership[43] (see below). His drift towards and final espousal of what appeared to be a massive retaliation missile strategy[44] should not be dismissed as a carbon copy of the American doctrine of the 1950's.

It was a strategy dictated by tactical considerations, and reflected the priority need for an effective deterrent as soon as possible. His statement at the time that the Army, Navy and Air Force had had their importance decreased[45] was relative. The accompanying quote was of crucial importance:[46]

'A reduction in the size of the Army does not prevent us from maintaining the country's defence capacity at the proper level. We shall continue to have all the means necessary for the country's defence – while reducing the minimal strength of the Armed Forces *we shall not reduce their fire-power: on the contrary, it will increase many times over in quality.*'

His policy presentation did, therefore, not entail disregard for the traditional branches of the Forces, but reflected rather a combination of military priority and economic considerations.

There is no doubt that Khrushchev was aware, or became aware, of the need for significant improvements of the domestic economy and the consumer goods sector. This is seen in his justification for the 1960 troop reductions, that they would entail great savings (about 16–17 milliard roubles).[47] And it is evident in his more explicit later admissions regarding the guns vs. butter quandary.[48]

But the comment relating to savings was again interlaced with the commitment that strategic capabilities and qualitative improvement would more than offset the apparent military loss.[49] The point was that the military could not expect significantly increased infusions of funds, and might in fact have to tolerate a lower level of budgetary allotments. The implication was that they must proceed with the introduction of qualitative improvements to replace and offset previous quantitative cushioning. This will be returned to later.

———

Khrushchev's gaining of ascendency had initially been accompanied by sizeable increases in the military budget: there was a 12 per cent increase in the military budget approved in 1955. This may be correlated with the fact that the first operational testing of an

ICBM took place in 1957. The implications of 'lead time' (of research and initial development) mean that Moscow was certainly acquainted with the imminence of the long-awaited delivery vehicle by 1955. It is therefore logical to see the 1955 budgetary increase as indicating the scale of the commitment to procure effective strategic delivery means, and as reflecting on Soviet perceptions of the need for such means.

The scale of this commitment is further emphasized by a considera-tion of the savings which accrued from the troop cuts of the later 1950's:[50] in 1955 640,000 were demobilized; in 1956–57 1,200,000 were demobilized; in 1958 300,000 were demobilized; and in 1960 1,200,000 were demobilized. The cuts decreased the size of the Armed Forces to 2 million, 423 thousand men.[51]

An unpublished Moscow exposition of 1966[52] provides indirect confirmation of Ulam's estimate, that previous high force levels were not out of proportion to the military's domestic and East European tasks. It also confirms that the cuts therefore had to be accompanied by extensive reorganization and qualitative innovations. It stressed that the demobilizations resulted in the Armed Forces personnel level falling below that of the USA 'in spite of the greater size of Soviet territory and the greater length of Soviet borders . . . .'[53] It implied that these two factors placed considerable demands on the Armed Forces.

The ensuing enforced attention to modernization continued to provide a prime focus of military concern through the years of our investigation. Mobility and dispersion criteria were emphasized more and more. So also were offensive operations, directed away from concentrated target areas (see also Chapter 5).

The aim was to provide force units with maximum independent capacity to overcome the effects of nuclear war. The first reorganiza-tion came in May 1954; the air defence forces were integrated into a unified command with status equal to that of the other services. Then, in 1957–58, the logistic services became subject to major upgrading and reorganization. Streamlined and effective logistics services were recognized to be a necessary adjunct to the new concepts and weapons.[55] The trend evinced a determination that the Armed Forces be moulded and dispositioned so as to decrease their vulnerability to a knockout nuclear blow.[56]

A side-effect of this stream-lining, and of the emphasis on military qualitative improvements, led to an exacerbation of the main difference between the views of the military and those of Khrushchev. The military considered the corollary to be increased effectivity through increased discipline. But Khrushchev's inclinations with regard to the place and role of the Party (described above) were not conducive to the effecting of such discipline.

The 1957 reassertion of political authority within the forces, and the stress on the Central Committee of the Party as the arbiter on questions of military science and military doctrine (see Chapter 8), was not inherently inimical to military needs. But in conjunction with the encouraging of self-criticism, and with the efforts to increase the military role and influence of the Party,[57] it did perturb the military. The trend could obstruct the execution of their professional duties. The autumn of 1958 saw the emergence of a number of military articles which complained of worsened discipline and lowered efficiency; political promotions and interferences were assigned the blame with considerable frankness.[58]

It was Khrushchev's reluctance to concede and respect a sufficiently precisely defined sphere of military professional autonomy which occasioned the one obvious difference in Party-Military relations prior to and following his ousting.[59] This therefore emerges as the one ascertainable reason for a possible military preference for his successors. His successors did not place the same stress on vague assertions of the 'role and influence' of the Party, assertions which inherently diluted the acceptance of the 'one-man-command' principle.[60]

However, it was only after late 1958 that this really appeared as an issue. The analysis of later events must await a survey of the reasons for the early harmony between Khrushchev and the military. The fact that this harmony persisted, the above issue excepted, through most of his era, provides an added rationale for an investigation of its causes.

On the one hand there was the persistence of a degree of fear and international tensions. Moscow continued to pursue efforts aimed at international disarmament agreements, and at the abolition of nuclear stockpiles.[61] (One presumes that expectations were minimal, since it would have meant a unilateral voluntary abdication by the USA of its position of supremacy.) In 1956 Moscow proposed to end nuclear testing. In 1958 she dramatically announced a (temporary) halt to her own testing.[62] In January 1958 she signed the US–Soviet agreement on cultural, scientific and other exchanges and contacts (the 'first step' towards a normalizing of relations).[63] And she stressed the potential benefits from further agreements in an era when war was no longer considered to be inevitable.[64] She now recognized that the hard line was only the dominant and not the exclusive factor in Washington;

she recognized a 'temperate' faction within the US hierarchy.[65] The result was recurrent gestures made in its direction, not least of which were hints as to the possible harvest from increased trade.[66] Finally, one may observe that the troop cuts were a further stimulant to efforts directed at easing the precariousness out of the Cold War confrontation.

Without detracting from other motives, one may distinguish reasons for military support of these policies. The more eased the relationships the less chance was there that the lack of effective strategic retaliation capabilities would prove fatal. And, of course, the less messianic the USA, the greater was the relative weight of the moral deterrent of the European-hostage concept. It would ease the strain of the period which remained before the USSR acquired a more secure deterrent.

The second and more basic cause of harmony lay in efforts aimed towards redressing the strategic imbalance. Progress reports and the initial procurement of missiles, as well as the moves towards Armed Forces modernization, brought closer the prospect of achieving effective nuclear strike and war-waging capability. The concensus clearly saw this achievement as the only real guarantee of security. But the prospect remained unrealized until some time in the 1960's (see following chapter). Technical difficulties were supplemented by considerations of economy. Further obvious infusions of funds, beyond those associated with the early budgetary increase, and those which accrued from personnel limitation savings, did not occur. Instead one saw the 'deliberate, systematic (and consistent)' deception of the West which was perpetrated by Khrushchev between 1957 and 1962.[67] Budgetary allocatory decisions made this policy strategically necessary. It was a very real complement to the easing of international tensions.

The psychological effect of the Sputnik successes was utilized. Khrushchev, who in 1955 had asserted that 'we cannot be intimidated by fables that in a new world war civilization will perish',[68] now felt able to proclaim (1958) that 'a future war would cause immeasurable harm to all mankind'. But the Malenkov parallel is misleading. The post 1957 assertions that war had become 'madness',[69] no longer permitted of the morale-deteriorating Malenkov corollary that the USSR itself might be destroyed. She might suffer 'immeasurable harm', but she would not be the one that was destroyed.

Scepticism no doubt remained about the extent to which American policy-makers (as opposed to the public) would be affected by the psychological up-grading of Soviet Strategic capabilities. Moscow would probably concede that they had access to relatively reliable balance of forces estimates. She may even have relied on this to produce a compromise US estimate of Soviet capabilities which was sufficiently above reality to inspire caution, while yet sufficiently below the psychological mirage to ensure against a catch-up effort such as would negate the Soviet progress(!). And Moscow appeared to succeed, until the feared 'backlash' occurred under Kennedy (see below, and Chapter 5).

In the meantime, in spite of occasional hints of hollowness such as sounded in the ineffectual Soviet threats at the time of the 1958 US landing in Lebanon, the USSR did acquire the desired super-power aura. This acquisition owed some debt to the encouragement to chance more assertive postures which was offered by Eisenhower's extreme caution during the Hungarian crisis of 1956. By demonstrating that the aggressive Dulles-tone was on leash, it decreased apprehension. It therefore encouraged faith in the viability of the psychological deterrent as projected, and engendered trust in the slow-paced build-up of a genuine deterrent which Khrushchev's policies envisaged. Temporarily Moscow had the pleasure of both having and eating the cake.

It is now appropriate to turn to the post-Zhukov military leadership, the 'Stalingrad Group'. The term was coined by Roman Kolkowicz.[70] He defined the group as coming 'almost without exception from the group of generals who were located at a single frontal sector (the Stalingrad Front) which was under Khrushchev's personal supervision during the six to seven months of the bitter battle for Stalingrad'. His thesis concerning Khrushchev's special relationship with the group was based on 'such empirical factors as close contacts under stress, opposition to common adversaries, and promotions to positions of influence that paralleled the Party leader's rise to power'.[71] His evidence regarding Khrushchev's rapport and harmonious working relationship with group members is impressive, and persuasive.[72] The rise to prominence of group members climaxed after Zhukov's ousting. It paralleled the rise of Khrushchev.[73] (And that of Khrushchev's protege, Brezhnev.)

Kolkowicz saw the group as splitting into two factions during the early 1960's. The one, including Marshals Malinovsky, Zakharov, Grechko and Krylov, is said to have 'viewed their obligations to the military establishment as paramount to others'.[74] The other, including Marshals Biriuzov, Moskalenko and Chuikov, was seen to exhibit overriding Khrushchev loyalties.[75] And there is evidence for some divergence along these lines. (Post Cuba) January–February 1963, for example, saw a number of articles on the 20th anniversary of Stalingrad in which authors 'belonging' to either faction seemed to differ on the relative prominence of Khrushchev and Malinovsky.[76]

But Kolkowicz may have over-elaborated on some of his themes, both with regard to group and intra group cohesion and with regard to the Party-group friction which he saw as emerging. One ought to be exceedingly wary of over-emphasizing apparent debate discrepancies. This all too easily leads to non-credible exaggerations of Party-Military and 'factional' antagonisms (see Chapters 2 and 8 for further comments).

Assertions such as Malinovsky's of 1961, that 'even if atomic weapons will play a prime role in a future war – nevertheless – final victory over an aggressor can only be achieved through combined operations',[77] need not be seen as anti-Khrushchev. They were fully compatible with Khrushchev's own thoughts, as described above, and as they emerge through Kolkowicz' own sections on the original Khrushchev-Stalingrad group rapport.

One is left with our previous conclusion: The only issue which provoked ascertainable abiding military oppositional concern was that caused by Khrushchev's vagueness. The vagueness is exemplified by his statement: 'The Party Program emphasizes that single command is a highly important structural principle of the Soviet Armed Forces. . . . At the same time we must always remember that Party leadership and a greater role and influence for the Party organizations in large and small units is the basic foundation of our military structure.[78]

This refers of course to the period prior to the Cuban crisis. After that crisis the military, and especially those sections most frustrated with the above, tended to switch allegiance to Brezhnev. As Khrushchev's erstwhile deputy, he was the one other political leader with close contacts with the 'Stalingrad group'. More importantly, he was as mentioned considerably more inclined to tolerate a more consistent sphere of military professional autonomy.[79]

But Cuban events were not crucial. What was pivotal was the fact that the conjuring aspects of Khrushchev's deterrence policies had been exposed. The Kennedy administration's drastic expansion of strategic weaponry outlays and procurements[80] had made any gradual or stealthy Soviet achieving of parity an impossibility in the short term. The US military budget was seen to increase from 40,992 million dollars in 1960–61 to 47,655 million dollars in 1961–62.[81] Parallel Soviet military budget increases were implemented (see Chapter 8). Yet these could not suffice to secure the desired parity; they did, however, contribute towards the early securing of some effective second strike capability (see below and Chapters 2 and 4).

It is to the strategic equation that a preliminary summary of the Khrushchev years must turn. The economic strain remained such as to strongly discourage increased military spending. And Khrushchev's awareness of this seems in fact to have grown towards the end (see footnote 48). There is little doubt that he saw the solution in the utilization and advance of early missile technology achievements. As described above, they entailed the promise both a of more reliable delivery-vehicle, and of potential capabilities offsetting those of the USA. Hence his 1960 espousal of a 'massive retaliation' strategy, according to which escalation of war was inevitable.[82]

But the early Soviet missile procurement-program was to prove highly inadequate. Missile degradation factors, to which we shall return, meant that her damage inflicting capability was low. The same factors applied of course to American missiles, and therefore in theory led to greater Soviet missile first strike survivability expectations. But the scepticism which was to emanate from a familiarity with degradation factor implications had probably not yet coagulated, and did probably not pierce the awe of missile novelty. And even if it had, Moscow certainly knew that the US strategic bomber-fleet alone retained sufficient penetration certainty to make the survival of her missiles a dubious proposition.

In other words: Moscow may have entertained overoptimistic expectations of her damage-inflicting capability.[83] But she must have realized that any such capability related only to first strike calculations. And she must have known that US superiority and deployment was of such a scale that the US would still retain second-strike retaliation means of greater power than her first strike capabilities. The USSR was checkmated.

Considerable advance was made towards the end of Khrushchev's tenure. More sophisticated, better protected, and in some cases mobile, rockets were finally to provide a more dependable deterrent with significant first strike survivability capacity.[84] But the achieving of this minimum aim only served to focus attention on the ultimate aim of parity with the US. Khrushchev's final campaign indicated that other needs precluded the assigning of funds to this end, and in fact demanded some re-allocation towards consumer interests.[85] The military was clearly dissatisfied.[86]

Cuban events must here be returned to, since they served as a catalyst for the late military 'opposition'. The events are logically explained as resulting at least in part from a Khrushchevian venture to secure a 'cheap' augmentation of strategic capabilities, and thus procure a more credible deterrent.[87] Intermediate-range missiles in Cuba would have a range covering the US heartland. They would therefore have the same effect on the strategic balance as an otherwise far more costly increase in ICBM numbers. There was the additional advantage of dispersal of potential targets that had to be covered by US forces. It appears reasonable to assume that the non-achievement of such considerable and anticipated benefits would, if only by highlighting their potential, lend greater urgency to the desire for their achievement through other means.

The fact that the late and apparently extensive 'opposition' emerged in public finally reflects equally on more general Party dissatisfaction with Khrushchev's economic and political schemes. One may draw a parallel with the Malenkov years, when the emerging Party opposition was powerful enough to provide protection.

The military opposition played second fiddle. The Party opposition, which was motivated by non-military considerations, was the determinant. This may be inferred from the fact that there was to prove little difference between the administrations' defence policies, except in emphasis. Khrushchev's final envisaged cutbacks were not implemented, and there emerged relatively more public appreciation of defence needs and requirements.[88] But Khrushchev's successors considered domestic demands equally acute, and gave them the same priority.[89]

Their first military budget was in fact cut by 4 per cent. Later increases did no more than parallel US military budget increases. Their achieving of 'strategic parity' by 1970 was to be primarily due to the slack in the US budget which was represented by the large proportion that was wasted on the Vietnam war (see end of Chapter 2).

The military campaign for increased conventional forces[90] was similarly not to result in troop augmentations following Khrushchev's ousting.[91] It was nevertheless then muted. The campaign may perhaps be seen as over-reaction to Khrushchev's final taking to extremes (if that it was) of his conceptions of both defence and budgetary priorities in general.[92] Subsequent events emphasize that it could not be interpreted to signify the emergence of any politically independent military power bloc.

The early evidence refutes speculation that Khrushchev was so obsessed with intercontinental missile needs as to ignore complementary conventional needs. To the contrary, even his later speeches affirmed that the imperialists could not be allowed to achieve or retain a superiority which permitted them 'to impose their will and policy'. He assured his audience that military requirements would not be jeopardized, nor would general armed forces efficiency be impaired.[93]

His tenure of office did from the beginning witness efforts towards a streamlining and modernization of the forces so as to make them suitable for nuclear war conditions. There is scant reason to doubt that he remained fully in accord, at least theoretically, with later assertions regarding the necessity for flexibility and mobility – 'the basic feature' of any utilization of nuclear strikes[94], and regarding the obsolescence of old defensive concepts.[95] His very reluctance to allocate significantly increased resources, together with his determination that the missile forces be given priority, spurred the development. He probably deserves prime credit for forcing the Armed Forces to recognize, and adapt to, nuclear warfare implications.

This comment must be extended to consider also the development of interventionary-type forces. Their significant emergence was precluded by allocatory priorities. But elements of such forces were procured under Khrushchev. It should be noted that this did not occur as a reaction to Cuban events. These events can at most be said to have crystallized attention on the glaring Soviet lack of ability to intervene, or show force, outside her continental environment.

The significant upgrading of the Navy, for example, of its strategic tasks, and of its commander, all took place prior to the Cuban events.[96] So also did the redefinition of the Navy's tasks: 'to give battle to enemy forces at sea and at their bases' (a far cry indeed from the previously unchanged limited and defensive naval strategy of World War II[97]).

One can conclude as follows: Soviet military concepts and capabilities under Stalin had remained largely conventional and orthodox, with a static continental role. Under Khrushchev considerable global strategic strike forces appeared. And there is evidence for seeing the general conceptual shift from continental restrictions to global perspectives as having occurred during his tenure and as having been spurred by his policies. The drawing of some of the consequences may have been slowed by his assigning of priorities. But it is clear that even the emergence of significant interventionary forces, after his ousting, owed its impetus to policies approved by Khrushchev.

NOTES

1. One of the first good examples was: Kolko, Gabriel, '*The Politics of War*. The World and United States Foreign Policy, 1943–45', Random House, New York, 1960. It formed the basis for much of the later work on the topic. For a good exposition of some of the economic factors involved, see Gabriel, Manuel, '*The German Peace Settlement and the Berlin Crisis*', Paine-Whitman, New York, 1960.

2. Ideological considerations and recent invasions increased the necessity for this in Soviet eyes. But control over East Europe had also been considered to be necessary by earlier Tsarist regimes.

3. Ulam, Adam B., '*Expansion and Co-existence*', Secker and Warburg, London, 1968.

4. *Ibid.*, p. 404. See also Ruban, M., Captain First Class, 'Soviet Military Construction in Post-War Period', *Kommunist Vooruzhiennykh Sil*, No. 13, July 1968, pp. 77–83: 'The total number of persons discharged was ... 8·5 million persons'. And see *Pravda*, January 15, 1960 (N. Khrushchev's report).

5. Ulam, *op. cit.*, p. 448. Mileykovsky, A. G., ed., '*International Relations after the Second World War*', Moscow, 1962.

6. Ulam, *op. cit.*, p. 447.

7. *Ibid.*, p. 448, quoting Mileykovsky, *op. cit.*, p. 364.

8. *Ibid.*, p. 455.

9. '*Documents on International Affairs*, 1949–50', RIIA, London, 1953, pp. 167–168; Ulam, *op. cit.*, p. 509.

10. '*Documents on International Affairs*, 1952', RIIA, London, 1955, p. 88.

11. Bell, Coral, '*Negotiations From Strength*', London, 1962, p. 99; Ulam, *op. cit.*, pp. 508 and 510.

12. Bingham, J. B. (Representative US Congress, and Member of the US UN Delegation), 'Can Military Spending be Controlled?', *Foreign Affairs*, October, 1969, pp. 51–66.

13. *Keesings Contemporary Archives* 1950–52, p. 11215.

14. *Keesings Contemporary Archives* 1952–54, p. 12740.

15. *Documents – 1947–48*, RIIA, London, p. 141.

16. E.g. in a talk sponsored by the Norwegian Institute of International Affairs (NUPI), Oslo, 9 May, 1969 (attended by author).

17. Djilas, Milovan, '*Conversations with Stalin*', Pelican, 1969 (Copyright by Harcourt, Brace & World, Inc., 1962), p. 141.

18. J. V. Stalin, *Pravda*, 2 August, 1952, 3 October, 1952 and 26 December, 1952 (for his letter to James Reston, in which he asserted that the US and the USSR could live peacefully in the coming years). The pronouncements can be seen to have constituted a redefinition of the concept of peaceful co-existence. Previous statements had considered it as a sometimes necessary expedient or compromise, but ultimately not durable as a basis for relations between incompatible social systems. See for example A. Zhdanov in *Informatsionnoe Soveshchanie*, September, 1947, Moscow, p. 27; or Lenin, in Pis'mo k Amerikanskim Rabocham, *Sochineniia*, XXIII, 20 August, 1918, p. 182, and in Ocherednye Zadachi Sovetskoi Vlasti, *Sochineniia*, XXII, March-April 1918, p. 440 (one must be willing to compromise if and when necessary to gain a 'breathing spell'). Stalin's 1952 formulations appeared to dilute the previous insistence on the temporary nature of 'peaceful co-existence' (and more so than had his obtuse, if positive, answers to Western journalists' questions in 1946 and 1947: *Isvestia*, 24 September, 1946; *Bolshevik*, No. 1, January, 1947.

Or see Shulman, M., *Stalin's Foreign Policy Reappraised*, Harvard University Press, 1963, Chapters 10 and 11: the process of redefinition of the concept of peaceful coexistence may be seen as having covered the period of 1949–52 culminating in the pronouncements and decrees which accompanied the 19th Party Congress.

19. Meray, Tibor, *Thirteen Days That Shook the Kremlin*, F. A. Praeger, New York, 1959, p. 28.

20. *Pravda*, 15 January, 1960.

21. *Pravda*, 11 April, 1960.

22. *Pravda*, 9 August, 1953.

23. Gus, M., as quoted by Dinerstein, Herbert, in *War and the Soviet Union*, Praeger, New York, 1959. See especially pp. 71 and 171.

24. *Pravda*, 9 August, 1953.

25. See e.g. Col. Nenakhov, L., *Voennaya Mysl*, Sept., 1953, p. 6; *Kommunist*, No. 8, 1954; *Pravda*, 27 January, 1955; *Krasnaya Zvezda*, 3 February, 1955; and Garthoff, R. L., *Soviet Military Policy: A Historical Analysis*, Faber & Faber, 1966, p. 43.

26. *Ibid.*, pp. 44 and 243.

27. *Pravda*, 21 December, 1954; *Izvestia*, 21 December, 1954.

28. *Pravda*, 9 February, 1955, announced Malenkov's replacement with Bulganin.

29. *Ibid.*

30. See e.g. coverage in Fainsod, M., *How Russia is Ruled*, revised ed., Harvard University Press, 1965, pp. 482–9; or Garthoff, *op. cit.*, pp. 51–4.

31. Most evident in subsequent Party efforts directed at reversing the process: see e.g. *Partinaya Zhizn*, August, 1958, pp. 15–23, and *Pravda*, 29 August, 1958.

32. An attack which gained Khrushchev's explicit support: see his *'Secret Speech'* to the 20th CPSU Congress, 1956.

33. *Voennaya Mysl*, March 1955, p. 6.

34. Adopted at the 22nd CPSU Congress.

35. At the 20th CPSU Congress.

36. See e.g. Olisev, B., Maj. General, in *Krasnaya Zvezda*, 3 August, 1955.

37. Although intimated in a February, 1955, article by Marshal Rotmistrov, this was first explicitly recognized by Emelin, V., in *Sovremennaya Voennaya Teknika*, Moscow, 1956, p. 131.

38. *Voennaya Mysl*, March, 1955, *op. cit.*

39. *Ibid.* provides the first indication of this need. The need finally received extensive treatment in the article by Marshal Sokolovsky and Maj. General Cherednichenko in *Kommunist Vooruzhiennikh Sil*, No. 7, 1966.

40. Garthoff, *op. cit.*, p. 50, suggests a further down-grading of the role of the Navy initiated by Zhukov in 1955 and the establishment of a separate long-range missile command. But naval priorities had in practice languished prior to this, and the latter might merely reflect the novel characteristics of the weaponry.

41. Malinovsky, R., Marshal, *Bditelnoe stoyat na strazhe mira*, Moscow, 1962, p. 25.

42. Western theoretical expositions on the subject were made available: see for example Kissinger, H., *Jadernoe Oruzhie i Vneshnaya Politika*, Moscow, 1959.

43. Kolkowicz, R., *The Soviet Military and The Communist Party*, Princeton University Press, 1967, pp. 224–238.

44. *Pravda*, 15 January, 1960.

45. *Ibid.*

46. *Ibid.* (This author's stress.)

47. *Ibid.*

48. *Pravda*, 15 February, 1964.

49. *Pravda*, 15 January, 1960.

50. *Pravda*, 11 April, 1960.

51. *Vneshnaya Politika SSSR na Sovremennom Etape*, Moscow, 1964, p. 205.

52. Tolnacheva, A. I., *Sovjetsko-Amerikanskie Otnoshenie 1956–63*, MGU thesis 1966 under the supervision of L. M. Papin (MGU's authority on Soviet Foreign Policy).

53. *Ibid.*, p. 26.

54. *50 Years of the Armed Forces of the USSR*, Voenizdat, Moscow, 1968, p. 511.

55. Mackintosh, M., 'Survival Strategy in World War III', *Survival*, ISS,

July–August, 1960, pp. 149–58. Mackintosh dates the reorganisation of the Logistics Services from 1957. It is probably more correct to date it from the June 1958 promotion of Bagramian to CINC of the Rear Forces (See '50 years . . . ', *ibid.*, p. 515).

56. Emelin, V., Colonel, *op. cit.*

57. See e.g. *Partinaya Zhizn*, August, 1958, *op. cit.*, and *Pravda*, 29 August, 1958, *op. cit.*

58. See e.g. Marshal Malinovsky's article in *Krasnaya Zvezda*, 1 November, 1958.

59. *Pravda*, 6 July, 1962, and *Pravda*, 4 July, 1965.

60. *Ibid.*, compare.

61. See e.g. Soviet Government Proposals of 10 May, 1955.

62. *Sbornik Osnovnikh Aktov i Dokumentov Verkhovnovo Sovjeta SSSR po Vneshnepoliticheskim Voprosam 1956–60 gg.*, p. 51.

63. *Mezhdunarodnaya Zhizn'* Vol. 2, p. 29, Moscow, 1959.

64. *Pravda*, 15 February, 1956, carried the relevant 20th CPSU Congress Resolution. And see *Mazhdunarodnaya Zhizn'*, *op. cit.*

65. Tolnacheva, A. I., *op. cit.*, p. 31.

66. *Mezhdunarodnaya Zhizn'*, 1963, No. 3, p. 43, pointed out that over 1000 types of goods were then included on the US embargo list concerning trade with the USSR.

67. Horelick & Rush, *Strategic Power and Soviet Foreign Policy*, University of Chicago Press, 1965.

68. *Pravda*, 27 March, 1955.

69. Kuusinen, O., *Pravda*, 23 April, 1960.

70. Kolkowicz, R., *op. cit.* The term is used in tribute to Kolkowicz' substantial scholarship. But it should be noted that group ties stretched back, before Stalingrad, to common school and Academy experiences. See Chapter 8.

71. *Ibid.*, pp. 279 and 281.

72. *Ibid.*, pp. 224–238.

73. *Ibid.*, pp. 241–255. The group also benefited by the purge of 250,000 officers inherent in the referred-to demobilizations.

74. Kolkowicz, R., *op. cit.*, p. 239.

75. *Ibid.*, pp. 239 and 263.

76. Malinovsky himself wrote a February 1963 *Pravda* article which minimized the role of Khrushchev at Stalingrad. And one may find contrasts with other articles 'campaigning' for the Party's leading role to be emphasized and for the military to 'know their place'. See e.g. three articles by General Jepishev, Cmdr. of the Political Control Apparatus, during the same period.

77. Speech to 22nd CPSU Congress, October 1961. See also Sokolovsky, V. D., Marshal, ed., *Voennaya Strategia*, 2nd ed., Voenizdat, Moscow, 1963, p. 374, and Kozlov, S. N., Maj. Gen., & others, *O Sovjetskoi Voennoi Nauke*, 2nd ed., Voenizdat, Moscow, 1964, p. 249.

78. *Pravda* and *Izvestia*, 6 July, 1962.

79. *Pravda*, 4 July, 1965.

80. *Ekonomika i Kapitalisticheskie Strany, 1962 g*, Moscow, 1963, pp. 18 and 30.

81. *Mirovaya Ekonomika i Mezhdunarodnie Otnoshenie*, Moscow, 1962, No. 2, p. 90.

82. *Pravda*, 15 January, 1960. See also Kolkowicz, R., *op. cit.*, for comparisons with similar doctrine advocated by and subsequently abandoned by the USA in the 1950's. (Although this was based on very different and more secure capability prognoses.)

83. Although the USSR clearly did realize that even then her forces' limitations were such as demanded their use to maximum effect, i.e. against cities, if they were to be effective at all. The USSR unlike the USA did not have the capabilities to afford contemplation of limited or varied target choice and strategy, such as relating to airfields and missile pads. See also explicit inference in Sokolovsky, *op. cit.*, 2nd ed., p. 84. And compare with later more sophisticated capabilities as reflected in Sushko & Kondratkov, *Metodologicheskie Problemi Voennoy Teorrii i Praktiki*, Voenizdat, Moscow, 1967, p. 147.

84. See e.g. Glagolev & Larionov in *International Affairs*, No. 11, 1963, p. 32, and testimony by Brezhnev and Kosygin in *Pravda* and *Izvestia*, 4 July, 1965, and see Chapter 3.

85. *Pravda*, 15 February, 1964, *op. cit.*
86. See e.g. Grechko, Marshal & 1st Dep. Min. of Defence, ed., *The Nuclear Age and War*, Voenizdat, Moscow, July, 1964.
87. See also Ulam, *op. cit.*, p. 669. Soviet sources in general concentrate exclusively on the explanation that missiles were installed at Castro's request to forestall perceived US invasion schemes. The outcome of the crisis, with the US pledging not to intervene, is hence seen as a victory which made the missile installations superfluous. See also *Pravda*, 11 February, 1963, for interesting comments.
88. *Izvestia*, 20 October, 1964, *Pravda*, 8 November, 1964, and *Pravda*, 4 July, 1965, *op. cit.*
89. See e.g. Kuarcz, J. F., 'The New Soviet Agricultural Program', *Soviet Studies*, Vol. XVII, No. 2, October, 1965, for a thorough analysis of one of their major initial civilian economy investment plans.
90. Such as in Grechko, *op. cit.*
91. Sokolovsky, V. D., Marshal, Press Conference for Western journalists, Moscow, 17 February, 1965.
92. *Pravda*, 2 October, 1964 – herein Khrushchev published designs for a drastic shift in resources away from heavy industry (a last desperate reaction to domestic economic disappointments?).
93. *Pravda*, 15 February, 1964, *op. cit.*
94. *Krasnaya Zvezda*, 6 June, 1964.
95. *Kommunist Vooruzhiennikh Sil*, No. 3, 1963, pp. 27–28. See also Khrushchev's own comments and assurances above. *Pravda*, 15 January, 1960.
96. *Pravda*, 2 February, 1962, art. by S. G. Gorshkov. *Pravda*, 29 April, *Izvestia*, 30 April, 1962.
97. Sokolovsky, *op. cit.* The stress is this author's. Compare re 2nd World War role, of which Sokolovsky testifies: 'Maritime operations had no decisive effects on the results'. See also McGuire, Commander, *Brassey's Annual* 1969, for exposition on the limited character of the Soviet Navy's tactical mobility at the time – on its reliance on short-range shore-based air support.

2

The Khrushchev Legacy: Deterrence vs. General Purpose Forces Debates

Discussion and analyses of the Debates follows. But it appears propitious to return first to a misconception which was referred to in Chapter 1. One of the best of the analysts who laboured under it was T. W. Wolfe. And it may be exemplified by his otherwise admirable 1964 analysis of the Khrushchev debates.[1] Against the background of definite Soviet inferiority in missile capability, and in consideration of the continental restrictions to Soviet conventional forces, he interpreted Khrushchev's theory of the inevitability of war escalation and 'massive retaliation' to mean tacit acceptance of Soviet strategic inferiority. He thought that Soviet ambitions had been curtailed, and that the USSR would therefore not seek to develop counter Force capabilities. He believed that financial and other considerations had forced Soviet leaders to accept the sufficiency of a limited deterrent.

The extent of Western credence for this theory is indicated further by a 1967 Hudson Institute Report.[2] Its relevant section was titled 'Exploit the Present United States – Soviet Union Strategic Position'. It contained this paragraph: 'There is reason to believe that the Soviet Union is in the process of trying to match a counter-force strategy of ours with a minimum deterrence position. This may be for reasons of economy, doctrinal trust in our restraint, an inclination not to make major provocations, a hesitance to indulge in an expensive or hopeless arms race, a belief in the efficacy of secret, or for some other reasons. In any case this may represent a mistake on their part'.

Moscow was clearly aware of the last point. By 1967 hardware and other evidence was already appearing as visible rebuttals to the report's tenet. And lead-time considerations (the time needed for the research and development of new systems) showed that the tenet's rejection had occurred already under Khrushchev.

As regards Wolfe's conclusions, they represented also a rather hazardous inference from Khrushchev's actions and speeches. As shown in Chapter 1 these might equally, and as it proved more justly, have been interpreted very differently. Economic necessities were certainly judged to preclude any concentrated early drive towards general forces capabilities. But this reflected economic priorities and had no necessary causal connection with long-term policies in the strategic field. Moves were made towards enabling Force units' mobile, flexible and independent operations under nuclear conditions. Together with the reviving and expanding of Naval capabilities, they supplemented the development of a reliable deterrent. The Khrushchev years saw the creation of the practical and theoretical nucleus on which more extensive General Forces would rely, and from which they eventually emerged.

One line of inquiry suffices to demonstrate why no other long-term aim ought in fact to have been ascribed to Soviet policy-makers. It relates to the credibility of a posture which permitted only all-out strikes or counter-strikes:[3] if your forces are such that only an all-out utilization of capabilities can ensure success, then how capable or willing can you be in deterring minor aggressions or taking initiatives? The knowledge that you can only inflict a maximum punishment in retribution for which you will yourself be destroyed does per definition crucially inhibit your freedom of manoeuvre. It also concedes to your opponent great low-risk freedom to initiate minor hostilities.

And this freedom can only be inhibited by fear that you will over-react to minor hostilities. A misinterpretation of the rationale or aim of your opponent's action might produce fear of a hostile strike, which might again induce you to launch a pre-emptive strike while your limited capabilities were still intact. The opponent might on the other hand feel forced himself to escalate to all-out action from fear that your fear might dictate such a pre-emptive strike.[4]

This situation is clearly ultimately intolerable for strategic policy-makers. The Soviet Union could not seek comfort in the power and protection of a friendly power. Her ideological (and chauvinistic) perceptions of herself demanded that she acquired means equal to those of her adversaries. She needed them both to ensure against the consequences or irrationalities of the above-mentioned fear, and to provide her with the freedom of manoeuvre and initiative upon which her chosen role was contingent.

THE DEBATES

Chapter 1 cautioned against such exaggerated estimates of debates' value as led to non-credible conclusions regarding group antagonisms. There are clearly vital questions that need answers before one can judge debate contributions. They may be summed up as 'How real are the debates?' and 'Do contributions represent genuine differences presented prior to, and thus meant to influence policy decisions? Or do they merely reflect different aspects of previously taken policy-decisions?'.

No absolute answers can be presented, but there are strong indications that the latter interpretation is the correct one. The research and development (lead-time) stages of weapon-systems procurement are difficult to quantify into exact periods. But the lead-time activation, and therefore the time of the original decision-making, may most often be judged to precede the appearance of relevant debates (even when these debates precede the first visible results of the procurement decision).

Naval developments provide one example: Major coverage of the potential benefits of interventionary and limited war-waging capacities, as well as of 'gun-boat diplomacy',[5] only emerged after the appearance of the nucleus of the necessary capacities.[6] The debate could admittedly be traced back further, for example to Admiral Gorshkov's 1963 references to US Naval capacities and to his hints regarding the necessity to counter them.[7] But then Gorshkov's own efforts might be traced back to yet earlier evidence, such as for example the upgrading of the Navy by 1962.[8]

One might comment that the decision to assign the Navy a definite strategic role, and therefore the decision from which all of the above flowed, must in fact have been taken at about the time of Khrushchev's crystallizing of his 'deterrence-doctrine'.[9] Prior to this one can certainly not find published evidence of any significant naval campaign. Military budget speculation provides a different but complementary example. Much has at times been inferred from military (Krasnaya Zvezda) pre budget-time articles on the importance of, and need for, heavy industry. But with regard to no budget can causal connections be drawn between such articles and budgetary allocations as finally published. This relates also to interpretations which saw the late Khrushchev era articles which demanded 'multi-million armies' and conventional force increments, as proof of a campaign hostile to the political leadership. Such interpretations must have accepted the post-Khrushchev developments as a political over-ruling of military aspirations. The point also relates to any credence conferred to rumours that the military desired a preventive strike against China in 1968–69 (on the basis that a strike would be easy within the near future, but possibly far more problematic in later years). Again developments would have to be judged as having demonstrated the finality of a political veto at the time. The conclusion must be that the political authority remained absolutely paramount (see also Chapter 8).

On the basis of discrepancies and occasional inconsistencies between articles, one can sometimes present a case for the existence of factional splits within the Party, as between 'moderates' and 'conservatives'.[10] One could with theoretical profit co-ordinate such inconsistencies with variations in style or content between different military articles, or between military and Party articles. But there is grave danger that the combining of too many inferences emasculate them of their possible value.

The main intent in pursuing debate contributions ought therefore not to be the unearthing of policy differences, a task perhaps made impossible by Soviet censorship practices. It ought rather to concentrate on the extent to which the articles help to explain and elucidate policy decisions already taken, and procurement programs already evident. Such a course has the added advantage of minimizing the danger of confusing 'declaratory' policy with 'action' policy.

The type of article justly demanding attention may be exemplified by Marshal Krylov's of 1966.[11] He then testified that the Soviet Union had only recently acquired the sophisticated means necessary to cut to a minimum 'the time required for putting missiles into combat readiness'. Now if previous command and control procedures techniques had not been sufficiently advanced to permit missiles' preparation and dispatch within comparatively limited time conceptions, then two conclusions follow: (a) The Soviet deterrent must have been even more vulnerable to extinction from hostile strikes than anybody might assume; (b) And, if so, then speculation that the Soviet Union might at any time have contemplated embracing first strike conceptions becomes very questionable. The USSR would under those conditions have reason to fear that the US intelligence/ information-processing/reaction time equation would permit a countering US strike before the contemplated Soviet strike ever got off the ground. (!)

The debate contributions surveyed below are therefore approached primarily with a view to their relevance to: the acquisition by the USSR of global perspectives and capabilities as concerns both strategic and interventionary-type forces (the actual procurements are analysed in Chapters 4 and 5); and to the evolution of the military's role in society, and its relationship with the Party (see also Chapter 8).

For purpose of simplification the debate contributions will both here and in the following chapter be divided into the following headings: The Strategic Missile Forces; Nuclear-Oriented Land and Air Forces; Naval Developments; The Military in Society.

THE STRATEGIC MISSILE FORCES

The priority development of these under Khrushchev[12] may be divided into two periods, prior to 1961–62, and after that date.

The first period can be seen as that of naively enthusiastic missile research and procurement policies. The degradation factors which detracted from missile effectiveness and reliability were, as intimated, probably not fully appreciated at first, and therefore encouraged over-optimistic expectations. Nevertheless, even over-optimistic expectations had to acknowledge the limited capacity of the early missile procurements vis-à-vis American capabilities. There resulted the partly illusory strength assertions, which were intended to psycho-logically bolster the deterrent image, and which we referred to in Chapter 1.

Research was also extended to the field of anti-ballistic missile development. Over-optimistic prognostications probably caused this to be seen as providing the missing link in the drive towards an imminent, secure, deterrent. If one considers the tentative BMD deployment of 1962,[13] and remembers lead-time considerations, then it seems reasonable to believe that Khrushchev entertained ex-pectancies of success by 1961, at the latest. Expectancies of success would of course have been further encouraged by a consideration of the supplementary benefits hoped for from the Caribbean missile installations.

One might see evidence for such optimism in an early 1962 Supreme Soviet decree: '(article 1): Starting in the academic year 1962–63 preconscription training for students in secondary schools and specialized secondary educational institutions is cancelled.'[14] This could be interpreted as reflecting satisfaction with military achievements and as being the first step towards consequent re-allocations in favour of the sluggish domestic economy (along the lines of Khrushchev's late 1964 efforts).[15]

But complacent estimates of the Soviet deterrent value were already being challenged by the large US strategic procurement increments of the early 1960's.[16] The optimistic house of cards was tumbling; the 1962 Cuban events drove the point home.

The second period saw the foundations attended to. Attention was directed at increasing the survivability prospects of existing missiles, through silo hardening, through launch mobility and dispersal schemes, and through the perfecting of control procedures.[17] This evaluation is supported by three considerations (which also reflect on the scale of the re-directed efforts). The first is negative; it is the lack of any ascertainable significant fund-diverting in favour of new military endeavours. The second may be found in the increased military budget allocations of 1963 and 1964 (see Chapter 8). The third relates to the apparent hiatus in BMD deployment which followed the initial procurements.[18] The released funds went to the protection and qualitative improvement of the missile forces.

The BMD hiatus probably also reflected Soviet appreciation of the unfavourable early cost-exchange ratios (of relative defensive-offensive systems' cost) associated with BMD. This appreciation must have provided a supplementary factor in the determining of priorities. But the hiatus serves to highlight the central interest of the later Khrushchev period.

Khrushchev's late 1964 espousal of a drastic shift of resources in favour of the domestic economy may be seen to reflect his belief that the second period had come to an end, and that the deterrent had been secured. This does not validate the belief of Wolfe and others. Domestic needs were clearly such as made Khrushchev intent on their satisfaction. But the intent was based on contemporary necessities as he saw them. It did not indicate satisfaction regarding the lack of more extensive counter-force capabilities. This interpretation emerges as the soundest reading of both his early speeches and associates, and of his later articles and procurement authorizations.

The first period may be symbolized by the following Malinovsky quotes. In 1959 he described as 'twaddle' the contention that war between major powers could be 'limited' or 'local'.[19] And in 1960 he elaborated on the complementary theme of the great destructive power of Soviet missiles.[20] It was contended that the Soviet Union 'could literally wipe off the face of the earth any country or countries attacking' her.[21] Or, as formulated by the 21st CPSU Congress: 'The traditional invulnerability of America is liquidated for all time'.

There was Khrushchev's 1960 assertion that the USSR had achieved a nuclear balance of cataclysmic implications, and that she could now afford and would henceforth pursue the policy of 'maximum retaliation' as her deterrent.[22] And Malinovsky followed up, by exhibiting the confidence in this deterrent which was inherent in the acceptance of US theories: 'the best means of defence is warning the opponent of our strength and readiness to destroy him at the first attempt to commit an act of aggression'.[23]

But the flaunting of Soviet capabilities subsided as its implicit claim to parity and part-superiority began to look more and more suspect. McNamara's calm assertion to the Senate Armed Service Committee of early 1962, that the US was 'fully capable' of destroying such 'Soviet targets' as it might select, carried considerably more conviction than Malinovsky's riposte:[24] 'Such boasting is to say the least reckless. Let us go so far as to grant that the forces are equal. We are prepared to agree to this in order not to fan war psychosis. But if our forces are indeed equal, the Americans should draw the correct conclusions from this and pursue an intelligent policy'. The USSR was still declared able to 'wipe out any target' and to possess forces 'sufficient to destroy any potential enemy'. He shortly thereafter felt compelled to return to the point: 'Do not touch us, imperialists, and do not threaten us, because you will fall into the pit you are so carefully preparing for us and will be consumed without trace in a nuclear hell'.[25]

A subtle difference could be detected between the uneasy demands for peaceful co-existence 'which precludes war'[26] and more confident later assertions like (1965): 'peaceful co-existence . . . is . . . an objective necessity resulting from the contemporary relation of forces between the two systems'.[27] The difference might be seen as a milder version of the graphic disparity between the blustering Soviet reaction to the 1958 Lebanon events and the more purposeful response to the 1969 events in that country. Whatever the value of this inference, public preoccupations were certainly to change with the crumbling of the camouflage increments to Soviet capabilities.

The mid-'50's had, as mentioned, seen hints that the USSR's strategic inferiority was of a scale to demand a first strike for any success to be envisaged.[28] And as late as 1962 there were warnings of US threats to strike first, warnings which invited the inference that the USSR might not survive such an attack, and might therefore have to strike first herself if she received relevant intelligence.[29] Marshal Sokolovsky's comment[30] to US discussions of counter-force and city sparing strategies was illuminating. He declared that such strategy and target choice discussions depended 'to a considerable extent on the delivery systems available, and their numbers'. He explained that systems that might be inaccurate were ineffectual 'against small targets like missile launch pads or airfields'. And, anyway, systems limited in numbers (of delivery-vehicles) could 'only be used against large targets like cities'. This is of course a concise characterization of Soviet capabilities prior to 1961–62.

The endeavours to escape from this quandary, and to secure the deterrent,[31] proceeded apace. Sokolovsky himself provided evidence with regard to later achievements (and aspirations):[32] 'missiles, which under today's conditions are absolute weapons, are emplaced in nearly invulnerable underground bases, on submarines, etc.'. He emphasized that 'the trend towards increasing this invulnerability is growing all the time'.

Previous admonitions on the need to protect against, and prepare for, nuclear eventualities had related primarily to land forces. This was the context in which the requirements for mobility and flexibility had been stressed.[33] But now it was missiles to which the admonitions were directed.

The new orientation was soon followed up: 'Foreign military analysts' were said to be 'talking through their hats' when they claimed that 'Soviet nuclear rockets are highly vulnerable and (therefore) designed for a first and not a counter-strike'; 'An aggressor would be unable to destroy all the counter-strike means with his first salvo, for these means . . . are dispersed. A considerable part of them is constantly on the move. Another, even greater part, is in a state of almost instant readiness to take off. It is physically impossible – to knock out all the counter-strike means simultaneously'.[34]

It remains of course doubtful that all this had yet been accomplished. Thus for example the previously referred-to 1966 article by

Marshal Krylov clearly indicates that 'instant readiness to take off' was not a quality the missile forces had acquired by 1963.[35]

But although articles a few years later were to carry greater conviction in assigning second-strike qualities to the missile forces, articles such as the above nevertheless serve as focusing the then current concern and endeavour.

NUCLEAR-ORIENTED LAND AND AIR FORCES

Previous sections invited scepticism regarding exaggerated inferences from the differing emphases of various articles. By assigning some credit to Khrushchev for re-organization schemes implemented during his tenure of office, and by granting some credence to his statements of concern for general armed forces efficiency, our investigation tends to minimize contradictions. The apparent differences, such as between the 1963–64 mass armies advocacies and Khrushchev's late 1964 contrary endeavours, may therefore be said to reflect primarily on the differences between purely military considerations, and considerations based on the wider concerns of the economy as a whole. The military emerges as a powerful interest-group, but as contained within the Party-dominated hierarchy, and with ultimate aspirations that are basically complementary to, rather than contradictory to, those of the Party establishment (see also Chapter 8).

The approach here pursued leads as mentioned to the assigning to Khrushchev of much of the credit for the transformation of the forces' perception and capabilities, from traditional to nuclear-oriented. The restrictions and priorities asserted by him, on the basis of his wider-ranging considerations, are seen as having resulted in a faster transformation than would have been possible on the basis of traditional partisan military considerations. By removing the cushions inherent in these, by cutting back force level and re-allocating funds, he enforced a stream-lining and modernization process which might not otherwise have occurred with the same pace and urgency.

He had enjoyed considerable military experience, and he had apparently established good rapport with military commanders. From this one may infer an understanding of military requirements and needs.[36] It was with his rise to power that one saw the first moves towards the building of mobile and flexible forces with considerable independent nuclear survival prospects and capacities.

The early re-organizations of the air defence forces and of the transport and logistics services have already been mentioned. Testimony with regard to armour further illustrates the efforts: 'The Soviet High Command apparently has proven to its own satisfaction that armour and the Guderian designs of battle are ideal for fighting a war under nuclear and non-nuclear conditions'.[37] As evidenced in Chapter 5, the apparent factor of tradition is in this context superficial. The operative word is 'nuclear'. And the crystallizing of this, and of the inherent awareness of the need for dispersion and mobility, was to become more pronounced as the 1960's progressed.

The military concern may be seen as epitomized by the following quote, cited by M. Mackintosh:[38] 'Even the appearance of atomic and hydrogen weapons and . . . rockets cannot ensure the swift destruction of the armed forces, and consequently a swift conclusion to the war, . . . A war cannot and will not be fought with these means alone'; Such weapons might in fact, it was declared, 'prolong' rather than shorten a war's duration.

While such expressions became more scarce during the following years, due to the emphasis on missiles and deterrence needs, they were nevertheless reflected also in Khrushchev's crucial 1960 promulgation. His espousal of a massive retaliation doctrine was (as quoted in Chapter 1) followed by explicit commitments in favour of the qualitative improvement of the older service branches. He promised that the qualitative improvements would more than offset quantitative restrictions.

These efforts gained impetus from the Kennedy administration's acceptance of McNamara's 'flexible response' doctrine and the consequent augmenting of US conventional and intermediate range capabilities. If only because of the resultant posture of US forces, one could now no longer rule out low-scale aggression. The argument that any direct confrontation between the super-powers would inevitably escalate to a nuclear conflict left considerable conceptual flaws as to the initial stages of the confrontation, – at least as long as one did not care to admit that one's own side might feel obliged to initiate the actual nuclear exchange. And this odious implication could only really be circumvented by securing, on the US pattern, forces capable of lower-scale responses. 1962–63 articles clearly reflected this need.[39] They also reflected the complementary need to be capable of rendering assistance to favoured national liberation movements. (They refrained from specific commitments; but the need had theoretical relevance, even if it may have had less practical substance.)[40]

The logical conclusion(s) could not be brought to fruition while doubts remained concerning the efficacy of the essential shield of a visible secure deterrent, and while economic restrictions remained necessary. The 'odious implication', all the more odious for its inhibiting of freedom and flexibility of action and response, had to be tolerated, – until the visible deterrent became such as to inspire confidence that it could not be challenged. A capacity to engage in medium-scale conflicts not supplemented by an effective deterrent could not be utilized without inviting destruction. An effective deterrent without a capacity to engage in lower-scale conflicts is inimical to your interests but it does at least guarantee against destruction. The priority concern defined itself. But Moscow was clearly aware of longer-term requirements, and the groundwork was, as indicated, laid.

A report of the principles of nuclear war, as approved by the Khrushchev-dominated 22nd Party Congress,[41] is worth quoting: 1. 'War . . . will inevitably assume the character of a nuclear missile war'. Consequently '*nuclear missiles constitute the basis of the fighting power of all branches of the USSR forces*'. Therefore 'we have created a new type of troops, the Strategic Rockets troops'; 2. 'Nuclear weapons . . . make it possible to achieve military results in the briefest time at any distance and over a huge territory'; 3. But 'the decisive role of nuclear missiles in war does not lessen the importance of other types of weapons. Complete and *decisive victory can only be achieved through joint actions*; nuclear missile warfare will be waged by mass armies of many millions'; 4. 'The very first mass nuclear strikes are capable of determining to an extraordinary degree the entire course of war'. Hence constant *preparedness, intensified training and mobility* became essential.

This may be supplemented by the following quotes,[42] equally representative of the Khrushchev-dominated consensus:[43] What counted was 'not the number of soldiers, but the quantity and quality of missile-nuclear weapons, rocket artillery, missile-launching aircraft and ships, especially atomic submarines, and also other technical means of combat', as well as '*nuclear stores in general*'.[44] On the other hand, while the 'strategic means will play the decisive role in the defeat of the enemy', there will be a 'theatre offensive following nuclear strikes . . . airborne landings in great depth and rapid advances (of infantry and armour) with the support of the air force (will) complete the destruction of the surviving armed forces of the enemy'.[45] Finally: 'the offensive constitutes the basic method of warfare . . . only a decisive offensive can bring victory'.[46]

The need for flexibility of operations under nuclear conditions, for mobility, is a recurring theme: '*Manoeuvre has become the basic feature*' *of any utilization of nuclear strikes.*[47] Another, interrelated, theme is the championing of more offensively-oriented thinking: 'in view of the striking power and range of present day weapons Soviet military doctrine regards the strategic defence as an unacceptable form of strategic operations in modern war'.[48]

Such quotes do not only reflect on the stream-lining and modernization of the armed forces. They certainly illustrate the development of a basis for flexible operational concepts and patterns, and thus for conflict varieties outside the restrictive all-or-nothing mould. But they furthermore reflect tendencies not consistent with the non-nuclear views of interventionary and flexible response forces which prevailed in the west.

The operative criteria may be summarized as: (a): An emphasis on nuclear capabilities not restricted to a strategic context, and in fact intimately associated with (b): Force units flexible not only with regard to independent survival capabilities but with regard to inter-service combined action potentials.

With the apparent support of both Khrushchev and his Minister of Defence, the Armed Forces were forced to transform themselves from World War II conceptual hostages to smaller but far more potent service branches and units totally oriented towards the task of combat under nuclear conditions.[49] As clearly demonstrated in Chapters 3 and 5, the operative criteria of (a) and (b) were to gain rather than lose in emphasis during the 1960's. By 1970 the Soviet interventionary and other forces had acquired considerable and varied flexible response capabilities, but near-exclusively within a nuclear context. This will be treated more extensively in later sections.

It here suffices to follow up a point previously mentioned. Khrushchev's policy of extensive personnel-cutbacks and cost-consciousness did, in the context of his own emphasis on increased fire-power and combat capacities, inevitably result in the squeeze which forced the drastic modernization process indicated above. One might well judge the resultant squeeze to have been so severe as to necessarily entail the early nuclearization of the non-strategic forces, at a time when the eventual inevitability of this process appeared not yet to be generally realized.

c

NAVAL DEVELOPMENTS

Early 1962 had seen confirmation of the Navy's definite upgrading and of her inclusion among Services assigned nuclear capabilities (see end of Chapter 1).[50] The assigning to the Navy of strategic capabilities related to the described awareness of deterrent-credibility deficiencies. It furthered the efforts towards dispersal which were component parts of the assigning of second-strike qualities to the deterrent. But it not only reflected temporary necessities. It soon became evident that it also represented, or occasioned, a more far-reaching awareness of naval potentials.

With regard to strategic implications, the subsequent period saw a number of pointed assertions and intimations about the value which the US derived from her fleet. A post-Cuba article[51] on the 'Turkish-US accord at the end of January to liquidate nuclear bases on Turkish soil, and similar developments with regard to Italy' ('following the settlement of the crisis in the Caribbean'), is illustrative. It emphasized that the partial US withdrawal 'by no means' signified 'the first stage of disarmament', but to the contrary 'a process of modernization of NATO's armaments'. The forces involved were declared to be more than offset by the new world-wide 'sea-based mobile launching sites' (Polaris) then being built. These were explained to represent not only an augmenting of US strategic power but a securing of this by making it less dependent on the whim of political allies.

The implications were pursued by Admiral Gorshkov.[52] After lampooning some US naval policies, such as the construction of aircraft carriers, which he evidently considered as sitting ducks, he went on to warn that: 'When Kennedy took over, the target date for building forty-one rocket-armed submarines was moved up three years. The number of submarines under construction in 1961 and 1962 was increased from 5 to 10. Beginning late in 1963 it is intended to commission one submarine every month. At the same time the construction of atomic anti-submarines is under way at an accelerated rate. Whereas previously three such crafts were started a year, in 1962 eight of them were started'. He noted that 'the Soviet homeland' had given the Navy 'the best rocket and nuclear weapons' (viz. above). But there was a clear implication that more would have to be procured.

The previous ignoring of naval potentials, presumably caused by a combination of strategic conceptions and economic necessities (see Chapters 1 and 5), was at an end. The use of the US Navy's dispositions as a guinea-pig qualitative yardstick for decisions of procurements emphasis and priorities not only reflected the US' status as opposing super-power. It also reflected on the scale of the naval efforts initiated and contemplated in Moscow.

These are treated more thoroughly in later sections, but it is proper here to mention also the complement to the building up of naval strategic capabilities. This is the emergence of interventionary-type forces. Their emergence may of course in itself be seen as complementing the general emphasis on developing mobile, independently sustained, units, attuned to the needs of potential nuclear conflicts, and with maximum operative flexibility.

On the one hand Sokolovsky proceeded from the afore-mentioned dismissal of the Navy's effective role during World War II to define the tasks of the 'new' Navy as follows: he identified 'The missions which the Navy will be assigned to perform in a future war' as long range; – 'to give battle to enemy forces at sea and (at their) bases' and 'to disrupt enemy ocean and sea transport'.[53] On the other hand there was the appearance soon after Khrushchev's ousting of 'high-speed landing craft', and 'marines' whose equipment 'included missiles'.[54] The interrelationship between the new strategy, which envisaged action against enemy bases, and the appearance of amphibious capabilities, is self-evident.

All in all, it is difficult to see Marshal Chuikov's assertion (that Western powers had acknowledged the ruinous effects of 'one-sided' military theories and were hence building up their ground forces together with their strategic capabilities) as reflecting more than at most a prod relating to allocatory decisions. It may in fact merely have reflected Party convictions. Khrushchev's orientation must, despite its overriding priority, surely be seen as moving away from, rather than establishing stereotyped dogmas.

THE MILITARY IN SOCIETY

Considering the survey of Khrushchev-related data in Chapter 1, as well as the extensive treatment of post-Khrushchev changes and developments in later Chapters (3 and 8), there is no need to dwell long on the theme here also. But it must again be noted that it represented the most visibly sensitive military-oriented topic of the

Khrushchev years. Attention must be redirected to the developing military frustration and concern regarding Khrushchev's reluctance to delineate clearly the admitted necessary – if limited – field of professional military autonomy. It must be reiterated that the vagueness of the Khrushchev-associated aspirations towards a more egalitarian yet Party-dominated society could not fail to cause unease in circles in which the professional desiderata affecting policy decisions were judged paramount.

ECONOMIC CONSIDERATIONS

These have been mentioned above as providing a main rationale for Khrushchev's emphasis on deterrence and strategic sufficiency. We shall return later in more detail to the military's involvement in economic affairs and related considerations (Chapter 8), but some evidence must be presented at this stage.

Khrushchev himself admitted the 'guns and butter' quandary. This was most explicit in a February 1964 speech: 'If we accepted an unreasonable reduction of military expenditures, if we started to build more housing and forgot about defence, we would be like blind men who cannot assess the real situation correctly'.[55] The implication worked both ways, and it was clear that while an 'unreasonable' reduction in military outlays was unacceptable, so also was any 'unreasonable' reduction in housing. Thomas Wolfe, who quotes the same speech, put it this way: 'In light of these words there was a palpably hollow ring to Khrushchev's denial in the same speech that the Soviet Union was being "forced to reduce armaments and armed forces because of difficulties in economic developments" '.[56]

One may further point for example to Sokolovsky's assertion that even the greater powers could not afford to keep such standing forces in times of peace as would be needed in times of war.[57] In other words: while one would of course ensure the existence of a strong professional core, one would have to rely on mobilization and extraordinary allocations to bring the forces up to a full-war standard. The inherent need for civilian training and civilian preparation for war-time roles and mobilization, was not resolved to the satisfaction of the military during Khrushchev's tenure. And it was hence another factor working against their acceptance of his tenets.

But as concerns the burden of the military on the national economy, it was, as our quotes have indicated, clearly admitted by Khrushchev and his associates. This leads naturally to the question as to how the Brezhnev-Kosygin regime later succeeded in closing the US–USSR disparity without resorting to drastically increased military budgets; why they succeeded when he did not? The answer may tentatively be indicated by the following.

On the one hand there were no immediate changes regarding the strategic balance; ABM developments remained in abeyance until the forthcoming advent of more favourable cost-exchange ratios. And allocated funds continued to be diverted to a higher priority ICBM procurement program aimed at parity with the US.

At the same time, as regards non-strategic systems and the development of interventionary-type forces, the lack of obvious increments in funds indicate that the necessary research allocations had already been enacted by Khrushchev. One must remember that the program was never precipitate, and what may be termed sizeable interventionary forces did not really emerge until 1970, – although the first procurements had been secured by the mid 1960's. Yet here continuing research and deployment (however gradual) requirement may be judged to have been as financially demanding as were the initiating efforts.

If one views the effective procurement potentials of the respective US–USSR military budgets as being of similar orders (a conclusion which will receive support in our later analysis), and if one acknowledges that no significant Soviet military budget increases occurred (this will be supported in the same analysis), then only one further factor remains to account for the closing of the disparities. And that is the Vietnam War.

Sources close to the US Administration have calculated that the cost of the Vietnam War amounted to 3 per cent of the US GNP and nearly one-third of the military budget. And they have shown that force personnel augmentations necessitated by the war amounted to between one-third and one-quarter of the total, depending on whether the basis excluded or included the troops engaged in Vietnam.[58]

There can be little doubt as to the relative correctness of these figures. And there can therefore be little doubt that in her so-called 'fight for freedom' in Vietnam the main US achievement was the final destruction of her own unchallengable world military superiority. Henceforth the fiction of comparable Soviet power was to become a reality. And, as will be demonstrated later, this reality of comparative parity was not of a kind which could be altered with ease by either side during the immediately following years.

NOTES

1. Wolfe, Thomas W., *Soviet Strategy at the Crossroads*, Harvard University Press, 1964; see also Wolfe, T. W., *Soviet Strategic Thought in Transition*, Rand Corporation Paper, May, 1964.

2. Rockett, Frederick C., *An Illustrative Study: Strategic Evacuation Plan*, Ch. V, A Report, The Hudson Institute, 1967.

3. The early post-war and later Eisenhower-Dulles deterrence postures were never as fragile, since the Soviet Union did not at the time have such counter-forces as would entail the suggested 'incalculable fear' syndrome. Neither was there ever an equal dearth of intermediate-type weapon systems.

4. As Garder, Michel (*A History of the Soviet Army*, Pall Mall Press, 1966, p. 207) asserted: 'There is no doubt that obsession with a preventive attack by the US must be very real in the USSR, which still has vivid memories . . . of 1941 . . .'.

5. See *Krasnaya Zvezda* issues the fortnight following, and referring to, the mid 1967 7-day war in the Near East. And see Timofeev, K., 'The Role of Navies in Imperialist Policy', *New Times*, 28th November, 1969.

6. *Ogoniok*, No. 25, June, 1965; *The Military Balance 1968–69*, ISS, London; and Chapter 5.

7. See e.g. *Izvestia*, 19 May, 1963.

8. *Pravda*, 29 April, 1962. Gorshkov's testimony regarding some emerging Naval strategic role and capabilities in *Pravda* 2 February 1962 pushes the time-estimate of the political decision back even further.

9. *Pravda*, 2 February, 1962, *ibid*. Compare the implications of this to earlier conceptions, as typified by Sokolovsky's reported earlier comment to Gorshkov that the Navy had become a 'totally obsolete' service branch under modern war conditions. See Giese, Fritz, Lt. Cmdr., October, 1959, '*Wehrkunde*', art., reprinted as 'Behind the Scenes of the Soviet Admiralty', *Military Review*, Fort Leavenworth, May, 1960.

10. See Chapter 9; and see e.g. Michel Tatu's admirable *Le Pouvoir en l'URSS*, Bernard Grasset, Paris, 1967.

11. *Pravda*, 19 November, 1966.

12. *Pravda*, 15 January, 1960. Note: The Strategic Rocket Troops became a separate service in December 1959.

13. Dr. J. S. Foster's (US Defence Dept.) 5 August, 1969 testimony to the House of Representatives Foreign Affairs Sub-committee, revealed that the US had evidence of tentative ABM deployments around Leningrad as early as 1962. See also *Krasnaya Zvezda*, 13 November, 1963; and *Pravda*, 19 November, 1964 for premature but interesting capability-claims.

14. *Vedomosti Verkhovnovo Soveta*, No. 7, 16 February 1962, p. 195; *Izvestia*, 15 December, 1963.

15. *Izvestia*, 15 December, 1963 and *Pravda*, 2 October 1964. The economy was affected by the drop in birthrates during the war and the consequent decrease in the number of 18 year olds available through 1960–70. The resulting premium on manpower did of course equally affect the military. One must caution against the view that civilian economy demands alone constituted sufficient reason for the realignment.

16. *Mirovaya Ekonomika i Mezhdunarodnie Otnoshenie*, Moscow, 1962, No. 3, p. 90; *Ekonomika i Kapitalisticheskie Strani* 1962, Moscow, 1963, pp. 18 and 30; *The Military Balance 1969–70*, ISS, London, 1969, presents a historical table of the quantitative growth of respective strategic missile strengths.

17. See Glagolev and Larinov, *International Affairs*, No. 11, November, 1963, p. 32, and assertions and retroactive implications of: *Pravda/Izvestia*, 4 July, 1965, and *Pravda* 19 November, 1966.

18. See testimony by Dr. Foster, *op. cit.*, and see Chapter 4 for extensive treatment.

19. *Pravda*, 4 February, 1959. Quoted also by W. D. Jacobs, 'Marshal Malinovsky and Missiles', *Military Review*, Fort Leavenworth, June 1960, pp. 15–20. Jacob's article also provides evidence which encourages scepticism concerning Kolkowicz' classification of Malinovsky as not in rapport with Khrushchev (see Chapter 1).

20. *Pravda*, 23 February, 1960.

21. *Krasnaya Zvezda*, 20 January, 1960.

22. *Pravda*, 15 January, 1960.

23. Malinovsky, *'Bditelno Stoyat na Strazhe Mira'*, Moscow 1962, p. 25. See also Garthoff, *op. cit.*

24. *Pravda*, 24 January, 1962.

25. *Pravda*, 23 February, 1962.

26. *Pravda*, 17 January, 1962.

27. Bochkarov and Sidelnikov, *Krasnaya Zvezda*, 21 January, 1965.

28. Emelin, *op. cit.*, p. 131.

29. *Krasnaya Zvezda*, 11 May, 1962. Article by Col. I. Sidelnikov which also contains an excellent summary of Khrushchev's doctrine.

30. Sokolovsky, *op. cit.*, 2nd edition, p. 84; see also 3rd edition, p. 235. And compare with Sushko and Kondratkov, *op. cit.*, p. 147, regarding the time when the USSR *had* finally acquired the capabilities necessary to permit such luxuries.

31. See *Pravda*, 11 February, 1963 for interesting post-Cuban comment by Y. Zhukov which clearly reflects (enforced) awareness of US strategic power and capabilities.

32. Sokolovsky, *op. cit.*, 2nd edition, p. 84.

33. Thus also those contained in Emelin, *op. cit.*, p. 131.

34. Glagolev and Larionov, *op. cit.*, p. 32 (article on 'Soviet Defence Might and Peaceful Coexistence').

35. *Pravda*, 11 November, 1966, *op. cit.*

36. R. Kolkowicz, *op. cit.*, pp. 224–238 (see also Chapter 1).

37. L'Heretique, *The British Army Review*, September, 1959, *op. cit.*

38. Quote taken from the *Military Herald*, June, 1958; see M. Mackintosh, 'Soviet Strategy in World War III', *Survival*, July–August, 1960, pp. 149–158.

39. See e.g. Kazakov, D., Major, in *Kommunist Vooruzhiennikh Sil*, No. 10, May, 1963.

40. *Izvestia*, 11 December, 1963 (illustrative article by Chief of General Staff, Marshal Biriusov).

41. As per I. Sidelnikov, Colonel, *Krasnaya Zvezda*, 11 May, 1962 (stress added).

42. From Sokolovsky, *op. cit.*; and S. N. Kozlov, Maj. Gen. (with Maj. Gen. Smirnov and Cols. Baz and Sidorov), *O Sovetskoi Voennoi Nauke*, 2nd edition, Voenizdat, Moscow, 1964.

43. Evidence for this may be seen in the wide publicity they were accorded. Thus e.g. Col. Korotkov (in 'The Development of Soviet Military Theory in the Post-War Years', *Voenno-Istorichesky Zhurnal*, No. 4, April, 1964, pp. 39–50), who described Sokolovsky's book as 'the most fundamental one'. Quote found (also) in Wolfe, 'Soviet Strategy . . . ', *op. cit.*, p. 268. And see same for treatment of the process: Kozlov's book's 1st edition evinced lingering scepticism re Khrushchev's deterrence/strategic supremacy doctrine; it was criticized for this by Sokolovsky; it thereafter soon reappeared in 2nd edition evidently more closely reflecting the operative consensus.

44. Kozlov, et al., *op. cit.*, pp. 297 and 390.

45. Sokolovsky, *op. cit.*, 2nd edition, p. 374.

46. Kozlov, *op. cit.*, p. 249.

47. *Krasnaya Zvezda*, 6 June, 1964, Col. Vorobev. (Stress added.)

48. *Kommunist Vooruzhiennikh Sil*, No. 3, February 1963, pp. 27–28 (Col. Gen. Shtemenko).

49. *Pravda*, 15 February, 1964 (Khrushchev).

50. *Pravda*, 23 February, 1962 (Malinovsky). See also Air Marshal Vershinen's *Pravda*, 19 November, 1964, article, for more specific references concerning the Air Force.

51. *Pravda*, 11 February, 1963.

52. *Izvestia*, 19 May, 1963.

53. Sokolovsky, *op. cit.*, pp. 242–3, 3rd edition. See also p. 344.

54. *Ogonyok*, No. 25, June 1965, p. 47. And see Chapter 5. *N.B. NATO Letter*

No. 9, September, 1970, pp. 20–22, asserted that the initial tentative procurement of Alligator and Polosny class landing vessels (as well as the initial marine infantry formations) could in fact be dated to as early as 1963. This of course more than confirms our dating of the origin of the Naval expansion effort, as well as our assigning to Khrushchev of credit for its orientation.

55. *Pravda*, 15 February, 1964.
56. T. W. Wolfe, 'Soviet Strategy . . .', *op. cit.*, p. 152.
57. Sokolovsky, *op. cit.*, 2nd edition, p. 410.
58. A. C. Enthoven (Asst. Secretary of Defence for Systems Analysis and other Defence Department posts 1960–69) and K. Wayne Smith (Staff member Rand Corporation and Special Asst. to Secretary of Defence 1960–69): 'What Forces for NATO? And From Whom?', *Foreign Affairs*, October, 1969.

3

The Acquiring of Counter-force Capabilities; The Military Debates 1965–1972

These years may be divided into two periods, with the first running through 1955–66. This may be seen as the continuation of the late Khrushchev period, as the years when the Khrushchev-inspired programs were brought to fruition. It was furthermore a period defined within similar parameters to that of the late Khrushchev years; of greatest relevance to our concern is the fact that the economic obstacles to military procurement increments remained similar.

While the new regime pledged itself to 'strengthen the country's defence capability',[1] and to arm 'the Army and the Navy with the most modern weapons of warfare',[2] it nevertheless soon felt obliged to acknowledge the need for further if temporary financial cutbacks. Its main rationale was without doubt the need for ambitious new investment plans for the civilian economy (with emphasis placed on the needs of agriculture[3]). The 1965 military budget was cut by about 4 per cent. And it was made clear that Armed Forces personnel increases would not be contemplated.[4]

The military budget cuts may have been offset through administrative economies, resulting from the centralization of defence industries.[5] Or they may have resulted from cuts in research allocations to uncertain projects. One thinks of possible parallels to the post 1962 hiatus in BMD developments (caused by a combination of deterrent priorities and initially unfavourable cost-exchange ratios; see below for elaboration). Or the budget cuts might, of course, have been illusory; they may have been compensated for by increments of 'hidden investments', that is, military research allocations under other budgetary headings. But no concrete evidence can be found for this supposition.

Which ever resource saving device was utilized, it did not appear to be of major consequence. As will also be supported by later quotes, Khrushchev's basic policies appear to have been kept intact. One may again refer to the gradual nature of the further expansion of inter-ventionary-type forces after 1965; it was a natural progression from initial investment efforts under Khrushchev, and did not reflect qualitative change or innovation.

Tendencies towards a too pedantic and possibly counter-productive Party supervision of military professional concerns were bridled (see below), and new efforts were aimed at decreasing international tensions. The fact that an eased international atmosphere would minimize the sacrifices inherent in the securing of the deterrent and would allow hope for a minimum cost gradual approach may be presumed to have been a motivating factor, as it had been in previous years.

The USSR proposed to reduce east-west arms budgets by 10–15 per cent.[6] She alluded to the planned Soviet budget cuts, and suggested that some of the savings might be diverted into aid to under-developed countries. She proposed a withdrawal of troops from foreign soil, and asserted Soviet willingness with relation to the Warsaw Pact if the US was willing to reciprocate with relation to NATO. She also suggested that foreign bases be liquidated, nuclear proliferation be prevented, zones be denuclearized, troop reductions be initiated, and a NATO–Warsaw Pact non-aggression treaty be signed (with observation posts in the respective territories to secure against surprise attack). There was, finally, the ending of polemics with China, and the initiation of Soviet-Chinese border talks.

When the significant military budget increases of our second 'period' were initiated in 1966, it was at a time when they could be justified, through references to the increasing American commitment in South-East Asia (the Soviet allocatory increases paralleled those of the US), and to China's new anti-Soviet bellicosity. And it must be noted that the more steady post 1964 Soviet economic growth, and the easing of the agricultural situation, had by then made military demands more tolerable.

The 1966 change furthermore coincided with the securing of the deterrent, an achievement which inherently encouraged the determination to close the still-remaining 'strategic gap'. It also probably reflected the yearning for increased development and procurement allocations for the non-strategic forces, the desire to acquire the advantages entailed by such capabilities. There was now less fear of a back-lash offsetting increment of US allocations. The Vietnam expenditures were so high as to make potential US legislative approval of further allocatory diversions in favour of the military most unlikely (excepting situations of too obvious challenge). The Vietnam expenditures also meant that the US military budget percentage that could be allocated to more future-oriented research was decreased. The auguries were therefore favourable for the USSR.

Suslov's assertion of 1970,[7] and the credibility it commanded, encapsuled the changes of the immediately preceding years. He stated: 'We believe with legitimate pride that the mighty Soviet industry is *now* capable of solving the most difficult technical problems of our time, and of guaranteeing reliably the steady and rapid growth of our homeland's economic potential and of strengthening dependably its defence capacity'. Counter-force capabilities had been acquired and the Armed Forces were assuming a new air of confident assertiveness. The need for propaganda-inspired exaggerations had been diluted, and possibly eliminated.

The following analysis of debates and developments will adhere to the scheme of Chapter 2. That Chapter's comments and cautions regarding debate-contributions' relative value remain relevant.

THE STRATEGIC MISSILE FORCES

The developments of our first period were referred to in Chapter 1. The developments of the second period are treated extensively in the next chapter. A comparatively brief synopsis will therefore suffice at this point.

The first years saw the rounding-off and satisfaction of the late

Khrushchev concerns. The strategic Rocket Forces remained pre-eminent.[8] But quantitative developments still awaited their qualitative transferral into forces with second-strike characteristics and prospects.

The process was spelt out in emerging claims regarding its completion. Brezhnev's mid 1965 assertion may be seen in this light; the USSR was then said to utilize: 'The most diverse types of launching of strategic rockets – surface, underground and underwater, both stationary and movable, including self-propelled. . . .'; this was said to ensure 'the manoeuvrability and invulnerability of our Army's missile forces'.[9] It was elsewhere elaborated that: 'The underground silos are carefully concealed from air and space reconnaissance and are securely defended against nuclear blows'.[10] And, of equal importance: 'missile launching controls are in underground command posts equipped with the latest electronic apparatus'.[11]

The latter statement related to often expressed fears that command-and control procedures had not kept pace with the sophistication of the equipment, and that this entailed acute dangers of accidents.[12] But this accident proneness was not the only dangerous consequence of the early 'sophistication-gap' between controller and controlled. There was also the inherent dilemma that either one facilitated early weapon utilization and accepted greater accident risks, or else one added cumbersome extra control procedures which militated against fast reaction prospects, and which therefore entailed a great risk of extinction on the ground by an enemy strike.

Marshal Krylov's 1966 testimony implied that such a sophistication-gap had existed, and that the Soviet Union had chosen to counteract it through the lesser evil of extra control procedures – in spite of the implicit ramifications for second-strike confidence predictions. He revealed that the USSR had now acquired more sophisticated and secure launching control and command facilities, and concluded:[13] 'Important changes (have now) occurred . . . the time required for putting missiles into combat readiness had been reduced to a minimum'.

The accompanying confirmation that the USSR possessed 'missiles which can be launched from mobile installations'[14] re-emphasized the related programs of hardening and dispersal of launch sites. The composite picture which emerges strongly indicates that the USSR had by 1966 acquired a secure second-strike capability.

There remained the question as to whether secure was sufficent. The answer was evidently no. Previous chapters presented evidence why a progression from the securing of the deterrent to the acquisition of counter-force capabilities must long have been considered by Moscow as inherently necessary. But one ought perhaps also to assign some causal effects to the noted ever-increasing US embroilment in Vietnam and to the once again deteriorating relations with China.

Certainly it appears that the decision to match US capabilities and operational flexibility must have been taken by 1966. This conclusion is supported both by the increased military budgets and by the great missile procurement increments which followed (see Chapters 4 and 8).

The thereupon changing strategic equation was dramatized in 1967, when there appeared a book which seriously discussed various selective target theories.[15] The USSR was evidently no longer forced into an all-or-nothing dilemma (with the 'all' having to be targeted on cities for even that to be effective)[16] due to inferiority. She could now afford the luxury of entertaining more sophisticated scenarios.

The change was further dramatized by assertions that the maintenance of the technical-military 'superiority' required that quality replace (and not merely complement) cost as a selection criterion relating to advanced weapon systems;[17] by cautions lest 'political organizations and their leaders . . . fail to use the emerging possibilities' inherent in the revolution in military affairs;[18] and by tentative claims (all too reminiscent of the aspirations of American conservative quarters) regarding the need to possess arms offsetting not only actual, but also potential enemy capabilities.[19]

The problems of strategic parity were replacing those of inferiority; but however gratifying this premise, it introduced problems of considerable gravity.

One of these related to over-simplistic military aspirations for superiority. The aspirations appeared oblivious of the implications of the fact that the USSR's previous inferiority mirrored the discrepancy between American second-strike capabilities and Soviet lack thereof. By the late 1960's the degree of offsetting second-strike capabilities was such that it could not be doubted by either power. In view of the sophistication of the respective technological bases, this made aspirations by either power for the re-establishing or establishing of superiority quite illusory. The only ascertainable result from further sizable arms increments had by then become a mutually offsetting arms race; any other envisaged result had become most dubious.[20]

Another problem related to military pressure for influence vis-à-vis the new military-political action options which were made possible by the new capabilities. The greater the emerging options for political utilization of military-strategic facilities, the less could the military remain satisfied with their traditional concern for autonomy only in matters relating to organization and the instilling of martial values.

The need for 'correct and timely' evaluations, and the increasing importance of 'initial decisions'[21] was seen to demand the establishment of a new 'supreme military-political organ'.[22] This organ would furthermore have to extend its area of concern to matters of economy. Not only were there extensive military implications inherent in and affected by more and more 'political' decisions. There were also military repercussions from economic decisions which affected the 'political' ones. The most obvious of these repercussions was followed up by Col. Gen. Shtemenko: 'The National economy will not have much time to reorganize during the course of military action . . . everthing needed for work in wartime conditions must be prepared in advance'.[23]

While this, and further implications, will be returned to in later sections ('The Military in Society' below, and Chapters 5 and 8), the Party attitude must here be indicated. There was implicit acknowledgement that military and political policy repercussions were becoming increasingly intertwined. But the implication which was drawn appeared at first glance to be diametrically opposed: the tasks involved in modern war conceptions were seen to be so complex that their solution had to 'fall completely within the competence of the political leadership'; – 'modern weapons are such that the political leadership cannot let them escape its control'.[24]

Yet this did not necessarily entail acute military-Party friction. There were warnings that separatist tendencies could not be condoned, due to the political and economic consequences which they would involve.[25] But these warnings might well be seen merely as preventive, or as reflections of the traditional Party jealousy of its prerogatives. The extent of the already existing integration of the military leadership into the Party-dominated hierarchy (See Chapter 8) does not encourage the inferring of antagonism from superficial contradictions. It is relevant to note that the above 'Party' reactions were presented by Military officers. And they conceded the need for improved military-political policy co-ordinating facilities.[26]

In other words: apparently irreconcilable military-Party articles might better be seen as reflecting functionally different aspects, audiences or situations. To the extent that policy-making (as opposed to executional or operational) decisions were arrived at within the integrated hierarchy, and to the extent that basic conceptual or programmatic differences did not appear to exist, to that extent must one caution against inferring antagonisms.

NUCLEAR-ORIENTED LAND AND AIR FORCES

The operative criteria of efforts undertaken during the Khrushchev years were in Chapter 2 defined as evolving towards:

(a) An emphasis on nuclear capabilities not restricted to a strategic context, and in fact intimately associated with

(b) Force units flexible not only with regard to independent survival capabilities but with regard to inter-service combined action potentials.

Developments during the latter sixties may be seen as a natural progression from, or evolution of, these criteria. They were molded by the squeeze between economically-determined personnel stringency and the political acceptance of the need for improved capabilities and greater flexibility. The squeeze was, as mentioned previously, at least in part responsible for the concentration on versatile forces which would be able to utilize the potentials of nuclear technology.

There was initially a straightforward following-up of previous efforts. Air Force developments testified to the role of missile technology (1965): missiles were said to have become 'the basic type of weapon of the strategic bombers, fighter-bombers, and all-weather fighter interceptors'.[27] *'All branches of the Soviet Armed Forces'* were in fact said to have been assigned *'nuclear rocket weapons,* perfected electronic equipment, and other material of the newest type'.[28] By 1970 Grechko could testify that the technical equipment of the Forces had undergone a radical change; that the Army had received far greater firepower per unit; and that it had acquired much increased mobility in general, as well as in conflict 'under atomic war conditions' (the peacetime simulation techniques were not specified). The fact that the core of the Air Force now consisted of all-weather and supersonic missile-armed planes[29] was indicative of the general situation, and not exceptional.

Superior 'speed, cross-country ability, durability and weapon capacity' became the by-word of the land forces;[30] the Air Force followed this up with the dictum that *all* pilots be capable of handling the most advanced planes from unsurfaced strips, regardless of adverse weather conditions.[31]

The stress on internal service flexibility was paralleled by increasing stress on the capacity to initiate and co-ordinate 'joint military operations' which involved different branches and services of the forces. The need for training and manoeuvre co-ordination and flexibility was as a consequence to receive prime attention.[32] This resulted in the placing of a premium on commander and troop education and specialization. Discipline and general capabilities were no longer enough. Expertise and special skills were becoming necessary rather than merely desirable.[33]

But this had the side-effect of increasing the difficulties associated with potentially necessary mobilizations. As troop sophistication demands increased, so did the training time needed before 'raw' peasants or townfolk could be inserted to augment or replenish ranks. And as the era came to entail decreased prospects for long mobilization periods, so there arose an increased need for extensive pre-mobilization training of the populace.

The Party's acceptance of the need for improved military-political-economic co-ordination was instrumental in the solving of the mobilization problems. The solution was to be one of the more pregnant novelties of the late 1960's. Its evolution was reflected by claims that previous distinctions between front and rear had become anomalies in the nuclear age: 'war will become all-embracing, intercontinental . . . the former distinctions between front and rear will no longer be preserved. . . . All branches of the Armed Forces will be required for total victory. . . . Everything needed . . . must be prepared in advance'.[34] It soon became clear that the 'everything' included the intensified training of civilians for insertion into wartime roles. This will be returned to below (the complementary interdependence between strategic considerata and investment and allocatory policies[35] is focused on in Chapter 8). But it must be noted that extensive programs to this end were initiated by 1968.

NAVAL DEVELOPMENTS

Naval procurement and matériel developments are analysed in Chapter 5. This section will therefore restrict itself to a presentation of some of the illuminating or explicatory pronouncements which accompanied the process of naval expansion.

It was soon made clear that the naval expansion would be continued by the Brezhnev-Kosygin regime. And it was made clear that US naval capabilities were indeed seen as the qualitative yardstick: 'More than one-third of the strategic nuclear offensive weapons in the possession of the US and NATO armed forces belong to the American Navy.... That is why our Navy ... is playing an ever-greater role in strengthening our country's ... might'.[36]

The evolution of the Soviet Navy towards a strategic equivalent to that of the US Navy, with its inherent second-strike advantages of dispersion and mobility, was confirmed by the early 1965 flaunting of the first submarine-fired strategic missiles.[37] Both the commitment and its irreversibility could by 1970 be accepted as indubitable; the surface cruisers then being built were so totally oriented towards missile and nuclear capacities that they no longer retained even a semblance of conventional armaments![38]

Therein lay the main qualitative difference between it and the quantitatively superior US Navy. The combat orientation, and the much more recent commissioning, of most of the Soviet vessels, certainly lessened remaining Soviet naval inferiority.[39]

Marshal Sokolovsky had defined the 'new' Navy's main tasks as long-range, directed both against enemy transports and Navies and against enemy bases.[40] He had noted that naval activities should no longer necessarily be contingent on land developments.[41] And he had defined the means, to the achieving of the tasks, as strikes from missile-carrying surface vessels co-ordinated with action by missile submarines and missile-carrying planes;[42] 'great possibilities' were seen to arise from the combination of a Soviet Navy 'with nuclear weapons (in general), atomic missile submarines, and long-range missile aviation'.[43] Naval fronts should furthermore be able to 'complete the destruction of enemy forces', 'taking advantage of the results of missile blows of strategic significance'; they should be able to 'occupy (the enemy's) territory'. Where possible, or appropriate, the Navy should correlate its actions with land and air fronts, but it should be capable of independent action.[44]

Sokolovsky's definitions of tasks and means commanded acceptance through the remainder of our period. A mid 1969 article by Fleet Admiral Kasatonov[45] is illustrative. He began by confirming that it was Soviet policy to 'build and further perfect an ocean-going fleet capable of solving strategic tasks of forward character'. He asserted that the core of such a fleet had by then been formed, and described its prime components as 'advanced missile-carrying vessels', submarines, and a vaunted 'naval aviation'.[46] He proceeded as follows: 'The Fleet structure (now) incorporates also the determined and unbeatable marine infantry. This is intended to be utilized over wide ocean expanses in troop-landing craft, to break through enemy shore defences and to solve tasks on the shore'. Here were the means for accomplishing Sokolovsky's 'tasks' vis-à-vis enemy bases.

Defensive and offensive strategic capabilities received the main focus of attention.[47] And the development of Naval interventionary-type forces was seen as a necessary complementary theme. But the USSR was also aware of the non-strategic potentials of interventionary-type forces; she was beginning to take an interest in the benefits that might accrue from local conflicts.[48] The initial 1964–65 procurements were followed by a steady expansion of amphibious marine landing capacities (see Chapter 5).

The importance attached to the development of interventionary-type forces was stressed by reports such as that carried by *Tass* in 1970. An exposition on the exercises and events of the world-wide 'Okean' manoeuvres included this passage:[49] 'In the Northern Fleet the firing (described as 'missile and artillery'), as well as the landing of marines on the shores of the Rubachi peninsula, were attended by the Minister of Defence of the USSR, Marshal Grechko, the Chief of the Main Political Administration of the Army and Navy, General Yepishev, the Commander in Chief of the Navy, Admiral Gorshkov, and the Commander in Chief of the Air Defence Forces, Marshal Batitsky.' (The list does of course also provide a graphic comment on the attention accorded to 'combined action' potentials.)

In conclusion; the development of amphibious marine and interventionary-type forces demanded considerable attention. And their training orientation, towards the utilization of missile (nuclear) strikes, increased the impact potential of their as yet limited numbers. It must be noted, with reference also to land and paratroop forces, that the 'clean' lack-of-lasting-fallout-effects nature of the *nuclear warheads* by then available *made it possible for forces to occupy targets very soon after a 'take-out' strike*.[50]

But the forces did not only have military punch. They also embodied considerable psychological pressure advantages even in situations which did not demand the full utilization of their combat capacities, and in peace. (Again, see Chapter 5.)

THE MILITARY IN SOCIETY

One might distinguish four interrelated but separate aspects. On the one hand there were the efforts to establish more advanced strategic research facilities, and the concerns relating to military-economic inter-dependencies. On the other hand there was the increasing need for pre-mobilization training for civilians, so as to permit their fastest possible insertion into more sophisticated wartime roles, and the general need for maximum war survival prospects. The first three have been referred to previously, and all will be treated more extensively in later chapters. But with regard to the last two aspects, certain preliminary data and comments fall within the present context.

The first of these will be treated first. Some military training or education of and for civilians had long been accepted. But its extent had if anything contracted under Khrushchev (viz. the early 1962 decree which cancelled preconscription training for students of secondary schools and institutions). And it was only after his ousting that the scope of the practice was significantly extended.

Previous sections described the military's acquiring of greater autonomy from 'Party' meddling in matters relating to organization and training; the stress on the need for 'one-man command' was relieved of the old accompanying, and partly contradictory, reminder of the 'role and influence' of the Party; the Party was to continue to give valuable 'assistance' – but in terms of support which might be called for rather than 'influence' which had to be accommodated or bowed to.[51] It soon became clear that the Party's acceptance of military training requirements incorporated acceptance of the need for increased pre-mobilization training.

Party and public organizations were directed to be 'more concerned with the military-patriotic up-bringing of school-children'.[52] And similarly: 'The YCL (Komsomol) committees are obliged to carry out more actively the work of military and patriotic education of Soviet youth and preparing them for service in the ranks of the Armed Forces'.[53]

There was to be established 'patronage over military units by workers, collective farmers and cultural figures' to help 'strengthen and expand the army's ties with the people'.[54] The intent is elucidated in testimony by Pavlov, then Komsomol First Secretary: 'Following the example of the Pacific Fleet, entire youth flotillas have been set up

in the Black Sea, the Baltic, and the North Sea. . . . In all corners of
the Soviet Union this summer, tents were pegged out for the 'Sons of
the Regiment' camps where juveniles learned about military technology and studied the heroic history of the USSR Armed Forces'.[55]

That such involvement of 'workers, collective farmers and cultural
figures' as well as 'youths' and 'juveniles' was taking on increasing
importance was clear. In May of 1966 DOSAAF, the organization
responsible for the training of civilians, held a major conference in
Moscow, and geared itself to much increased activities.[56] In 1967 the
military service was cut to two years.[57] In 1968 decrees were introduced which not only extended the scope of pre-mobilization
training, but which made the previously voluntary participation
obligatory.[58] Three advantages accrued. The number of trained
reservists would rise; the decrease in the number of draftees, caused
by the post-war demographic pattern, was offset; while the efficiency
of the regular forces was secured through the assigning of boot-camp
type and initial training responsibilities to DOSAAF. See Chapter 8
for a further analysis.

With regard to general survival prospects, the basic concern
complemented that of the military-economic interdependence. It
could be defined as follows: ' . . . to create the conditions for the
uninterrupted operation of units of the National economy if nuclear
war should break out'.[59] Civil Defence, which constituted the means
for the fulfilling of this task, was not a novel conception. But it was
now to receive increased, if strictly limited, attention. Shelter-
building facilities were focused on the protection of essential components of the National economy and administration. The populace,
on the other hand, became the target for educational campaigns
intended to promote realistic self-help prospects.[60]

Civil Defence was in 1965 defined as 'a system of state-wide defence
measures being carried out throughout the country for protecting the
populace and National economy from the weapons of mass destruction, and also for rescue work in the zone of a possible strike'.[61]
'Every city and inhabited point' was to be given protection.[62]

The limitations affecting the populace were stated frankly.
'Planned and systematic' training would be given to 'workers,
employees and the general public'.[63] But 'first of all attention is being
focused on the *preparation* of the entire populace, on the ability to
help oneself and help one's neighbours'.[64]

Both sources made it clear that the program was encountering some
opposition from enterprise managers and their ilk who disliked the

loss of time involved in the training of their personnel. And such opposition might be seen to relate equally to the other civilian training endeavours treated above. Yet in spite of this the programs were plainly of considerable scope and importance.

It remains only to suggest that the encouraging of some military training of the civilian population may not appear inimical to Party interests as interpreted by its leaders. It may in fact appear conducive to the furthering of Party interests. The programs may be seen to answer modern military necessities. But their enactment was probably part-motivated by considerations of further-ranging advantages which would accrue from a more disciplined society. Factories, not to mention Party cells, could on occasion also do with more discipline.

Among the many Soviet works on strategy of the late 1960's and early 1970's, special mention must be made of Marshal Grechko's 1971 pamphlet 'On Guard for Peace and the Construction of Communism'.[65] Soviet strategists describe it as being for the 1970's what Marshal Malinovsky's 'Vigilantly on Guard for Peace'[66] was for the 1960's, namely, the most authoritative guide to, and synopsis of, official thinking. A selection of illustrative quotes may therefore usefully serve as a chapter conclusion.

War is a 'many-faceted and complicated socio-political phenomenon which influences the entire life of society;' 'the scattered placement (of the productive forces) will significantly raise the defence capability of the Soviet motherland and make our industry less vulnerable' (Chapter 2, Section 1).

'History knows many revolutionary jumps ... however, never before ... with such rapidity and on such a scale.' 'Nuclear weapons ... have become the determining factor in the revolutionary changes in military affairs.' 'On the basis of achievements in mathematics, cybernetics and electronics, automated control systems have been developed.' 'At present the Army and Navy are qualitatively new Armed Forces' (2·2).

'Strategic Missile Troops comprise the basis ... of our Armed Forces' (2·2).

'The operational and tactical missile units comprise the basis of the Ground Troops. This is a qualitatively new branch of arms which is the basic means for employing nuclear weapons in combat and operations.' (2·2).

'The Airborne Troops have developed rapidly. Their mission is to wage combat in the enemy rear using nuclear attack means, to make rapid use of the results of nuclear strikes . . .' 'The capabilities of military air transport . . . have risen significantly.' 'Our Air Force is equipped with . . . fundamentally new combat aircraft . . . such as the vertical take-off and landing aircraft and aircraft with a variable wing configuration.' (2·2).

'The Soviet Navy . . . has emerged from the coastal waters . . . and has repeatedly demonstrated its increased combat capabilities with great conviction.' 'The naval missile carrying aviation . . . is one of the basic strike forces of the Navy . . .' (2·2)

'The Rear Services . . . have been completely motorized (and their) organizational structure . . . has been completely changed.' (2·2)

'A particular feature of the present day officer corps in the Armed Forces is its youth. At present more than 65 per cent of the officers on the regimental level are under 30.' (2·2)

Combat training is emphasized (3·1), as is the psychological training and indoctrination of the troops (3·2). Practical training and exacting, realistic, manoeuvres are spotlighted. (3·4)

'The complex military equipment requires the mastery of related specialities in order to achieve interchangeability of the members of crews, teams, squads.' (3·3)

'High discipline' is essential (3·6), as is 'loyalty to proletarian internationalism' and the defence of 'the entire socialist community' (4·1). '. . . departure from (socialist) unity is intolerable' (4·2). '(Warsaw Pact collaboration) has been manifested . . . in the creation of the United Armed Forces and the United Command . . . joint measures are carried out . . . military consultations are organized . . . (and there is) close contact of the political bodies in the allied armies . . .' (4·2) 'The Warsaw Pact (furthermore) serves as the main centre for coordinating the foreign policy activities of the fraternal nations' (1·1).

The book ends by reiterating and stressing the need for patriotic and international indoctrination.

NOTES

1. *Izvestia*, 20 October, 1964. See also 23rd Party Congress' (1966) assurances as per Col. V. V. Larionov in *Kommunist Vooruzhiennikh Sil*, No. 22, 1966; and *Krasnaya Zvezda*, 22 September, 1965.
2. *Pravda*, 8 November, 1964 (Malinovsky's 7 November Anniversary Speech).
3. See especially Kuarcz, Jerry, in Soviet Studies, October, 1965, *op. cit.*
4. Sokolovsky, V. D., Marshal, Moscow Press Conference for Western journalists, 17 February, 1965.
5. *Izvestia*, 4 March, 1965.
6. *Pravda*, 8 December/*Izvestia*, 9 December, 1964.
7. *Pravda*, 7 November, 1970 (stress added).
8. *Pravda*, 19 November, 1965. The article also expounds on some of the operative characteristics of ICBMs. E.g.: their reliability is explained to be 'a function of the flight altitude measured in 100s of km.s and the speed permitting a rocket to cover a distance of more than 10,000 km.s in 30 to 35 minutes'. One might further point to Krylov's as yet somewhat premature claims regarding BMD capabilities, in *Pravda*, 19 November, 1964, and the accompanying, belaboured, true but still rather hollow assertion that 'the creation of the Soviet strategic rocket troops has put an end for ever to the trans-oceanic imperialists' reliance on the inaccessibility and invulnerability of their territory'.
9. *Pravda*, 4 July, 1965 (Speech to Military Academy graduates).
10. Ogoniok, No. 2, 1965, *op. cit.*
11. *Ibid.*
12. Expressed strongly e.g. by Herman Kahn during his 1969 lecture tours; this author was a guest at his seminar with Norwegian international affairs specialists in Oslo on 9 May, 1969 (arranged by NUPI).
13. *Pravda*, 19 November, 1966.
14. *Ibid.*
15. Sushko and Kondratkov, *op. cit.*, p. 147.
16. Sokolovsky, *op. cit.*, p. 84. See Chapter 2.
17. *Kommunist Vooruzhiennikh Sil*, No. 18, August, 1969 (Article by Maj. Gen. Cherednichenko).
18. Col. Bondarenko in *Kommunist Vooruzhiennikh Sil*, No. 24, December, 1968, and Cols. Bondarenko and Rybkin in same, April, 1969 issues (No. 7 and 8).
19. *Krasnaya Zvezda*, 25 September, 1969 (Article by Maj. Gen. doktor nauk, and Professor Lagovsky). There had been previous admonishments that 'the stern dialectics of development are that the struggle for superiority must be waged continually' (Bondarenko, in *Kommunist Vooruzhiennikh Sil*, No. 17, September, 1966), but Lagovsky's pregnant implication had not been spelt out before.
20. Exhibiting awareness hereof, *Pravda*, 20 January, 1969, did in apparent contradiction to Bondarenko's implication (above footnote) affirm Soviet interest in Strategic Arms Limitation Talks. Note also the pregnant assertion in *Kommunist*, No. 14, September, 1970, p. 11: 'Maximalists' who refused to acknowledge the potential benefits or usefulness of partial measures and who insisted 'on a futile all or nothing formula', were 'doing a disservice to the cause of peace' (!). And see end of Chapter 4.
21. Grechko, in *Voenno-Istorichesky Zhurnal*, No. 6, June, 1966.
22. See *Krasnaya Zvezda*, 30–31 March, 1967 (Article by Lt. Gen. Zavyalov), and *Kommunist Vooruzhiennikh Sil*, No. 7, April, 1966 (Article by Marshal Sokolovsky and Maj. Gen. Cherednichenko).
23. *Nedelia*, No. 6, 31 January–6 February, 1965. There had as early as 1957 been assertions that the strategic leadership was 'duty-bound to act as consultant in questions concerning the state's economic life which . . . influence the nation's defence capabilities', and it was then also stated that 'military economists' must in

fact be added even to regular 'planning organs . . . within the state's administration' (see Chapter 8). But the post late-'6o's strategic equations obviously added further aspects, and hence greater urgency, to the basic motivating factors.

24. *Krasnava Zvezda*, 5 January, 1967 (Article by Maj. Gen. Zemskov).

25. *Krasnaya Zvezda*, 6 April, 1967 (Article by Col. A. Babin).

26. *Krasnaya Zvezda*, 5 January, *op. cit.* For further elaboration, see chapter 8.

27. *Ogoniok*, No. 25, June, 1965. The concentration on and scope of this conversion was indicated by Egyptian MIGs' inability to counter Israeli 'strafing' capabilities during the 6-day war of 1967; the omission was recognized and rectified with the subsequent reintroduction of some artillery capability to supplement fighter missile capacities.

28. *Krasnaya Zvezda*, 17 May, 1969 (stress added).

29. *Pravda*, 23 February, 1970. And see *Newsweek*, 'Periscope', 21 September, 1970, for evidence that the Soviet swing-wing jets were by then being mass-produced.

30. *Pravda*, 23 February, 1965 (Malinovsky).

31. *Krasnaya Zvezda*, 17 May, 1969, *op. cit.*

32. *Pravda*, 23 February, 1965 (Malinovsky). For the trend, see e.g. *Pravda*, 26 January, 1968 (Air Chief Marshal Vershinen) and *Krasnaya Zvezda*, 17 May, 1969, *op. cit.*

33. See e.g. *Izvestia*, 20 November, 1969 (Col. Gen. Grigoriev), and *Pravda*, 19 November, 1969 (Marshal Krylov).

34. *Nedelia*, No. 6, 1965, *op. cit.*

35. See e.g. *Krasnaya Zvezda*, 22 November, 1966, editorial.

36. *Pravda*, 14 July, 1965 (Fleet Admiral Gorshkov).

37. *Pravda*, 23 February, 1965 (Malinovsky).

38. Bundeswehr's *Soldat and Technik*, No. 10, 1970, pp. 566–70. Concise article on 'Neue und Modernisierte Kriegsschifftypen der Sowjet-Flotte' surveys also new Kresta II cruiser, and presents pictures which are unequivocal. Compare with other surveys in same, No. 11, 1969, p. 626. The then surveyed vessels' only remaining cannons were so small (57 mm.) as to rule out any conception of conventional war. *Note* also the new 3,500 ton gas-turbine rocket-destroyer (NATO code-named KRIVAK DDG) which 'appeared' in the spring of 1971, – embodying theory's total practical implementation. No equivalent vessel is either serving or (as yet) projected for service with any western navy.

39. See extensive interview with SACEUR (NATO) General Goodpaster, *Aftenposten*, Oslo, 29 October, 1970.

40. Sokolovsky, *op. cit.*, 3rd edition, pp. 242–3.

41. *Ibid.*, p. 341.

42. *Ibid.*, p. 246.

43. *Ibid.*, p. 344.

44. *Ibid.*, p. 340.

45. *Krasnaya Zvezda*, 27 July, 1969 ('Nadezhni Forpost Rodini'). See also Kasatonov in *Starchina Sersjant*, No. 7, 1969, for further treatment of the extensive Naval quantitative and qualitative build-up, and for descriptions of the extending of Naval operational patterns until these came to cover all major oceans.

46. Krasnaya Zvezda, *ibid.*: He further confirmed that 'an important role in the securing of bases and combat operations is executed by aid vessels of various types' (i.e. electronically equipped merchant and fishing vessels).

47. As to defensive, Sokolovsky, *op. cit.*, 3rd edition, p. 363, focuses on the crippling of the hostile aircraft carriers and missile submarines, – because of their strategic capabilities.

48. This clearly emerged from the Soviet media's treatment of the aftermath of the 1967 Arab-Israeli conflict. See also Chapter 5.

49. *Tass*, 29 April, 1970.

50. See Chapter 9 for further exposition as to why one could by the late 1960's envisage local nuclear conflicts *not* entailing escalatory probabilities.

51. Article by Grechko in *Voenno Istorichesky Zhurnal*, No. 6, June, 1966, supports the conclusion. See also Col. Gen. Yefimov, Asst. Chief of Chief Polit. Administration of Soviet Army and Navy, *Izvestia*, 16 November, 1965; and *Pravda*, 6 July, 1962 and 4 July, 1965, *op. cit.*

52. *Izvestia*, 16 November, 1965 (Yefimov).

53. *Komsomolskaya Pravda*, 15 June, 1965.
54. *Izvestia*, 16 November, 1965, *op. cit.*
55. *Pravda*, 27 June, 1965.
56. *Krasno-Znamennoe Oboronnoe*, DOSAFF izdat, Moscow, 1971, re: 'Postanovlenie TsK KPSS i Soveto Ministrov SSSR 7 Maia 1966g.'
57. The new law on military service also provided for the retirement at 60 of all officers up to four star rank (with the proviso that 5 year extensions could be granted when necessary).
58. They had been foreshadowed by articles such as, Maj. Gen. Zemskov's in *Krasnaya Zvezda*, 5 January, 1967, on the need for an extension of para-military training for civilians, in schools and outside.
59. *Krasnaya Zvezda*, 22 November, 1966.
60. See Chapter 4 for further details.
61. *Pravda Ukrainii*, 28 October, 1966 (Article by Head of Civil Defence, Marshal Chuikov).
62. *Krasnaya Zvezda*, 22 November, 1966, *op. cit.*
63. *Pravda Ukrainii*, 28 October, 1966, *op. cit.*
64. *Ibid.*
65. A. A. Grechko, *Na Strazhe Mira i Stroitelstva Kommunisma*, Voenizdat, Moscow, 1971. The book is the focus of the series Reshenia XXIV S'ezda KPSS v Zhizn (which also includes I. I. Yakubovsky's *Boevoe Sodruzhestvo*, on the Warsaw Pact, and A. A. Epishev's *Kommunisti Armi i Flota*, on military-political questions).
66. R. Malinovsky, Bditelnoe Stoyat na Strazhe Mira, *op. cit.*

4

Soviet Strategic Procurements: Their Implications for Foreign Policy[1] (Late 1960's-1970's)

There are two main prerequisites of military concern which determine the credibility and thus the effects of a nation's foreign policy commitments. One is the nation's ability in a last resort to provide sufficient military support for the fulfillment of pledges. The second is the awareness of others of its capacity to provide such support. If this is doubted (whether rightly or wrongly), other nations will feel neither the confidence nor the apprehension which they might otherwise be induced to feel (depending on the quality of their relations with the power in question).

Until the mid 1960's the USSR totally lacked the capacity of the USA to intervene effectively in areas outside her immediately adjacent environment. The Soviet Union's capacity to defend the homeland and these adjacent areas carried some credibility, as did her capacity to inflict punishment on her strongest adversary, within a first or pre-emptive strike scenario. Yet even this capacity was inhibited by the knowledge of the far greater and more reliable US capacity to bring destruction to the USSR land mass.

The USA therefore retained a marked psychological advantage, a position of superior bluffability. That is to say, a US bluff could logically be carried further. (This might, for example, be seen as having been of relevance to the 1962 Cuban crisis sequence of events.)

The 1960 Kennedy presidential campaign gave wide publicity to statistics which purported to demonstrate a developing missile gap in favour of the USSR. The comparison did not include all US delivery vehicles capable of reaching the USSR (e.g. bombers). It did however include Soviet medium-range missiles covering Europe. But the deterrence value of these missiles was strictly limited to whatever value the US set on the preservation of Western Europe. In a setting of developing US isolationism or xenophobia this value could easily become, or be thought to have become, negligible. The reliability of the statistics was therefore dubious. They were misleading as indicators of relative strength. Their acceptance testified to the popular credibility of Soviet 'massive retaliation' at the time, a credibility buttressed by the psychological impact of the Sputnik successes; it did not testify to facts.

The consequent priority on ICBM development by the Kennedy administration therefore did not close the gap. To the contrary, it temporarily exacerbated it. The real gap, with the US in the position of superiority, had narrowed with the Soviet attainment of limited missile capabilities. But the emerging US quantitative superiority was such that it minimized, and possibly eliminated, any chance that the unprotected Soviet first generation missiles might survive a hostile strike.

The limited Soviet capabilities of the late 1950's had been psychologically up-graded in the hope of inducing a US belief in a new situation of genuine balance. The policy represented an attempt to gain a bargaining position which could otherwise only be claimed following the climax of on-going procurement endeavours. By *appearing* to possess offsetting super-power capabilities, the USSR hoped to erect a smoke-screen which would permit her to effect these capabilities at a less financially demanding pace, while at the same time permitting the early enjoyment of the fruits which would accrue from the efforts.

But the design backfired. The resultant exacerbation of Soviet vulnerability sparked the more open final Soviet drive to redress the balance. This drive was initially directed towards the qualitative improvement of her missile complexes. Protective measures were instituted; her missiles were acquiring 'second-strike character'. The process of qualitative improvements was immediately followed by quantitative increments. The USSR was clearly determined to effect irrefutable counter-force capabilities.

The first part of the drive had succeeded by the mid 1960's. The second part was completed by the late 1960's. The second-strike character of the respective US and Soviet forces was thereafter to minimize the de-stabilizing potential of force increments by either. The balance of the 1970's could no longer be upset as easily as in the days of primitive first-strike type missiles.[2]

It is intended in this chapter to trace and analyse the Soviet development of strategic arms and capabilities. No exhaustive summary of military and technical innovations is attempted. Rather, the analysis will concentrate on factors which have implications for foreign policy choice and scope, whether separately or in conjunction with each other. Available data is believed sufficient to make tentatively valid assertions. But before pursuing this attempt it is appropriate and necessary to echo John Craven's caution regarding the difficulties of both critical analysis and rebuttal when information as to (e.g.) a weapon system's effectiveness lies in the classified field.[3]

A further difficulty, which relates to such data as is released, must also be noted. This is exemplified by the reported 1969 Pentagon paper on 'Improving the Acquisition Process for High Risk Military Electronic Systems'. An analysis of previous weapon (system) developments led to the conclusion that achieved operational efficiency had been consistently proved much inferior to theoretical and planned-for efficiency.[4] One must caution against inclinations to view 'achievable' as meaning 'that which is achieved'.

STRATEGIC OFFENSIVE CAPABILITIES

Some preliminary statistics must be introduced.

1. Growth of inter-continental and submarined-launched ballistic missiles:[5]

(Mid-year) (strengths)	USSR–ICBM	USA–ICBM	USSR–SLBM	USA–SLBM
1959	Some	None	None	None
1960	35	18	None	32
1961	50	63	Some	96
1962	75	294	Some	144
1963	100	424	100	244
1964	200	834	120	416
1965	270	854	120	496
1966	300	904	125	592
1967	460	1054	130	656
1968	800	1054	130	656
1969	1050–1350[6]	1054	160–200[9]	656

(Mid-year) (strengths)	USSR–ICBM	USA–ICBM	USSR–SLBM	USA–SLBM
1970	1300–1440[7]	1054	280–350[10]	656
1971	up to 1500[8]	1054	up to 400[11]	656
Nov. 1971[12]	1520	1054	475	656
Mid 1972[13]	1550	1054	580	656
SALT agreement 1972[14]	1618	1054	650	656

2. Estimate of Comparative Strategic Strengths – as per SALT agreement, 1972:[15]

	USSR	USA
ICBM	1618	1054
IRBM & MRBM (medium-range)	700	0
Cruise missiles	100	0
SLBM	650	656
Sea-based cruise missiles	358	0
Long-range bombers	190[16]	512
Medium-range bombers	500[17]	70

2b. Anti-ballistic missiles – mid 1972:[18] Number of launchers: USSR – 64; US – 0.

3. Total Offensive Force Loadings – mid 1972:[19] USSR – 2500; US – 5700.

But US quantitative superiority must be related to yield inferiority; in terms of megatonnage the USSR was estimated to have achieved parity already by late 1967.[20]

3b. The backbone of Soviet ICBM forces by mid 1970 consisted of 'over 300' SS9 with warheads of 20–25 megatons,[21] and 900 SS11 with warheads of one megaton plus[22] (similar to US Minuteman ICBM loads). Multiple warhead re-entry vehicle capacity was being assigned to both models; some SS9s were developed for a fractional orbit bombardment system (FOBS) or a retrofired depressed trajectory ICBM.[23]

There are clearly discrepancies between different force estimates. Not only do different sources provide different estimates,[24] but one can often find inconsistencies between figures provided by the same source.[25] The discrepancies may perhaps be seen to illustrate the degree of uncertainty of intelligence estimates. The Pentagon's preferral of the higher figures may be taken to reflect an inclination to present the maximum of any probability range estimate of enemy forces available at any one time. The inclination could be seen as a logical precaution on the part of officials responsible for a nations' defence. That it is also one with inherent dangers will be documented later.

With regard to SLBM figures it must be noted that the remaining Soviet inferiority was due to the fact that her older nuclear and diesel submarines had only 3 missile tubes each. But she was rapidly converting to 'Y-class' nuclear missile submarines, each with 16 tubes (analogous to US practice). This force rose from 4 operational units in early 1969 to 'at least' 17 operational units by late 1970, with another 15 'in various stages of assembly and fitting out', and with production proceeding at the rate of 7 – 8 (i.e. 112–128 missiles) a year.[26] Through 1971 and 1972 the conversion program proceeded 'at an ever increasing rate'. By early 1972 it appeared that the USSR would equal US SLBM levels by 1973 at the latest.[27] A similar development related to the quality of the missiles available. The reach of early Soviet SLBMs had been inferior to American standards. But by 1970 she was converting to new types of comparable quality.[28]

The bomber figures are of doubtful relevance to strategic balance calculations and prognostications. Their main rationale is found in high estimates of the degradation factors which affect missile prospects, in estimates relevant to early missile generations, but questionable today. The USSR appears to be ahead of the USA in the development of a new 'low level supersonic folding-wing bomber' generation.[29] But the above comment remains applicable. While some such bombers may be procured, as yet another 'insurance', one would not expect large production runs (see section on degradation factors, below).

As regards the US quantitative stagnation after 1967, it partly reflected a strategic decision of sufficiency. It also reflected a dearth of funds. It was not divorced from the fact that one-third of the military budget became diverted to the conduct of the Vietnam war (see Chapter 2); Congress was all too leery of allocating supplementary funds.

The slow Soviet quantitative growth until 1967 reflected priority concentration on the development of second-strike characteristics (hardened silos, mobile launching pads, initial ABM endeavours, etc.). The consequent effecting of strike survival expectations mitigated Soviet vulnerability, and gave her a security she had not possessed since the war. But her quantitative inferiority nevertheless still detracted from the public credibility of her deterrence. Soviet expositions on the subject had never allowed room to doubt her determination to counter US capacities. And it was therefore no surprise that the qualitative securing of her existing forces was followed by the quantitative increments necessary for them to effectively counter US capabilities (and the US 'bluffability' advantage). By 1970 she had manifestly succeeded. Her momentum was furthermore leading to a position of apparent superiority[30] ('apparent', since the USA's earlier effecting of second-strike force characteristics ensured against critical vulnerability; a constellation of mutual checkmate had emerged).

There were a number of qualitative innovations and developments that must be noted in any consideration of the strategic balance. One of these was the development of silos which were capable of withstanding, and offering protection from, comparatively close-proximity nuclear explosions.[31] This is considered further in the section on defensive developments below.

Then there was the improvement of missile control facilities. Early procedures and techniques had been primitive. As a consequence of this safety considerations had dictated that allowance be given for considerably longer missile preparation times than warranted, or envisaged by technological theory. But by the mid 1960's the USSR had perfected sufficiently sophisticated facilities to cut reaction and missile preparation time demands to a respectable minimum.[32]

Missile technology itself also made impressive progress. Liquid fuel missiles which needed fuel changes every few days were replaced by missiles which needed fuel changes only every few months, and these were finally themselves replaced, by solid fuel missiles which were exempt from fuel-changing restrictions. Power and accuracy factors showed parallel improvements; by the mid 1960's they permitted missile trajectories which had previously been ruled out by prohibitive cost implications.[33] Early missiles had been forced to follow high 'minimum energy' trajectories, with peak altitudes of perhaps 800 miles.[34] The more flexible trajectory choice associated with later missiles posed considerable problems for the opposing defence; a lower trajectory cut down the time avaiable for detection, identification and reaction.

The USSR pioneered mobile solid fuel ICBMs.[35] The speed and accuracy of modern satellite detection techniques might have been thought to make their ground immunity uncertain. But authoritative Soviet expositions testified to a positive conviction both with regard to these missiles' survival prospects and with regard to their offensive potential.[36]

Another Soviet innovation was the development of an orbital or sub-orbital bomb.[37] The advantage of these bombs lies in the fact that their low orbital altitude of about 100 miles poses defensive problems not fully alleviated by the contemporary development stage of 'Over-the-Horizon Radar' (again, see following sections).[38] But the further development of OHR promises to eliminate their relative immunity. And as regards fully orbital bombs, satellite course predictability makes their interception relatively easy.[39] Their military value is low even within first-strike contexts: synchronization difficulties ensure that a large percentage would at any one time have orbital locations which defied immediate firing; they could therefore not be effectively utilized. The main potential of these bombs therefore appeared to be psychological, and related to popular unease or fear of 'bombs overhead'.

Another qualitative improvement, effected by both powers, had more pregnant implications. This was the development of sophisticated decoys (PENAIDS, or penetration aids), intended to multiply enemy identification problems in order to ensure the unintercepted arrival on target of a missile. But by 1968–69 the value of PENAIDS, as originally conceived, was becoming dubious. High speed short-range ABMs (such as the American Sprint), and more sophisticated 'floating' long-range ABMs (such as introduced by the Soviet Union in 1968),[40] had been developed, together with associate radar facilities. The former envisaged interception only after the atmosphere had separated the warhead from the dummies (differences in weight and density entail differing re-entry times); the latter allowed for interception prior to the release of the dummies. The cost of effective dummies was approaching the point when 'one might just as well use several warheads on each missile'.[41] Or, as USIS put it: 'As opposed to other methods of penetration, MIRV is regarded as more certain, since defence against it must necessarily utilize ... ABMs for each individual MIRV warhead'.[42] The difficulties encountered by PENAIDS designs had given birth to, or at least provided an impetus to the development of MIRVs.

The research and development of MIRVs (Multiple Individually-targeted Re-entry Vehicles) was at first considered a US preserve. But by 1968 it became clear that the USSR was equally determined to produce such weaponry.[43] US sources by 1969 testified to 'very successful' Soviet MIRV tests, and confirmed that the Soviet testing did concern MIRVs and not merely the less sophisticated non-individually targeted MRVs (Multiple Re-entry Vehicles 'dropped' during descent).[44] It was at the same time stated as a fact that 'Both the USA and the USSR already have a limited number of rockets capable of delivering multiple warheads ready for use, and both are continuing their development'.[45] The American sources quoted may have had reason to inflate estimates of Soviet progress, so as to fore-stall Congressional pressure to cut back research and development funds. If so, they were successful. By 1971 the US began tentative deployment, and extensive MIRV deployment by both sides was clearly imminent.[46]

The principle of MIRV may be diagrammed thus:

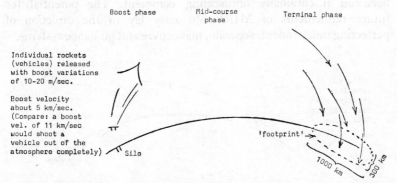

Boost phase

Mid-course phase

Terminal phase

Individual rockets (vehicles) released with boost variations of 10-20 m/sec.

Boost velocity about 5 km/sec. (Compare: a boost vel. of 11 km/sec would shoot a vehicle out of the atmosphere completely)

Silo

'footprint'

1000 km

300 km

Note: The effect on spread by a difference of 1 m/sec. in boost velocity equals

$$\left(R = \frac{v^2 \sin}{g(=\text{about } 10)} \left| \frac{dR}{dV} = \frac{2V}{g} \right| dR = \frac{2 \times 8000\ m}{10} \right) = 1600 \text{ metres!}$$

A very considerable spread, or 'footprint', may hence be effected with only very minor velocity variations between individual vehicles at the time of their release.

There were apparently some variations between US and Soviet concepts. That of the USA saw a single guidance and propulsion system controlling the velocity of a 'bus' from which re-entry vehicles are released sequentially. The bus re-aligns its trajectory and velocity each time in accordance with the desired targeting of the next-to-be released vehicle:

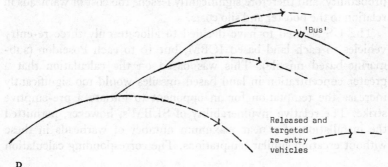

'Bus'

Released and targeted re-entry vehicles

As opposed to this, there were indications that the USSR was pursuing the concept of having each individual warhead equipped with a separate guidance system. American comment labelled this concept 'more cumbersome' and less sophisticated.[47] This might perhaps be seen as a partisan comment, since the Soviet concept's effectiveness as such remained unchallenged. But it may merely have been an intentionally obfuscating comment. The potential for future refinements of MIRV obviously lay in the direction of perfecting independent, separate, manoeuvre and guidance systems.

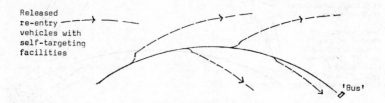

Released
re-entry
vehicles with
self-targeting
facilities

'Bus'

A prime advantage of the MIRV concepts is that the early flight trajectory ejection of independently guided re-entry vehicles make it possible to minimize or discount the danger that an anti-ballistic missile fired from the opponent's territory might destroy the booster prior to dispersal. This had been a real danger of the 'old' MRV concepts.

MIRV target accuracy achievable with present technology is thought to lie inside a 0·25 nautical mile (350–400 metres) radius from the target ('achievable' ultimate accuracy is considered to lie within a radius of 30 metres from a target!'.[48]) This should be related to the impact, or kill-probability, calculation of yield $\frac{2}{3}$/accuracy – which correlates the effects of warhead and yield. As evinced by the formula: improved accuracy permits smaller warheads for constant impact probability, and therefore significantly lessens the cost of warheads in relation to the booster and silo costs.

The US seemed to have decided to allocate only three re-entry vehicles to each land-based ICBM, but 10 to each Poseidon (sub-marine-based missile). This was based on the calculation that a greater concentration in land based missiles would too significantly increase the temptation for an opponent to initiate a pre-emptive strike. The relative invulnerability of SLBM's, however, permitted the installation of a near maximum number of warheads in these without creating similar temptations. The corresponding calculation on the part of the USSR might be presumed to effect similar deployment decisions in the Soviet Union, although the greater size of the SS9 increases the maximum number of warheads which could theoretically be carried.

One could therefore anticipate an early 1970's multiplying of either side's offensive missile capability by a factor of between 3 and 10. This invites a consideration of so-called 'overkill'. The situation today may be illuminated by relating existing strategic force levels to such as are considered to guarantee the destruction of either super-power. The Soviet Union appeared to have acquired considerabe 'overkill' capacities; US Secretary of Defence Laird testified in the spring of 1969, to the US Senate, that 200 nuclear warheads of one megaton each would assure the killing of 55 per cent of the US population.

Laird claimed on the same occasion that it would take 1200 US one-megaton warheads to destroy 45 per cent of the USSR population, due to the more scattered pattern of Soviet industrial and population centres.[49] The comparison might well be suspected of being based on 'maximum efficiency' criteria with regard to Soviet, and 'minimum efficiency' criteria with regard to US capabilities. But even so it sufficed to ascertain that the US retained considerable 'overkill' capacities of her own, if not on the basis of ICBM numbers alone, then certainly when account was taken of her bomber and Polaris forces. (Senate Armed Services Committee member Gore shortly thereafter reportedly estimated that there were 48 American strategic weapons for each of the USSR's largest cities . . . !)[50]

But although prima facie calculations strongly confirmed both powers' 'overkill' capacity by the late 1960's, there remained uncertainties. There were a number of 'degradation factors' which negatively affected estimates of the dependability of the missile forces. One related to the fact that a number of missiles would probably be unusable, due to undiscovered technical and other faults, and would therefore not be available when needed. A second degradation factor related to missiles which for various reasons, although technically up to standard, were nevertheless not prepared or available for immediate firing. A third factor concerned launch facilities which were not ready for action, whether due to unpreparedness or personnel or equipment. A fourth factor hinged on the unknowns of in-flight reliability: undiscovered faults could negate the in-flight reliability of a percentage of the missiles. Then there was a fifth factor, which related to second-strike calculations: how large a percentage of one's forces would remain intact and available after an initiating strike by an enemy? And, finally, there was the calculation of what percentage would succeed in penetrating a hostile BMD.

Each of the first four factors might conceivably detract from effective missile numbers by, say, five to twenty per cent. The fifth factor could detract a significantly larger percentage; its exact size would depend on one's own missiles' vulnerability, on enemy intentions, and on enemy missiles' yield and accuracy. (It was with this in mind that Secretary of Defence Laird warned that the Soviet SS9 was capable of destroying even strong silo-protected US ICBMs, and that the USSR might therefore infer that she could cripple US capacities for second-strike retaliatory action.[51] Suffice it here to note that the warning was intended as a spur to ABM deployment. The spectre was overly alarmist even within a scenario restricted to land-based missiles – see below –; it was certainly misleading in its ignoring of US submarine-based second strike forces). With regard to the sixth degradation factor, ABM developments are treated below. But for illustrative purposes one might see it as detracting another 5–20 per cent from effective strength.

One can understand how military calculations of guaranteed deliverable weapons might, by maximizing degradation factors, leave a 'reliable' number of possibly only one-tenth of the theoretically available missiles. The full conversion to MIRV, with its multiplying of utilizable warheads, would then appear to be necessary in order to secure second-strike capability confidence.

High estimates of degradation factors, which decrease missile cost-effectiveness expectations, have the further consequence of up-grading bomber cost-effectiveness expectations. Competitive such have been suggested to emerge if the 'deliverable' missile force percentage is judged to be as low as or lower than 30 per cent.[52] Calculations along these lines would lead to pressures for the continuing R & D of bombers which would be considered out-performed and out-dated when faced with more optimistic estimates of missile degradation factors.[53] It must be said, however, that the sophisticated super-power missile generations of the early 1970's were most unlikely to be encumbered by high enough degradation factors to favour bomber production. The contraction of bomber capacities that occurred during the early 1970's lent support to this assertion.[54]

Finally, to sum up Soviet postures and capabilities as she entered the 1970's; the Soviet Union considered that she had achieved strategic parity; she furthermore felt confident that she could secure its continuation, and that she could therefore demand that this parity be recognized as the operative base for any potential SALT discussions and agreements.[55] She clearly felt confident that she had secured forces commensurate with any need and that she could maintain this stance.[56] Her strategic targeting options were no longer restricted to counter-city prospects; she could afford the luxury of integrated counter-force, counter-city and counter-administration foci forces; she had secured capabilities which allowed her to contemplate an impressive scale of hypothetical strike option choices.[57]

STRATEGIC DEFENSIVE CAPABILITIES

Before analysing the BMD problem complex, a few words must be said about the radars on which it depends. A hostile ICBM can only be detected by land-based radar during one of a few specific periods of its flight, as indicated by the following diagram:

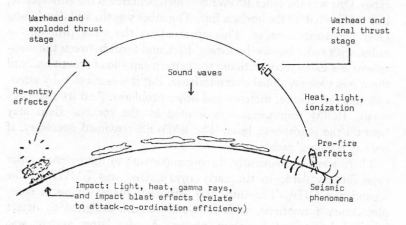

The limited range of detection possibilities must be related to the wide range of natural cosmic disturbances, such as meteors, which can induce false radar readings. The problems involved are clearly immense. This was why a number of scientists of the late 'sixties believed that decoys or multi-warheads would add a hopelessly confusing factor to BMD radar tasks, and make BMD designs utopian in practice.[58] And, as if this was not enough, one could conceive of yet another difficulty: an 'advance' high altitude enemy atomic explosion could theoretically succeed in blacking out ground radar capabilities completely.

But the problems were belittled by government scientists. And the embarking on the path of BMD deployment indicated that the belittling was backed up by considerable confidence. One reason could be found in progress towards the development of airborne and satellite radars. Such radars promised to go beyond the detection of the firing and burnt-out phases, and to actually track a missile's flight path. Lookdown radars of this type would not only be advantageous vis-à-vis 'regular' ICBMs, but would also facilitate defence against low trajectory and submarine-fired missiles, and against MIRVs (by monitoring their early separation spread and the paths of their re-entry vehicles). Evidence presented by Jane's Weapon Systems in 1971 confirmed Soviet success in the development of an airborne early warning system.[59] The further development of this, and of parallel US systems, could be expected as the 1970's progressed.

In the meantime the radars utilized through the late '60's remained the backbone of strategic defence endeavours. There were two main types. One was the older BMWES, which penetrated the atmosphere, but was limited by the horizon line. The other was the still developing Over-the-Horizon radar. This operated on the same principle as radio, with radar beams 'bouncing' back and forth between the ionosphere and earth relay stations; the pattern capable of repetition until the waves took on global characteristics. But it was affected by atmospheric false echoes, meteors and other problems. And its efficiency versus ICBM trajectories was limited by the rockets' short stay beneath the ionosphere level. The BMWES remained necessary, if only as 'back-up' radars.

There were consequently three components to the defence radar capability available in the early 1970's. One was BMWES. The second was OHR. The third was airborne; planes flying in complementary formations, with infra-red censors designed to detect missiles' boost and burn-out phases. As the latter system was

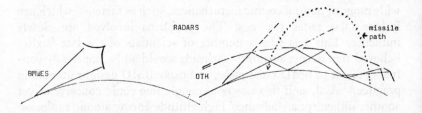

perfected, in conjunction with emerging satelite capabilities, it appeared likely that the first component (at least) would be phased out.

But detection by a radar facility is not the only problem with which a defence must wrestle. The definite screening and identification of the detected object remains problematic. And there is the related difficulty associated with the subsequent transmitting of data and interpretation to the officer or body entrusted with the responsibility to decide on the response. Finally, there is the process of sending the decision back through the same channels, of coordinating its implications into the mechanisms of the defence, and of initiating corresponding actions. These procedures must all be taken in sequence. And they must be completed within the remaining flight-time of the ICBM (under 20 minutes) for ABM utilization to be possible. One does not need to be an expert to perceive the complexity of the problems involved.

Through the early 1960's this constellation of problems was to cause the US to doubt the potential efficacy of a BMD. It clearly motivated her early concentration on other means of protecting her retaliatory capacities, and her early spurring of defence in-depth concepts. She concentrated for example on increasing the PSI (blast overpressure in pounds per square inch), or blast resistance, of silos.[60] By 1969 there were reports that silos capable of withstanding 2–3000 PSI could be constructed; this meant that they could survive even close proximity nuclear explosions.[61]

But Secretary of Defence Laird's 1969 testimony, that the Soviet SS9 had the correlated power-accuracy potential to destroy missiles in silos, indicated emerging doubt as to the ultimate efficacy of silo-strengthening (possibly also on grounds of cost). The doubt is partly explained by a consideration of the previously presented impact calculation of yield $\frac{2}{3}$/accuracy 2. The formula entails that an improvement in accuracy by, say, a factor of 2, has the same effect as a ten-fold increase in warhead yield, or as a ten-fold improvement in silo blast resistance capacities.[62] The formula took on increased relevance with the development of sophisticated ICBM generations.

BMD scepticism was, however, deeply rooted. The depth of the scepticism was indicated by US Secretary of Defence McNamara's last official prediction: in an all-out nuclear exchange in the mid '70's either power would be capable of inflicting about 120 million fatalities on the other, *regardless* of which country struck first.[63] BMD sceptics retained confidence in the viability of a second-strike capability (the acknowledged viability of which was recognized as the best deterrent) without a BMD.

Their logical premise presumably related to the impact blast effects notation on our diagram on stages of detection possibilities. It suggests that even if detection fails, then the unmistakable first arrival of a hostile missile would be guaranteed to activate reaction procedures. The implications are not as illogical as they appear to be at first glance. Quite irrelevant of the take-out capacities of more powerful and accurate rockets, attack synchronization problems are of such a scale as to make any concept of ideally coordinated first-strikes untenable. The greatly differing geographical locations of launching sites as well as of ultimate targets, and the widely spread multiple and independent nature of count-down and targeting procedures, ensure that missile arriving times would vary considerably. This entails a guarantee of sufficient reaction time for a significant percentage of land-based forces to be activated. One can logically expect a sizeable land-based force to survive, and to supplement (the already sufficiently powerful) Polaris and other forces, so as to provide continued double-ensured second-strike capabilities. BMD deployment therefore appeared to be unnecessary and superfluous.

Yet in spite of the outlined reasons for scepticism regarding BMD radar potentials, and in spite of the given reasons for confidence in second-strike capabilities even without a BMD, the USSR nevertheless early demonstrated a contrary conviction. She pursued BMD development.[64] She clearly considered pro-BMD considerations and rationales to be of greater validity. These considerations and rationales will be treated below.

What was considered to be a primitive ABM (the 'Griffon') was shown at the 7 November, 1963, Moscow military parade. Shortly thereafter an article in Krasnaya Zvezda conveyed the definite impression that a partial and probably experimental BMD deployment had already been implemented.[65] The following year's parade unveiled the improved solid fuel 'Galosh', the missile presumed to form the core of early BMD deployment patterns.

There was visible evidence of some deployment by 1966.[66] What appeared to be the protective domes of a BMD battery's radar complex could then be glimpsed from the Leningrad road north-east of Klin, about 65 miles from Moscow. And what appeared to be elements of a long-range BMD radar warning system, such as the huge aerial arrangements, could be seen from the Minsk road, about 50 miles from Moscow.

Initial American reports specified only Moscow and Leningrad as centres of BMD activity.[67] But it appeared logical to assume that initial deployment patterns extended also to the protection of at least some ICBM sites. Confirmation that deployment patterns did extend beyond Moscow and Leningrad was given by implication in a McNamara statement of 1967.[68] And it received indirect support from a London Institute of Strategic Studies assertion that existing Soviet ABMs were intended for area defence, in particular of the North-Western USSR.[69]

The same source[70] characterized the Galosh missiles as having ranges of 'several hundred miles' and being equipped with 'nuclear warheads in the 1–2 megaton range'. The ABMs were in other words programmed for early and high-altitude interception of incoming missiles. The power of their warheads appeared to be sufficient to disrupt the homing equipment of hostile missiles at some distance beyond that affected by the immediate blast consequences.[71]

There was no evidence that initial deployment encompassed also greater thrust short-range missiles such as the 'Sprint'. (This was the missile envisaged as the back-up to the longer-range 'Spartan' in the limited US BMD authorization of 1969). And there was, furthermore, no evidence of any significant expansion of the early deployment patterns during the remaining 1960's.[72]

Yet this was not logically explained by perceived Soviet misgivings regarding BMD potentials. Dormant BMD deployment expansion designs were more logically explained by economic allocatory decisions subject to, and expected to, change with the late 1960 advent of more favourable cost-exchange ratios (see below). A related secondary rationale for the BMD development hiatus was to be found in the evident priority initially accorded to ICBM procurements and improvements.

Throughout the period Soviet BMD research (as opposed to deployment), continued unabated. It received funds far in excess of equivalent US programs.[73] One tangible consequence was the unveiling of a more advanced and sophisticated version of the Galosh ABM in 1968.[74] This missile had the capacity to 'float' for a while after its take-off until it had definitely identified its target ('controlled float'); its propulsion would then be re-ignited, and it would be guided towards the target.[75] There was also the parallel deployment of new large and improved Anti-Ballistic Missile radar complexes, presumed to give sophisticated guidance to the aforementioned ABMs.[76]

A more basic consequence was revealed when the US in 1969 'acknowledged' that the experience accruing from early Soviet research and development efforts provided the basis for a substantive Soviet BMD technological lead. President Nixon crystallized the situation: 'The Soviets have already deployed an ABM system which protects to some degree a wide area centred around Moscow. We will not have a comparable capability for over four years. We believe that the Soviet Union is continuing its ABM development directed either towards improving this initial system or more likely, making substantially better second-generation ABM components'.[77]

One should here expand by refuting also the belief that the referred-to development hiatus was based on apprehension that further deployments would precipitate increases in US arms procurements. The USSR stressed that she considered any such action-reaction sequence to be unnecessary as she saw no necessary causal connection. The view warrants credence in view of the fact that she never once objected to early US BMD procurement efforts. Prior to the entertaining of President Nixon's 'Safeguard' concept for initial US BMD deployment[78] she furthermore never indicated that she might consider any potential US BMD program as a danger which demanded increases in Soviet strategic offensive forces.

Kosygin expressly propounded the belief that a BMD was a stabilizing development, that it was therefore desirable and that it was not something one was interested in banning.[79] The late 1960's ABM furore in the US may have instilled an appreciation of the negative psychological ramifications that might be associated with BMD deployment extensions, and this may therefore have emerged as a factor deterring such extensions. But if these psychological aspects came to command appreciation, they certainly did not command agreement.

A further indication that the USSR did not consider BMD developments as necessarily affecting the relative strategic balance could be seen in a 1964 statement by Major General Talensky. He argued in favour of BMD deployment since this would 'make (the state's) defences dependent chiefly on its own possibilities, rather than merely on mutual deterrence' ('that is, the goodwill of other states').[80] The statement indicates support for the view that if BMDs prove to be effective,[81] and costs turn out to be surmountable, then one could and ought to effect a decrease in expected casualty rates through a reallocation of funds. If a BMD was initiated through the reallocation of some of the funds otherwise oriented to offensive arms one might for example effect a decrease in the number of expected fatalities from 120 to 80 million. Since the resultant figure would appear to be equally 'unacceptable', there would be no logical reason why the BMD endeavours need lead to a fuelling of the 'arms race'. (See below for a more comprehensive discussion.)

It is necessary at this point to present more exact cost and efficiency measurement data. One can only judge such as have been presented by the USA. But one can probably presume that Soviet data with regard to scientific developments parallel those arrived at by the USA for similar projects.

The US Department of Defence presented the following calculations in 1967. Posture A related to limited BMD deployment and Posture B to a more extensive programme. Either programme calculation was based on intended early 1970's deployment schedules. [82]

	Posture A US $ Bill	Posture B US $ Bill
Radars (MAR, TACMAR, PAR, MSR) Investment costs:	6·5	12·6
Missiles (Spartan & Sprint, no number given) Investment costs:	2·4	4·8
Total DOD (Dept. of Defence) Investment costs:	8·9	17·4
AEC (Atomic Energy Commission, fabricating warheads at est. cost of US $ 0·5 mill. each. The Postures represent 2,000 and 4,000 warheads respectively) Investment costs:	1·0	2·0
Total investment costs (excl. R & D)	9·9	19·4
Annual operating costs:	0·38	0·74
No. of cities with local defence (i.e. protected)	25	50

The estimates invited comparison with the approximately $50 billion which had been spent on normal air defences since the Second World War, and with $1·9 billion projected for these defences for 1968. [83] The first figure included accumulated operating and turnover costs and might for fairness of comparison purposes possibly be halved. But even so, the figures showed that an effective BMD would reduce fatalities to a greater degree and at less costs. [84]

The US Defence Department release went on to present the

relevant 'cost-exchange' ratios.[85] (These ratios measure the relationship between the cost of the offensive forces which would be needed
to offset an enemy's increased defensive capability, and the cost of the
defensive forces which would be needed to offset enemy offensive
deployments.) The cost-exchange ratios had until then greatly
favoured the offence. Now, however, this appeared to be changing.

For a BMD able to restrict US fatalities from the otherwise
expected minimum of 100 million down to 20–30 million, the cost-
exchange ratios incurred by Soviet attempts to offset the reduction
through offensive increments would look like this:

	*Cost-exchange ratio**
40 million	1 : 4
60 million	1 : 2
90 million	1 : 1

* Related to a Soviet second-strike (i.e. US first-strike).

The Soviet offensive increment needed to raise US casualty
expectations to 40 million would therefore cost only one-quarter of
the US effort. But the offensive increases necessary for the USSR to
force a return to the previous status quo hostage, of 100 million
expected US fatalities, would cost more than the US BMD program
which decreased the casualty expectations. The following year the
US Defence Department Posture Paper altered the figure of 100
million. It now anticipated that 120 million US deaths would result
from any early 1970 exchange, even if the USA struck first.

It was clear that BMD research had reached the state when a limited
decrease in casualty expectations could be effected at less cost than
that of the offensive increment necessary to effect an equivalent
increase in enemy casualty expectations. It was clear that an invariance of the 'value for money' effect of defensive versus offensive
weaponry now existed for a scenario embodying sizeable changes in
casualty expectations. It was clear that it was only beyond that level
that offensive increments became cheaper.

There remained sceptics who not only doubted BMD operational
efficiency, but who believed that the cost of any potentially efficient
system would increase far beyond prognostications.[86] This did in fact
seem likely, as previous (offensive) weapon systems had invariably
proven more costly than anticipated.[87] But no convincing evidence
was presented as to why a BMD system's eventual costs should
exceed estimates to a greater degree than any other new weapon
system's costs.[88] The BMD estimates might be presumed, if any-

thing, to have passed a more sceptical scrutiny than was usual, since they were presented by a Secretary of State who opposed the system's deployment (on political grounds).[89] It appeared reasonable to presume (as did, for example, Dr. Brennan), that the cost-exchange ratio would in fact become more favourable to the defence. Further technological advances were more likely to be achieved in relation to new weapon-systems than in relation to older ones.[90]

Two further statistics which appeared in the Defence Department's 1968 Posture Statement merit reproduction.[91] They are to some extent based on unverifiable assumptions (e.g. with regard to the powers' chosen emphasis of attack). But they provide as accurate a graphic representation of BMD potentials as is available. The first was confined to a US–USSR context:

		SOVIET FIRST-STRIKE	
		US Retaliation at USSR Cities	
		Expected	Expected
	Soviet	US Fatalities	USSR Fatalities
US Program	Response	(in millions)	(in millions)
(Some) ABMs	None	120	120
Sentinel	None	100	120
(Limited BMD System)	PENAIDS	120	120
Posture A	None	40	120
(More Extensive	MIRV & PENAIDS	110	120
(BMD)	+ 100 ICBMs	110	120
Posture B	None	20	120
(Even more	MIRV & PENAIDS	70	120
Extensive BMD)	+ 550 ICBMs	100	120

		US FIRST-STRIKE	
		USSR Retaliation at US Cities	
		Expected	Expected
	Soviet	US Fatalities	USSR Fatalities
US Program	Response	(in millions)	(in millions)
(Some) ABMs	None	120	80
Sentinel	None	90	80
(Limited BMD System)	PENAIDS	110	80
Posture A	None	10	80
(More Extensive	MIRV & PENAIDS	60	80
BMD)	+ 100 ICBMs	90	80
Posture B	None	10	80
(Even more	MIRV & PENAIDS	40	80
Extensive BMD)	+ 550 ICBMs	90	80

The US first-strike was postulated as aimed at strategic targets, while the USSR first-strike was presumed aimed at both strategic and city targets. It must, of course, be noted that the actual strategic balance at the time would more properly have been represented by an inverting of the first two columns (so as to evaluate US attempts to offset Soviet BMD programs through increased offensive forces).

The graph reflected Secretary of Defence McNamara's concern to show that a Soviet BMD program could be offset through offensive dispositions, and that it would therefore not necessarily warrant the building of a US BMD system. But the graph's most unequivocal evidence led elsewhere. It confirmed that a BMD could significantly reduce casualties.

The second graph related to US fatality rates expected from potential Chinese attacks during 1975–80.[92] The number of intercontinental missiles the US expected the Chinese to possess by the mid 1970's was presented as a factor of X. X was not specified but could be presumed to represent 10.[93]

Expected US Fatalities (*in millions*)	*No. of Chinese Missiles* X	$2 \cdot 5x$	$7 \cdot 5x$
Without Sentinel (Limited BMD)	7	11	15 (23)
With Sentinel	1*	1*	1–2 (1)

* less than one, and possibly none.

It was therefore clear that even a limited BMD would succeed in cutting fatalities from possible Chinese attacks of the 1970's to a 'negligible' level. It must be reiterated that these figures were presented by officials who opposed BMD deployment, on political and psychological grounds. They were therefore not subject to the naive optimism that sometimes surround calculations of the import of new weapon systems.

Before turning to our Strategic Debate analysis, a few words must be said regarding super-power civil defence (shelter) programs, – the more so since they could be seen, and most often were seen, as necessary adjuncts to any effective BMD. At the same Senate hearings which examined the Johnson administration's conception of initial BMD deployment (the Sentinel system), General Wheeler of the Joint Chiefs of Staff declared the following (as to potentials): 'A full fall-out shelter program should be able to preserve the lives of some

22 per cent of the population. We are talking in terms of 40 million fatalities in the time frame of 1970'.[94] (With relation to a BMD:) '... (if we did not have civil defence programs) the Soviets could defeat our anti-ballistic missile defences by the tactic of shooting away from the (defended) target rather than shooting at it'. That is, 'they could rely on the fall-out drifting on to the target'.[95] There was, however, no corresponding budgetary allotment of consequence.

In the USSR the same belief was expressed, that active civil defence and shelter programs could limit the effects of a nuclear (and/or chemical or bateriological) exchange, and thus contribute to national survival.[96] By 1970 she had implemented comparatively extensive programs. But they were not of the scale envisaged by Wheeler, and did therefore not entail the strategic consequence he had referred to. Because of this they will be dealt with rather in our analysis of military-civilian integration (Chapter 8).

THE STRATEGIC DEBATE

It appears proper to begin by reiterating our earlier conclusion, that the USSR had by the late 1960's achieved a dynamic equilibrium with the USA as regards strategic capabilities. There were still American individuals who insisted that the US was superior, and who demanded that the government ensure that she retain this superiority. The novelty emerged from the fact that one could now find Soviet authorities or individuals who insisted on the obverse, that Soviet superiority had been achieved, and that it must be retained (see Chapter 8). While superficially contradictory, such verbal and in part psychologically inspired claims might perhaps be seen as a natural outgrowth of a situation wherein both powers were assured of confidence in their ability to destroy the other.

The major debate here referred to accepted the basics of this confidence, and concerned itself instead with the dangers that might be inherent in the dynamism of the equilbrium.

On the one hand, there were the firm proponents of BMD deployment, such as Dr. Brennan. They drew from the revealed data the conclusion that the new cost-exchange ratios invalidated all previously elaborated rationales for the continued pre-eminence of offensive forces. They claimed that the powers' relative positions could now be maintained through vigorous defence programs. And they went on to see the traditional offensive-oriented 'assured destructability' concept as having become 'assured vulnerability'. Stressing the emerging 'invariance' in offensive/defensive procurement costs, they concluded that 'one dead Russian equals one live American'. They demanded that US policy give precedence to the latter, and re-orient her strategic thinking accordingly. As concerned arms limitation talks, they based themselves on the new cost-exchange ratios, and demanded that the desired effects be brought about through reductions in offensive, rather than limitations in defensive, armaments. They saw a clinching argument in the 'fact' that a major war was less likely to be initiated if both sides possessed a 'heavy defence'; this argument related to the view that escalatory war was more likely than immediate all-out war.

The presence of a BMD was seen to limit the potentials for accidental war, as it promised to provide protection from limited attacks. Yet another desirable consequence was seen in the fact that it would eliminate 'counter-city' blackmail possibilities of limited missile exchanges, by providing that any successful strike would have to be part of a major effort. By increasing the 'threshold', one guaranteed that the initiation of hostilities entailed greater necessary consequences; this was considered in practice to mean a more secure deterrent.[97]

Then there were the equally convinced BMD opponents (see footnote 86). They tended, as indicated, to raise doubts regarding both BMD cost and efficiency. Yet this seemed to be a secondary consideration. They did not so much refute the above reasoning, as question one of its implicit premises. That is, they doubted whether a potential BMD deployment would or could be effected as merely a different way of ensuring the same relative security. They related impressions from the US efforts to counteract initial Soviet BMD endeavours through offensive increments with the belief that decision-making authorities had followed, and would continue to follow, the advice of 'hawkish' military advisers. They saw no reason to hope that BMD deployment could be initiated on the basis of a diversion of offensive funds. To the contrary, they were convinced that such deployment would necessarily be accompanied by both 'normal' offensive increments, and by additional offensive increases intended to offset enemy BMDs. In other words, they thought that the premise of a status quo with regard to relative security would drown in a psychologically misguided but inevitable arms race of ever-increasing proportions.[98]

Rather than view BMD as qualitatively different, they viewed it as what might be called a negative offensive increment. They thought it represented yet another cycle in the action-reaction syndrome of offensive increases, a syndrome encouraged by lead-time (research and development) considerations. They saw the post-war period as having proved that the powers not only augmented their forces in reaction to actual increases by the other, but that they also augmented them in reaction to anticipated increases by the other (on the principle of preparing for the worst).

It was feared that the original Soviet BMD development had been motivated by the early '60's (and later shelved or postponed) American designs for new supersonic bombers. The main reason for the Soviet development no doubt related to her resolve to gain strategic parity with the USA; it was part of her over-all effort to secure her deterrent. But one cannot dismiss the possibility that feared American designs may have influenced the urgency, if not the basic decision. Other action-reactions focused on by the sceptics were such as: US MIRV development in response to Soviet BMD efforts; massive Soviet ICBM build-up and Soviet MIRV endeavours in response to the US MIRV program; and, finally, US BMD in response to the Soviet offensive advances'[99]

The main fear was that the advent of overkill and possibly multiple overkill capacities might not be accepted as guaranteeing the survival of second-strike capacities. They feared that it might rather be seen to make possible a 'first-strike', a strike so massive that it ruled out any major retaliation. They feared that if a power could conceive of crippling enemy capacities to such an extent that the surviving enemy force levels could be viewed with equinamity – as insufficient to penetrate its BMD –, then it would be subject to a temptation to strike. While a BMD might by one side be seen merely as a tool to limit fatality expectations, the other side might all too easily be jittery, and react by introducing MIRVs in order to maintain the credibility of its deterrent. Finally, a nation having acquired a population-defending BMD might, with the acquisition of MIRVs, feel that it could survive the retaliatory forces retained by the other after a MIRV attack. The inherent temptation to attack would be reinforced by apprehension if the other side also possessed both weapons systems, to the extent that a pre-emptive strike might be considered *necessary* in a situation of mistrust in the other's intentions.[100]

One might further highlight the fears by postulating, as did William C. Foster, a full mutual conversion to MIRV, with each booster containing a mean of 5 re-entry vehicles.[101] Hypothetically this would mean that one booster rocket would suffice to destroy 5 enemy silos, each containing 5 warheads, i.e. a total of 25 warheads. The 'temptation' aspect is self-evident (at least as long as the invulnerable Polaris/Poseidon type forces are conveniently forgotten).

The psychological insecurity objection here outlined formed the basis for most BMD opponents' views. A number of other points were also raised, but most of these could, as indicated, be refuted with greater ease. As concerned, for example, the objection that current BMD designs would become outdated: certainly, but so would current offensive system designs, and no cogent reasoning was presented as to why this should be significantly more so with regard to the BMD. As concerned the objection that while cost-exchange and efficiency prognostications might point to one conclusion, one could not rely on this proving correct without inconceivable operational testing: this appeared equally applicable to offensive systems' penetration capabilities versus a BMD. Any analysis of the pros and cons had to allow the potential validity of BMD opponents' fear of a psychologically-induced vicious circle of arms (and cost) escalation.[102] But by 1969/70 certain facts, and counter- 'uncertainty factors', had to be considered. We shall treat the latter first.

Following France's successful building of missile-firing nuclear submarines, there emerged evidence that the stage had been reached when the relevant technology had become widely available. In other words: A number of technically-advanced nations could by the late 1960's effect the production of a Polaris-type submarine, provided only that they were willing to invest the necessary funds.[103]

This meant that the super-powers would relinquish their privileged position if they did not implement a BMD, the technology of which would remain their preserve for the foreseeable future.[104] Their positions would be relinquished, since any nation which possessed even one primitive 'Polaris' with ten nuclear warheads, would in theory be assured of the capability to destroy the ten most populous cities of a super-power.

Any second-rate power thus capable of inflicting unacceptable destruction could bluff, act, and blackmail as if it was a super-power. Any fear as to the potential irrationality of the USA or the USSR would of necessity be multiplied by any such situation.

This uncertainty, and the fears induced thereby, can be seen as reflected in the apparent fact that the USSR had at some time prior to 1969 deployed ABMs in such patterns as to also protect against potential Chinese attacks. (See above for US Defence Department's efficiency predictions regarding a US 'anti-Chinese' BMD). This was revealed in President Nixon's testimony:[105] 'Today their (Soviet BMD) radars are also directed towards Communist China'. It must be noted that his evidence may have related merely to additional east-directed BMD radar facilities around Moscow, or it may have teetered on logical inference only, – logic overcoming evidence? Yet the logic was irrefutable. If a Soviet anti-Chinese BMD was not a reality prior to Nixon's announcement, it could safely be presumed to be imminent.

There was another dimension to the uncertainty, that of a genuine accident. The position by the late 1960's was such that some leading scientists considered it very much an accident that an accident had not occurred ('Dr. Strangelove')![106] That many if these scientists enjoyed access to classified material lent credibility to their assertion. The fact that they considered the danger of accidents to be less acute by 1969, with the introduction of more sophisticated multiple control measures and equipment, did not mean that the possibility either was or could be eliminated.[107]

One might therefore with some confidence declare that the uncertainty complex associated with a no-BMD situation, was *more* acute and dangerous, than the uncertainty problems focused on by BMD opponents. Our analysis of attack synchronization problems indicated that even the conceivable massive attacks of a post-MIRV era would be most unlikely to destroy an opponent's second-strike capability before it could be activated. First-strike take-out success could not logically be expected by either super-powers' strategic experts, – even without considering degradation factors and other difficulties surrounding any initiation of attack. The temptation aspect therefore becomes less important and is probably in reality negligible.

This did not mean that 'arms race – temptation' uncertainties should or could be completely discounted. It did mean that a different, and quite possibly more ominous, uncertainty, made some BMD deployment appear essential. And, on the practical side, there was the fact by the late '60's of the existing Soviet BMD deployment, and of the authorization of some US deployment by the US Congress. The USSR seemed already to have made the decision that she must protect herself against second-rank power capabilities, and against accidents. The USA seemed at the very least to have indicated that she leaned towards the same conclusion.

However, even if the decision to effect a limited BMD deployment was thus taken, probably irreversibly, on grounds of overall security considerations, a number of worrying factors nevertheless remained. One related to the referred-to spiralling military costs. The spiralling did appear to be encouraged to a frightening extent by military authorities' tendency to over-react, in their desire to counter enemy programs which they conceived of as threats to their deterrence capabilities. To anyone sceptical of a nation's strategic analysts being *proficient* enough to perceive the impossibility of a successful pre-emptive attack, even if this impossibility was dictated by both logic and technology, to him there remained indeed a dangerous 'temptation' factor inherent in any 'arms race'.

There were therefore reasons for hoping that BMD deployments would be effected to the extent necessary to eliminate no-defence uncertainties, – but that they would not be effected to the extent where they might mistakenly be conceived of as endangering the other super-power's ultimate deterrent. There was clearly a need for an agreement to accept the existing relative strategic balance, if possible with a lowered level of 'guaranteed' casualty-inflicting capacities.[108] The necessity to accept some approximation of the existing relative balance situation was stressed by Kosygin in a meeting with US Senators Gore and Pell on 19 November, 1968.[109] He presented three prerequisites to any proposed arms limitation talks: (1) peaceful co-existence; (2) detente; (3) avoidance by either power of attempts to acquire positions of greater ('superior') relative strength.

The third point referred to President Nixon's ambiguous election campaign pledges that he would only negotiate with the USSR from a position of strength. Soviet advocacies of the necessity for *USSR* superiority (see also Chapter 8), represented a clear warning not only that the Soviet Union could also play the escalating arms race game, but that Soviet Military pressures for such would not be resisted without a curtailing of the parallel US tendencies. The era of US strategic superiority had to be recognized as at an end, and as 'non-resurrectable'.

Hence the SALT (Strategic Arms Limitation Talks) initiated in Helsinki in November, 1969, engendered considerable expectations. At least their very opening indicated widespread appreciation of the NEED for agreement(s). . . . This appreciation was further confirmed and encouraged by the tentative agreements of 26 May, 1972 (See Foreword).

Overkill. Two factors must be delineated: one, the overkill capacity necessary to ensure kill capability in the minds of defence planners maximizing all factors potentially detracting from such a capability; and two, the popularized ludicrousness of 'killing the enemy x times over'. The latter is preposterous. The former is not, although it can often be seen to be in danger of becoming the latter. . . .

A maximization of degradation factors (re. missile effectiveness prognostications) implied that the early 1970 missile numbers might, even when correlated with contemporary conversions to MIRV capabilities, yet conform merely to the requirements of the first type of overkill. One could envisage degradation percentages of such a scale as to make the consequent warhead number necessary within the logic of cautious defence planners. But such degradation factor estimates appeared to be inappropriate to the sophisticated missiles then available. If numbers had been further multiplied, as implied in the questionable US prognostications which postulated 2,500 Soviet ICBMs by 1974–75,[110] then the logic would have become shaky indeed.

It appears safe to assert the powers would then have engaged in procurements which relate to the second overkill category. The present semi-balanced large-scale offensive forces, complemented by a limited BMD, may well be reasonable and necessary. But multiplications of offensive capacities justified by 'hostile' BMD system expansions could only lead to a higher level of mutually offsetting offensive-defensive increments; the basic balance would remain unchanged.

There could be little doubt with regard to either power's capacity to effect the increases in its own forces necessary to offset increments in those of the other. Logic drove towards a recognition of the present balance. Acceptance of this premise carried the promise that the balance might in future be retained at a lower level (through limited BMD expansions, accompanied by offensive contractions).

It had to be in thus lowering, *without altering*, the offsetting balance between the super powers, while simultaneously assuring their security and relative positions vis-à-vis lesser powers, that one might envisage ultimate SALT success. The argument and process was contingent upon acceptance of the fact that attack degradation and synchronization problems, when juxtaposed with defence dispersal and 'second-strike' characteristics, entailed that neither power could achieve a 'credible first-strike' force through any conceivable force augmentations of the foreseeable future. The limited SALT agreement of 1972 finally provided implicit acknowledgement thereof by the superpowers.

Over-reacting dilemma. A few additional comments ought to be made concerning this related quandry, some aspects of which have been dealt with previously. On the one hand there are the mentioned inducements to an arms race psychosis which are inherent in long lead times. Research and development time demands are such that present achievements may be said to have been determined by debates of 5 years or so ago; the present debates determine the postures and capabilities some 5 years hence. It is in this context that the above conclusions take on crucial significance.

The same may be said with regard to another aspect: this is the psychological inheritance of the past Soviet obsession with the need to achieve balance and offsetting capabilities. The obsession with the need to eliminate the weaknesses of vulnerability might cloud the realization that the task has basically been achieved. There is a danger of being so intent on reaching parity, as to pass it, and threaten an obverse imbalance – with all its arms race connotations. Or to put it differently: there is a danger of over-consciousness of the strategic quagmire of the vulnerable, to the exclusion of strategic considerations affecting the non-vulnerable, with the result that when the latter position is attained, it may not be accompanied by the appropriate thought and plan level.

There were, however, indications of appropriate political leadership appreciation, – as seen for example in the initiation of SALT negotiations. And this was of greater import than cruder military endorsements of the need to pursue no longer realizable, but destabilizing, superiority designs. (See Chapter 8).

The 1971–72 slowdown in Soviet missile procurements reinforced the impression of political appreciation, paved the way for the 1972 agreements, and encouraged a psychological climate which augured well for future agreements of substance.

NOTES

1. This chapter will be primarily concerned with Soviet strategic developments. But Western (US) parallels will be considered whenever such consideration appears conducive to greater clarity, and to a more meaningful appreciation of the context. Some of the conclusions which emerge pertain as much to a more general East–West strategic framework as to specific Soviet conditions.

2. For evidence regarding the scenario-definition at the beginning of the paragraph, as well as for an analysis of the 'debates' relating to the described process as a whole, see Chapters 1, 2 and 3.

3. *Adelphi Papers*, No. 46, The Institute for Strategic Studies, London, March, 1968.

4. See 'Weapon Systems: A story of Failure', *Washington Post*, 26 January, 1969.

5. *The Military Balance* 1969–70, same for 1970–71 (both I.S.S., London), and Statement of Secretary of Defence Laird on the *Fiscal Year 1972–76 Defense Program and the 1972 Defense Budget*, before the House Armed Services Committee, 9 March, 1971.

6. *The Military Balance* 1970–71 asserted 1050; a Pentagon leak reported in the *Guardian* of 29 October, 1969 asserted 1350.

7. *The Military Balance* 1970–71 asserted 1300; Laird's 9 March, 1971 St., *op. cit.*, asserted 1440.

8. In Laird's Statement, *ibid.* (estimate).

9. *The Military Balance* 1970–71 asserted 160; Secr. of Defence Laird asserted 200 in an Associated Press Annual Meeting, 20 April, 1970.

10. *The Military Balance* 1970–71 asserted 280; Laird's 9 March, 1971 St., *op. cit.*, asserted 350.

11. In Laird's Statement, *ibid.* (estimate).

12. Statement by Secr. of Defence Laird on *FY 1973 Program and Budget*, 15 February, 1972.

13. *Ibid.* This figure includes a limited number stationed in IRBM/MRBM fields, and therefore probably targeted on targets not in the US.

14. SALT agreement, Moscow, 26 May, 1972, *op. cit.*

15. *Ibid.*; figures not supplied are taken from Laird, 15 February, 1972, *op. cit.* and from *The Military Balance* 1971–72, I.S.S., London.

16. Laird's February, 1972 Statement, *ibid.*, notes that 50 of these are tankers and reconnaissance aircraft.

17. The Military Balance 1971–72, *op. cit.*, notes that the Soviet Naval Air Force operates another 300 medium-range bombers, capable of delivering nuclear weapons.

18. Laird's February, 1972 Statement, *op. cit.*; May, 1972 SALT agreement, *op. cit.*

19. *Ibid.* These figures are accompanied (in Laird's statement) by the notation 'figures for USSR as computed – should not create impression of precise intelligence' (!).

20. Testimony of Deputy US Secretary of Defence Gilpatrick, in *New York Times*, 3 December, 1967.

21. President Nixon, *Message to Congress*, 18 February, 1970.

22. Laird's 9 March, 1971, Statement, *op. cit.*

23. *Ibid.*

24. See footnotes 6–11; or compare with figures provided by yet other sources, – e.g. Capitaine Raoust, in *Revue de Défence Nationale*, April, 1969, Paris.

25. *The Military Balance* 1969–70 allows for 1,054 Soviet ICBMs in 1969; the 1970–71 edition allows for 1,050; *Strategic Survey* 1969 (also of ISS) allows for 1,200.

26. See e.g. (Senate Armed Services Comm. member) Senator Jackson's closing remark in the US Senate debate on ABM authorizations, 6 August, 1969, and the estimate given by Laird in his 13 October, 1971 Washington Press Conference.

27. Testimony by Secr. of Defence Laird to October, 1971 Press Conf., *ibid.*; see also 1972 SALT agreement, *op. cit.*

28. Bundeswehr's *Soldat und Technik*, No. 7, 1969, p. 381, and Laird, *ibid.*

29. *Jane's Weapon Systems*, November, 1971, London (see editor's introduction).

30. Azovtsev, N., in *V. I. Lenin i Sovetskaya Voennaya Nauka*, Voenizdat, Moscow, 1971, asserts present and insists on future 'superiority'.

31. E.g. *Ogoniok*, No. 2, 1965, *op. cit.*

32. Marshal of the Soviet Union and CINC Strategic Rocket Troops N.I. Krylov, in *Pravda*, 19 November, 1966.

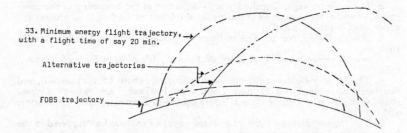

33. Minimum energy flight trajectory,
with a flight time of say 20 min.

Alternative trajectories

FOBS trajectory

34. US Secr. of Defence McNamara to Washington D.C. Press Conference, 3 November, 1967.
35. *Pravda*, 19 November, 1966, *op. cit.*
36. See e.g. Marshal Bagramian et al., *Istoria Voin i Voennovo Iskusstva*, Section 4, Voenizdat, Moscow, 1970.
37. *Izvestia*, 4 July, 1965, and *Izvestia*, 8 November, 1965; also *Pravda*, 19 November, 1966.
38. McNamara's November, 1967 Press Conference, *op. cit.*
39. Quite apart from their vulnerability to enemy destruction, they were also becoming vulnerable to other types of interference. By late 1971 Soviet hunter satellites had the capacity to close in on and lock on to both high and low altitude satellites. See e.g. report in *The New York Times*, 2 January, 1972.
40. See treatment in 'Non-Proliferation Treaty', *Hearings of the US Senate Foreign Relations Committee, 1st Session, 1969*.
41. Rathjens, George W., 'The Dynamics of the Arms Race', in *Scientific American*, April, 1969, pp. 15–25.
42. USIS release, US Embassy, Oslo, 17 September, 1969.
43. A rocket of a multiple warhead type was shown at the 7 November, 1968, Moscow military parade. No specifications were announced; – as noted by *Strategic Survey, 1968* (ISS, London), Soviet testing of a multiple re-entry vehicle was reported to have occurred in August, 1968.
44. Dr. John S. Foster, Jr., US Defence Dept., Director of Research and Engineering, in testimony to the House Foreign Affairs Committee, US Congress, 5 August, 1969 (text released by Pentagon same day). Another official US Government account is less categorical, but does confirm that the SS9 certainly at least 'possesses MIRV homing and control equipment, which in a few years will possess sufficient accuracy for the destruction of US Minuteman III rocket silos'. The same source further affirms the much greater size of USSR MIRV warheads. (USIS release, *op. cit.*)
NOTE. Perhaps it ought to be noted here that probably the most useful definition distinguishing MIRV from MRV (and one inherent in the above description and the following diagram), at least for defensive identification and monitoring purposes, is that which defines MIRV as a missile the re-entry vehicles of which have a lateral variation from the flight plan exceeding a certain number of degrees, – a definition of little additional conceptual value, but possibly essential within a context of arms limitation and control posts.
45. USIS Release, *ibid.*
46. Presidential Special Advisor Henry Kissinger, in his Moscow Press Conference of 26 May, 1972, confirmed expectations that the USSR would also have mastered MIRV technology before the lapse of the interim SALT agreements (signed the same day); see also US Secretary of Defence Laird's testimony to the Senate Armed Services Committee about Soviet MIRV testing (*New York Times*, 9 June 1972; *Reuters*, 20 June, 1972).
47. *Newsweek* ('Periscope'), 16 June, 1969, quoting US 'intelligence' sources and official 'analysis'.
48. Dr. Brennan, presentation of evidence released by Pentagon, *op. cit.*
49. But see discussion in *The Military Balance 1970–71*, which concludes: 'To an unmeasurable extent, however, that advantage may be offset by the greater ad-

ministrative and ideological centralization of the Soviet system, and its consequently greater vulnerability to the destruction of a few centres of control'.

50. Quoted by *The New York Times*, 10 April, 1969. See also e.g. Secretary of Defence McNamara in his 'Posture Statement' of 1967, p. 68, regarding the number of tactical warheads in Europe. And e.g. Secretary of Defence Laird in *'Hearings on Military Posture'*, Comm. on Armed Services, House of Representatives, 1969, Part I, p. 2467, regarding the number of Polaris and ICBMs.

51. Secretary of Defence Laird, *ibid*. The Hearings concerned BMD authorization. See also testimony by Dr. Panofsky, Professor and Director of Stanford Linear Acceleration Centre, Stanford University (in 'Authorization for Military Procurement, Research and Development Fiscal Year 1970, and Reserve Strength', Part 2. *Hearing before the US Senate Committee on Armed Services*, GPO, Washington, 1969, pp. 1129 and 1175): 'It is consistent with known technical intelligence information on their high yields and accuracy on target, that each SS9 missile could destroy a Minuteman launch control centre and/or silo'. And see footnote 44.

52. *Hearings on Military Posture*, Comm. on Armed Services, House of Representatives, 1969, Part II, p. 4241.

53. 'Military Procurement Authorizations for Fiscal Year 1967', p. 55, *Hearings*, Senate Armed Services Committee, GPO, Washington, 1966. See also, Bingham, J. B., 'Can Military Spending be Controlled?', *Foreign Affairs*, October, 1969, pp. 51–66.

54. See Laird's February, 1972 Statement, *op. cit.*

55. *Pravda*, 7 March, 1970 (Art. 'Vashnaya Problema').

56. *Pravda*, 3 February, 1971.

57. Sokolovsky, ed., Voennaya Strategia, 3rd edition, *op. cit.*, p. 235; Sushko, N. Y., and Kondratkov, T. R., *'Metodologicheskiye Problemy Teorii i Praktiki'*, Voenizdat, Moscow, 1967, p. 147.

58. Richard Garwin and Hans Bethe, 'Anti-Ballistic Missile Systems', *Scientific American*, March, 1968. Their questionable quoting of McNamara (p. 31) leaves considerable room for misinterpretation (see 'Authorization for Military Procurement . . . Fiscal Year 1970', *op. cit.*, Part 2, p. 1340). But otherwise, the article is both good and instructive. 'Authorization for Military Procurement . . . Fiscal Year 1970', *op. cit.*, Part 1, furthermore contains more optimistic evaluations of radar possibilities, as well as useful graphs of the various relevant radar types, pp. 173–181. In this context it should be noted that the use of relay stations necessitated by 'Forward Scatter' may be made superfluous through the development of 'Back Scatter' (what might be termed a 'self-relaying' beam).

59. *Jane's Weapon Systems*, November, 1971, London.

60. That the USSR followed the US example and secured (at least some) 'hardening' of all their ICBM silos was testified to by Secretary of Defence Laird in *Hearings on Military Posture*, Comm. on Armed Services, House of Reps., 1969, Part 1, p. 2467.

61. Dr. Brennan, Hudson Research Institute, *op. cit.*

62. See also Strategic Survey 1969, ISS, *op. cit.*, pp. 30–33.

63. US Dept. of Defence *Posture Statement* for 1968 (including fiscal 1969). He must have known the formula presented above.

64. Dr. J. S. Foster, Jr. (US Defence Dept.), 5 August, 1969, testimony to the House of Representatives' Foreign Affairs Subcommittee, revealed that the US had acquired evidence of a tentative BMD deployment around Leningrad as early as 1962, and that this had been followed by evidence of some 1964 deployment of an improved ABM in the same area. It seemed that this development was not followed up, and one might therefore conclude that it represented initial experiments rather than a fully-fledged 'system'.

65. Marshal Boriuzov, *Krasnaya Zvezda*, 13 November, 1963, and *ibid*.

66. When this author visited Moscow.

67. As regards the Moscow BMD complex, President Nixon was in 1969 reported as testifying that it encompassed at least 67 Galosh ABMs — *The New York Times* 15 March, 1969.

68. Secretary of Defence McNamara, at a San Francisco *Press Conference*, 18 September, 1967, revealed that there had been initiated offsetting increases in US ICBMs targeted on ABM defended 'cities and areas'.

69. The Military Balance, 1968–69, *op. cit.*

70. *Ibid.*
71. *US News and World Report*, 6 February, 1967, p. 36, produced a report according to which the USSR had succeeded in producing 'the so-called X-ray effect in intense proportions', with the described result being a neutralizing of ICBM guidance equipment and even fissionable material at considerable distances from the ABM detonation. See also *Technology Week*, 2 January, 1967, pp. 10–12, according to which this effect would not be hindered by present US warhead shielding materials.
72. US Defence Dept. Posture Statement for 1968.
73. See 'Non-Proliferation Treaty', *Hearings of the Foreign Relations Committee*, US Senate, 1st Session, 1969, p. 419, for Secretary of Defence Laird's testimony regarding Soviet BMD R & D and ABM testing. In a nationally televised Washington interview, 9 February, 1969, Laird asserted Soviet BMD research allocations to be four times those of the USA, and expanded by claiming that this represented a seven times greater relative effort when related to differences in GNP.
74. *Ibid.* ('Non-Proliferation Treaty'). Laird's Statement of 9 March, 1971, *op. cit.*, postulated operational deployment during 1971.
75. 'Safeguard Anti-Ballistic Missile System', *Hearings before Subcommittee of the Committee on Appropriations*, House of Representatives, 91st Congress, 1st Session, 1969, pp. 10–11. And see Laird's 1971 St., *ibid.*
76. 'Diplomatic and Strategic Impact of Multiple Warhead Missiles', *Hearings before the Subcommittee on National Security Policy and Scientific Developments of the Committee on Foreign Affairs*, House of Representatives, 91st Congress, 1st Session, 1969, p. 244.
77. President Nixon's News Conference, 14 March, 1969, announcing the Administration's intention to proceed with the deployment of a modified Sentinel BMD system, the 'Safeguard' system. See *Keesings Contemporary Archives*, 1969–70, p. 23289. Also see Secretary of Defence Laird, 9 February, 1969, interview, *op. cit.* By this time there was also concern that a very large-scale expansion of BMD capabilities might be imminent through the conversion of anti-aircraft defences (such as the Tallin line) by the introduction of advanced BMD radars. See e.g. Laird's 1971 statement, *op. cit.*
78. Approved by the US Senate after the defeat (6 August, 1969) of (1) the Senator Margaret Chase Smith amendment; (2) the Cooper-Hart amendment, *op. cit.*
79. Statement by Kosygin at Press Conferences in London, 10 February, 1967, and New York, 26 June, 1967. See also *Adelphi Papers*, No. 65, February, 1970, ISS, London, footnote 13 of article 'Parity, Superiority or Sufficiency'.
80. Major General N. A. Talensky, in *'International Affairs'*, Moscow, October, 1964.
81. One might here interject a supporting quote from Dr. Brennan, *'Hearings on Military Posture'*, before the Committee on Armed Services, House of Reps., 1969, Part 1, p. 2189: 'One major Russian scientist who *is* closely associated with the Soviet missile program has said (to Americans) that effective missile defence is on the whole probably realizable'. The stress is Dr. Brennan's. See also Sokolovsky, ed., *Voennaya Strategia*, 3rd edition, p. 361.
82. US Dept. of Defence 'Posture Paper' for 1967, p. 49. See also subsequent Senate Hearings.
83. See Annual 'Military Procurement Authorizations for Fiscal Year . . . ', *Hearings before the Committee on Armed Forces*, US Senate, US Govt. Printing Office, Washington, D.C.
84. A view forcefully propounded by Dr. Brennan at the 1968 Oslo Conference, *op. cit.*
85. US Defence Department, 'Posture Statement' for 1967, p. 53.
86. Garwin and Bethe, in *Scientific American*, March, 1968; Rathjens, same April, 1969; and see Senator Jackson's Senate Speech of 6 August, 1969, *op. cit.*, for a useful list of scientists opposing BMD deployment. Also, see R. L. Rothstein, 'The ABM, Proliferation, and International Stability', pp. 487–503, *Foreign Affairs*, April, 1968, and C. M. Herzfeld 'BMD and National Security', *Annals of the New York Academy of Sciences*, New York, 1965. Herzfeld's critique that 'any defensive system can really do no more than raise the entrance price which an attacker must pay in order to destroy a target' may of course, in the view of later developments and

our analysis, be seen as misconceived and in fact providing a basic rationale for BMD deployment (!).

87. Wm. C. Foster testified, e.g., to development and production costs of an ICBM missile increasing from US$ 3·3 million in 1960 to US$ 8·75 million in 1965, in 'Prospects for Arms Control', pp. 413–33, *Foreign Affairs*, April, 1969.

88. D. G. Brennan, 'The Case for Missile Defense', pp. 433–49, *Foreign Affairs*, April, 1969, and testimony of same to US Senate, see 'Authorization for Military Procurement . . . Fiscal Year 1970 . . . ', *op. cit.*, Part 2, pp. 1338–50. (Testimony by, e.g., Rathjens, is to be found just before that of Dr. Brennan; testimony by other leading scientists are to be found in the same volume).

89. US Defence Department, 'Posture Statement', January, 1967, *op. cit.*; and see 'Military Procurement, Authorization, for Fiscal Year 1970', Part 2, pp. 1410–14, and elsewhere.

90. Dr. Brennan, 'Authorization for Military Procurement . . . Fiscal Year 1970', *op. cit.*

91. US Defence Department's *'Posture Statement'*, January, 1968, p. 64.

92. *Ibid.* The figure in brackets are alterations introduced by Secretary of Defence Clifford in presenting the same graph in 1969; see 'Authorization for Military Procurement . . . 1970 . . . ', *op. cit.*, Part 1, p. 32.

93. As it was presumed by Dr. Brennan at the 1968 Oslo Conference, *op. cit.*

94. Military Procurement Authorization for Fiscal 1970, *op. cit.*, pp. 253–4.

95. *Ibid.*, p. 257 (this author's explanatory insertion).

96. Marshal V. I. Chuykov, *Izvestia*, 15 June, 1967, and same in *Rodina*, 3 January, 1968.

97. Dr. Brennan, *op. cit.*

98. See especially Rathjen's article in *Scientific American*, April, 1969, *op. cit.*

99. See *ibid.* for a good exposition of this belief.

100. See e.g., Dr. J. S. Foster's Congressional testimony, 5 August, 1969, *op. cit.*

101. Wm. C. Foster, *Foreign Affairs*, April, 1969, *op. cit.*

102. As regards the costs, see, e.g., *'World Military Expenditures*, 1966–67', The Economics Bureau of the US Arms Control and Disarmament Agency, Washington, 1969; or synopsis, thereof, by A. Alexander, 'The Cost of World Armaments', *Scientific American*, October 1969, pp. 21–7. See also Chapter 8.

103. Dr. Herman Kahn, Director of the Hudson Research Institute, at a 9th May, 1969 seminar arranged by the Norwegian NUPI, and attended by this author, presented this as the definite conclusion of his Institute's specialists.

104. *Ibid.*

105. President Nixon, as reported by *The New York Times*, 15 March, 1969 (per the President's *News Conference* of 14 March, 1969). And see Secretary of Defence Laird's testimony, 'Safeguard Anti-Ballistic Missile System', *Hearings before Subcommittees of the Committee of Appropriations*, House of Reps., 91st Congress, 1st Session, 1969, pp. 10–11.

106. Herman Kahn, *op. cit.*, and *Why ABM?*, by Herman Kahn and other Hudson Institute analysts, Pergamon Press, 1969.

107. *Ibid.*

108. It is interesting to refer to the US Draft Treaty of 29th April, 1965, to the Geneva 'disarmament negotiation'. It suggested a reduction in offensive strategic forces by cutting a substantial percentage from the forces of either side in each of two stages. The reductions would be effected so as to preserve the relative balance. The proposal came to nought (as was probably expected) and was not followed up. Yet the indicated thought process gestated . . . – see 'Authorization for Military Procurement . . . Fiscal Year 1970', *op. cit.*, p. 1345.

109. US Embassy, Moscow, News Conference, 19th November, 1968.

110. US Secretary of Defence Laird, *Hearings on Military Posture*, Comm. on Armed Services, House of Reps., 1969, Part 1, p. 2467.

5

The Development of the Navy and the Emergence of Soviet Interventionary-type Forces; The Soviet Navy's Acquisition of Global Capabilities and Perspectives

By 1970 the Soviet Navy had assumed a strategic role of considerable significance. The quality of her new vessels did to a considerable degree offset American superiority in numbers and tonnage. The Soviet Union had furthermore developed interventionary-type forces of notable importance. She had achieved world-wide mobility. And she had acquired a flexibility of operation and response which covered the gamut from strategic warfare to interventionary activity in areas not adjacent to the USSR.

Russian desires for such capabilities had been longstanding. One may for example point to the fact that she kept a naval squadron in the Mediterranean throughout most of the period from 1769 to 1830. But at no time had she previously had the capacity to sustain more than a very limited presence in foreign waters.[1]

Even the sizeable second world war fleet had to restrict its operations to territorial waters, where it could rely on land-based air-cover, and concentrate on defence against potential hostile landings.[2]

The Cold War saw a considerable build-up of the submarine fleet.

But it was not oriented to the disruption of the West's control of the seas. The submarine production centred on smaller types with restricted action radii. Operational emphasis remained restricted to defensive anti-invasion conceptions and tasks.

Yet Soviet recognition of the theoretical NEED for more extensive capabilities was evident as early as the time of the Spanish Civil War.[3] The viability of this assertion is evinced also in Stalin's remark about the post-war Civil War in Greece. Despairing of breaking Allied communication lines, due to the fact that they were protected by the world's 'most powerful' nation, he concluded that '. . . we have no navy. The uprising in Greece must be stopped, and as quickly as possible'.[4]

One may postulate two reasons why the recognition of the advantages of greater naval capacities did not result in relevant procurement programs; – why the naval expansion that did occur was neither in quantity nor quality such as was desired by Soviet leaders. The first, basic reason lay in insufficient priority, dictated by budgetary stresses similar to those which later constricted Malenkov.[5] The second reason was supplementary, but served to preserve the low naval priority even after the budgetary inhibition had been eased. It lay in the naive and over-optimistic early missile procurement and capabilities prognoses, prognoses which temporarily blinded planners to naval needs.[6]

But the situation changed drastically in the 1960's. The early 1962 upgrading of the Navy[7] coincided with emerging awareness of missile unreliability (high 'degradation factors' minimized effectivity expectations) and vulnerability ('first-strike characteristics'), an awareness which was encouraged or forced by the Kennedy-administration's procurement policies (See Chapters 2 and 4). The consequent efforts to provide the missile forces with second-strike qualities, through silo-hardening, increased launch mobility and dispersal, and more sophisticated missile control and dispatch procedures,[8] incorporated the build-up of the Navy. Far from having become superflous in the modern age,[9] the Navy was now recognized as an important ingredient of a balanced and secure strategic posture.[10]

Once the basic decision had been taken, however, it was evidently extended to encourage the development also of non-strategic naval capabilities, (see below). And the changes and procurement developments were soon reflected in strategic promulgations of note.

The New Navy was no longer to be a mere adjunct to the other service branches. A high stress was placed on inter-service co-ordination and support, but the Navy was clearly to be capable also of independent operations.[11] She was assigned definite strategic defensive and offensive tasks, but was further to be capable of interventionary-type action against enemy bases and presumably, by extension, other targets.[12] And it is significant that such action, whether of a strategic or a non-strategic nature, was to be accomplished by personnel trained to operate under and to utilize nuclear conditions and technology. It was clearly accepted that modern requirements made a mockery of traditional nuclear/conventional distinctions; troops and officers were trained to utilize the implications of such sophisticated nuclear technology as was making possible 'clean' take-out strikes rapidly followed by physical occupation.[13]

Finally, there emerged a complementary awareness of the potential peace-time psychological advantages accruing from the mere existence of navy capacity.[14]

These development trends will be traced in more detail below. But it appears propituous first to turn to the other aspects of the trilogy of Soviet maritime assertions:[15] (a) A navy with a striking power surpassed only by that of the USA; (b) A merchant marine among the world's largest and most modern, and the largest and most modern fishing fleet in the world; (c) A unique program of oceanographic research.

THE MERCHANT MARINE

The 1960's saw the emergence of a large, modern and specialized Soviet merchant navy. Its dynamic development is indicated by the fact that it rose from 2 per cent of world tonnage in 1960 to 6·5 per cent in 1967 (about 12 million tons d.w.); it is further indicated by the achieved and projected annual tonnage increase rate of 1 million tons d.w.[16]

The fact that a significant proportion of the Soviet grain purchases from Canada (and, to a lesser extent, Australia) of 1963 and thereafter had to be transported in foreign vessels,[17] highlighted early Soviet tonnage limitations. There was clearly a prima facie case for such merchant marine expansion as would facilitate minimal self-sufficiency in Soviet export-import transport capability.

But having identified this basic strategic consideration one must proceed to reflect further on some of the related desiderata.

There are the purely political implications of an awareness in foreign ports of modern Soviet ships frequenting the harbours. The implications are abstract and any defining of their scope must be contentious. But one should not under-estimate the impact of the emerging 'normalcy' of previously unknown routines. This will be returned to below.

Then there are the more concrete advantages which accrue from not having to submit cargo to foreign scrutiny, whether such might be deemed undesirable for strategic, moral or other reasons. The military relevance was demonstrated during the 1962 Cuban crisis when merchant vessels, evidently constructed to accomodate military needs, were utilized for the transport of missiles.[18] And one may perhaps presume a continuing utilization of this military capacity, with relation e.g. to arms exports.

The ability to carry military hardware did of course also entail ability to accomodate military personnel. The Naval transport capacities later developed provided more potent means, but did not obviate the advantages of supplementary merchant marine facilities. These remain an important adjunct to Soviet strategic capabilities.

THE FISHING FLEET

Captain Raoust succinctly delineated the relevant factors of contemporary and abiding significance. After describing the Soviet merchant fleet as 'the most modern in the world' and as operating on 'all seas', he continued: 'In a normal period 400–500 fishing vessels are concentrated in the North Atlantic. They may repair to Havana where a base has been specially constructed with the aid of Soviet capital and technicians; – ... as with the merchant fleet ... (it) is utilized equally for military-political ends such as ... control of occidental maritime activities. ... But above all ... sonars utilized for the detection of fish may also no doubt be utilized to detect larger objects. It is not implausible to infer that Moscow knows the deployment of American Polaris submarines nearly as accurately as Washington'.[19]

A NATO source goes further: 'The Soviet 'fish-factory' ships and trawlers now range over the world's oceans, and it is significant that a large proportion of them are outfitted for intelligence gathering. They carry comprehensive monitoring equipment and highly sophisticated electronic gear. Their speed is often in excess of that usually associated with such craft. It is not unusual for such a trawler to attach itself to NATO formations during exercises as an . . . extremely persistent observer'.[20]

A determining of the extent and utility of data thus derived by the USSR necessarily rests on educated guesswork. But that it is substantial may be inferred from Fleet Admiral Kasatonov's assertion that: 'an important role in the securing of bases and combat operations is executed by aid vessels of various types' (i.e. electronically-equipped merchant and fishing vessels . . .).[21]

THE OCEANOGRAPHIC RESEARCH PROGRAMME

The same Revue de Defence Nationale source[22] stated categorically that by 1968: 'the number of (Soviet) research vessels (of various types) . . . is greater than the combined number of ships performing analogous missions for all the other nations of the world'. Accepting this correlation as accurate, the import is clearly relevant to an investigation of Naval capabilities.

Most scientific data, such as relating to ocean floor contours and ridges, ocean currents, ocean salination and temperature levels, and ocean marine life, may be utilized by Naval authorities engaged in sub-surface activities. Furthermore, as with the fishing fleet, one might expect the presence on board of electronic and other equipment intended for the discovery, tracking and supervision of hostile vessels. Such vessels might be photographed, their electronic equipment (radio, sonar, radar et al) tapped, and their activities audited.[23]

It was presumably knowledge of this activity which prompted Admiral Rickover to suggest that the USSR would by the mid 1970's possess the knowledge and techniques necessary to destroy the US Polaris fleet.[24]

This appears to be an exaggerated evaluation of an emerging situation of US loss of non-vulnerability. A glance for example at the National Geographic Magazine's charts over the Indian Ocean (1967), the Pacific Ocean (1968), and the Atlantic Ocean (1969) floors would indicate that a proportion of a nuclear submarine fleet ought to succeed in finding a safe haven among the myriad ridges (North-South in the first, East-West in the latter oceans).

But the programme's aid to Soviet anti-U-boat tracking and killing capabilities and its general contribution to such knowledge as required by the expanding surface fleets must nevertheless be of a considerable scale.

E

THE NAVY

The qualitative and quantitative innovations which signified the end of the defensive strategy previously in operation were plainly evident by 1965–66. The Navy Day propaganda of July 1966 stressed the Soviet Union's new stature as 'A Great Naval Power', and announced the end of the 'complete domination of the seas by the traditional naval powers'. The assertion was hasty with regard to contemporary force balances, but significant as a statement of intent. It reflected the substantial infusion of funds into Naval expansion, and the priority rating of such. Both of these developments may, in view of development-time demands, be dated back to early 1962, if not before.

This dating of the initiating efforts is also suggested by a consideration of the basic requisita that had to be provided even before any particular procurement design could be envisaged. General ship-building, dock, and dry-dock facilities had to be expanded and modernized. And the communication networks within, to and from ports had to be improved.[25]

Yet even the amphibious forces development had by 1963 reached the stage when suitable landing vessels (of the Alligator and Polosny classes[26]) were being produced, and a marine infantry formation had been established.[27]

By 1965 the developments were referred to extensively in the Soviet press. One now possessed 'high speed landing-craft (carrying) ground units and marines with all their light and heavy equipment, including missiles'.[28]

By 1967 there were the first public demonstrations of mock amphibious manoeuvres and operations (with Polosny craft, each carrying two amphibious tanks and four amphibious armoured personnel carriers).[29] And there were the first public parades of specialist naval infantry ('marine') forces.[30]

The trend was thereafter evinced by more and more frequent and detailed articles dealing with amphibious operations, training and techniques.[31]

As concerns the regular surface, and the strategic fleet, qualitative innovations will be returned to below. But their implication (if not their scope) was forced on world awareness by the 1967 sinking of the Israeli ship *Eilat* by a missile from an Egyptian-manned Komar class Patrol boat. It is noteworthy that the sinking immediately sparked off

NATO efforts to develop similar weaponry for member navies.[32] 'The seriousness of the Styx missile problem is evident in that no surface-to-surface missile system with an adequate range is in general service with the US Navy or the navies of Allied countries. Naval . . . forces must drastically alter operating procedures'.[33]

But quantitative developments must here be referred to. Mediterranean trends were among the most easily ascertainable, and were illustrative. According to one authoritative source (1967):[34] 'Between 1963 and 1966 Soviet Mediterranean forces increased tenfold'. Soviet submarine operating days in the Mediterranean were asserted to have increased by 2000 per cent during the same period. A 1969 survey ascertained that 'the number of Soviet vessels in the Mediterranean varies between 25 and 60 and has included vessels which can land tanks and a helicopter cruiser'.[35] Another survey of the same year evidenced the fact that the overall Soviet naval expansion had already made her navy 'larger than all the Navies of Western Europe put together'.[36]

The Soviet Navy's combat potential clearly remained severely restricted when compared to US Naval capacities. But it had equally clearly already acquired a status which enabled it to entertain a far wider policy option spectrum than ever before. This may be illustrated by the following survey.

Four credible potential action-initiating scenarios relevant to a Navy such as the late 1960's/early 1970's Soviet Navy may be delineated:

The first type is illustrated by the limited 1961 British landing in Kuwait; – a landing in support of a friendly regime feared threatened by foreign intervention (in this case from Iraq).

The second type of action-initiating scenario may be exemplified by the 1958 US venture in Lebanon; – a landing to stabilize a perceived friendly regime at a time of internal political disintegration, the consequences of which are feared. Analogous operations might be initiated to encourage or stabilize the fortunes of friendly power factions engaged in utilizing the political disintegration. (This can be illustrated by hypothesizing Soviet ships in Latakia at the time of a Syrian C.P. coup attempt. Their presence could be decisive for the success of such an attempt. Quite apart from limited interventionary support potentials, the mere providing of an escape route could be sufficient, in that it would encourage coup leaders to 'hang on' through the crucial hours/days following a seizure. . . .)[37]

The third type may be seen as 'gun-boat diplomacy', a modern example of which was provided by the DRK's seizure of the Pueblo in 1968.[38]

The final action initiating scenario is that encompassing symbolic actions designed to lend conviction to national policy; – manoeuvres, deployments and redeployments are tools at hand.

These may be contrasted with three types of action-deferring scenarios for which the resources of such a Navy suffice:[39]

The first type may be represented by the 10th July, 1967, arrival of 8 Soviet warships to Alexandria and Port Said, immediately after the Arab-Israeli War, and their possible role in deterring any design for crossing the Suez Canal that Israel may have envisaged. (The Soviet Admiral in charge announced that his command might join the Egyptian armed forces in the face of aggression across the canal). Or one may point to the analogous Soviet Naval presence in Alexandria at the time of the sinking of the *Eilat,* as possibly having been instrumental in deterring Israeli reprisal schemes.

The second type can be illustrated by referring to the spring 1969 unrest in Lebanon, and contrasting it with the similar situation of unrest in 1958. In 1958 the USSR had protested vociferously but to no avail against the US intervention; in 1969 she merely warned mildly that any similar sequence of events would be opposed. The consequent US denial of intent appeared to be genuine, but any such intent would otherwise certainly have been strongly affected.

The final action-deterring type of scenario may be sketched through reference to the deployment of one Soviet Naval Squadron west of and one east of Libya at the time of the 1969 revolution. This would necessarily have caused concern to any Western intervention scheme, had such been envisaged. . . . Or one might refer to the US dispatch of 7th Fleet elements to the Bay of Bengal when Bangla Desh ceceded from Pakistan in December 1971; it was answered by the northward dispatch of elements of the Soviet fleet in the Indian Ocean. The war ended before the ships reached the Bay of Bengal. If it had not, the Soviet response would certainly have affected US plans.

As this survey indicates: a belittling of Soviet capabilities was not only becoming militarily dubious, but it might be seen per se to represent a misconception. It appears clear that *the political value arises from the mere capacity to assert a presence, and is not contingent on relative military strengths* (except at a time of general conflagration). An elaboration of the second action-deferring scenario, for example, must acknowledge that political considerations would have exaggerated the effectiveness of a militarily inferior Soviet flotilla stationed between interventionary force vessels and the coast. It is the political value which is strategically relevant in times of peace.

The capacity to show face was therefore a crucial extension of earlier capabilities. By the late 1960's the emerging forces already sufficed to initiate significant supporting and diversionary action.

A final example of illustrative and clarifying value may be found in the impressive scale of the Soviet link-up manoeuvres around the Norwegian coast, after the intervention in Czechoslovakia. The size and character of the forces involved, including amphibious forces, escorts and air-cover, was impressive enough to cause serious concern in the Norwegian government. This was evinced by the subsequent address to Parliament by the Minister of Defence. He dwelt at length on the fact that 'the Soviet Navy, which is today the second largest in the world, is constantly being expanded with, (inter alia), new rocket cruisers, nuclear submarines, helicopter carriers and amphibious landing vessels. The increase in amphibious capacity, that is in landing vessels, coincides with the establishing and expanding of marine infantry'. This was followed by a documentation of recent Soviet manoeuvres in the North Barents and Baltic Seas.[40] The psychological novelty of finding oneself potentially interred BEHIND established enemy front-lines necessarily enforced a profound re-evaluation of policy concepts. . . .

The last part of the decade witnessed a dynamic furthering of these trends. Three strands might be differentiated: Missile developments; amphibious and interventionary capability patterns; and world-wide mobility and flexibility achievements.

The dynamic aspect is perhaps that on which attention ought to focus with regard to all three. It may tentatively be documented with the following quote by Lord Balniel, British Minister of State (opening the Parliamentary Debate on Government Policy of 19th November, 1970):[41] 'Five years ago the average number of Soviet vessels (in the Mediterranean) was 3 surface warships, 3 submarines and 10 auxiliaries. This year it was 24 surface ships, at least 13 submarines and 24 auxiliaries. . . . Five years ago there were no Soviet naval vessels in the Indian Ocean. This year there were 7 surface warships, at least 4 submarines, and 9 auxiliaries. . . . The Soviet Union builds a nuclear submarine every 5 weeks'.

As concerns missile developments, the 1967 missile sinking of the *Eilat* was soon demonstrated to have been not merely indicative of experimental endeavours, but to have been illustrative of a conscious, all-embracing and novel combat orientation program. By 1969 it was clear that the Soviet Navy had engineered a near-total conversion of its vessels' armaments from artillery to rockets. Developed vessels only retained such small calibre cannons (57 mm) as could not effectively be utilized under conditions of general combat; they could no longer even theoretically engage in so-called conventional conflicts.[42] It became abundantly clear that (nuclear) missile technology would be utilized even in local combat constellations, where these vessels were involved.

By 1970 new warships were apparently no longer equipped even with symbolic concessions to old conventional theories; the Kresta II class destroyer had no ascertainable conventional armament at all, – only missiles.[43]

Even the limited helicopter complement (one or more) of these vessel types appeared uniquely oriented towards missile technology considerata, as they were most probably conceived of as helping to provide 'self-contained target location beyond the radar horizon .[44]

And it was within this context, of ever-increasing evidence of unprecedented qualitative innovations towards the effecting of a totally missile-oriented fleet, that the world-wide 'Okean' manoeuvre of that year took on increased significance. The manoeuvre deployment patterns,[45] when co-ordinated with missile radii data,[46] strongly indicated that a prime exercise aim related to deployment and dis-positioning for global atomic warfare. And if this correlation of the evidence is accurate, as appears indubitable, the 'Okean' may well be seen to augur a new naval era. It will be returned to below.

As concerns interventionary capability patterns one ought perhaps to turn first to the helicopter carriers which were being produced by the late 1960's,[47] as they impinged on a wide gamut of strategic thinking.

Their initial assignment related to the defensive strategic purpose of submarine tracking and killing.[48] Their contingent of 36 heli-copters were hence presumably oriented towards this role, as well as towards the performance of tasks analogous to those of the helicopter(s) of the regular cruisers. But they could clearly also be utilized by the marine infantry for purposes of sea-borne landings – in which case they would probably be divided into 3 echelons of 12, in accordance with traditional Soviet tactical preferences (see below). The limited character of the force potential lessened the likelihood of its use against organized land forces of significance. But it entailed consider-able consequences within scenarios such as were traced above.

The helicopter-carriers had furthermore been developed after a lengthy and sceptical consideration of the modern role and utility of traditional aircraft carriers. Admiral Chabanenko had declared these to be 'extremely expensive giants of very doubtful efficiency';[49] his Cmdr. in Chief Gorshkov had stated flatly that they were 'eight times the cost of an atomic submarine', and strongly implied that they were in reality much over-rated sitting ducks.[50] The cost scepticism was borne out by relevant US estimates;[51] the effectivity scepticism must, in view of the referred-to combat re-orientation programme, have been borne out by achieved missile performance standards.

Yet there was no doubting Soviet awareness of the need for air-cover for distant operations. It had to the contrary been emphasized ever since the inception of the naval expansion efforts.[52] But overall cost-effectiveness considerations had evidently dictated reliance on 'long-range missile aviation' based on land.[53]

In consideration of this strong awareness (footnotes 52 and 53), it would be logical to assign considerable causal influence, as relating to the helicopter carriers, to new aviation developments. It was in 1967 that an all-jet Soviet VTOL (vertical take-off and landing) fighter was first unveiled in public.[54]

And it therefore appeared most probable that some advanced version of this VTOL was intended for assignment to the helicopter carriers by the early 1970's. The need for the traditional type of aircraft carriers would be obviated. The sought-after advantages of air-cover flexibility would be provided by the helicopter carriers, and, by later generations of 'mini-carriers', – vessels of superior mobility and flexibility.

Meanwhile the general emphasis on amphibious capacity was, as already mentioned, becoming ever more pronounced, with self-evident implications also for the auxiliary tasks of expected future 'helicopter-carriers'. One may again with profit turn to 'Okean', in conjunction with which there were extensive amphibious exercises on the Rubachi Peninsula.[55]

The landings of marines were specifically stated to have been co-ordinated with missile firings, and to have been witnessed by an impressive array of prominent Armed Forces personalities.[56]

One must again emphasize the implied 'nuclearization' of the forces involved: '*All branches* of the Soviet Armed Forces are now equipped with *nuclear rocket* weapons, perfected electronic equipment and other material of the newest type'.[57]

The amphibious forces themselves were to be operationally

flexible. They plainly entailed potentials for local interventionary-type activities. But they were also assigned a definite strategic-oriented role. They were to utilize (clean) nuclear take-out strikes against hostile points, and be able to proceed quickly to occupation of the site(s) and remaining facilities: 'In maritime regions . . . naval fronts . . . will take advantage of the results of missile blows of strategic significance . . . complete the destruction of the enemy's forces, (and) occupy his territory'.[58]

Attention must now be reverted to the mobility and flexibility factor. A NATO source indicated the tendency: 'The Russians have intensified their surveillance of all maritime activities west of Bornholm. From a tentative start some years ago, there is now a constant and wide coverage of the Danish Straits and all waters leading to it by Naval and specialized surveillance vessels'. And it appended a chart of 'Soviet Naval Exercises 1960–70' which displayed the increasing outward thrust and extending of regular Soviet manoeuvre patterns: from the Baltic and Arctic Seas, to the North Sea, to Icelandic waters, and then to mid-Atlantic manoeuvre settings.[59]

Soviet sources were themselves equally candid in describing the extending of their naval activities into distant oceans and ports.[60] Fleet Admiral Kasatonov was quite explicit in a 1969 exposition on the extensive naval qualitative and quantitative build-up, an exposition which went on to describe the extending of naval operational patterns until these came to cover all major oceans.[61] Other sources were similarly unequivocal in asserting Soviet rights,[62] and in emphasizing that the developments would be continued and were not to be regarded as transient phenomena.[63]

A 1970 chart[64] over recent Soviet manoeuvre patterns in the Mediterranean does as a consequence take on increased significance. It clearly indicated that short tours of duty and frequent rotations between the Northern, Baltic and Black Sea Fleets were standard. It appeared that the Mediterranean Fleet was not a separate unit of defined ships and crews. One might infer from this that Mediterranean duty was seen as a compensation or reward for more trying duties elsewhere, because of its advantages of climate and ports of call, and because of the professionally stimulating(?) prospect of shadowing the US 6th Fleet. But a primary or auxiliary rationale obviously related to a program to train rapidly expanding Navy personnel cadres in as diversified tasks as possible.

'Okean' can again be seen as a turning point, this time as the first manifestation of the world-wide nature and range of the new Soviet

Navy. Over 250 ships participated, deployed over every major ocean, as well as up some of the major rivers, of the world.[65] In the north: 'Ships and submarines moved back and forth between the Atlantic and the Mediterranean in a display of rapid redeployment and reinforcement available to meet the requirements . . . meant to tell NATO that the Soviet Navy can operate wherever circumstances dictate, be that by their choice or NATO's '[66]

And it finally served also to highlight Soviet awareness of political considerations and of the psychological import of political appearances. The manoeuvre was not wound up by the prompt return of participating vessels to their home bases or routine patrols. Instead they dispersed to a variety of 'neutral' harbours around the world; a flotilla of smaller warships even went up the Danube to Vienna . . . ![67]

CONCLUSION

Combat potentials: The qualitative novelty of its combat orientation not only mitigated residual quantitative inferiority, but did, in conjunction with the high priority quantitative expansion efforts, entail Soviet Naval potentials of an order far above that generally appreciated.[68] By 1971 the Soviet Navy had become powerful enough to sow seeds of apprehension in the minds of some US military leaders. It had acquired sufficient firepower to cause at least some doubts about the American military capability to defy it.[69]

Peace-time implications: Two quotes may serve to synopsize our tenet: – 'Navies are not created solely to fight other navies. Sometimes we loose sight of this fact. Navies are also instruments for the projection of national power, when circumstances require us to be strong in distant places'.[70] And: ' . . . it is no longer possible to keep military and political considerations in separate water-tight compartments . . . whatever may be the military assessment of the significance of the Soviet Fleet in the Mediterranean . . . the presence of this fleet is having a profound effect on men's minds . . . it is contributing significantly to the rise of Soviet influence'.[71] There was therefore a considerable kernel of truth in, for example, the propagandistic Soviet assertion that her Mediterranean Fleet was 'preventing the US 6th Fleet from carrying out with impunity the aggressive designs of the Pentagon and from lording it in the area in the same unceremonious fashion as previously'.[72]

And therein lay the essence of a very changed international situation indeed.

Note: – Naval bases considerata are dealt with in the following Chapter, on 'Geo-Political Determinants of Soviet Strategic Policy'.
– The emerging Naval leadership is treated briefly in Chapter 7.

_____

RELATED AIR AND LAND DEVELOPMENTS

The Soviet stress on inter-command unity and flexibility of operations and training,[73] and the related stress on the need for Armed Forces units to effect the specialization and mobility required for nuclear combat conditions,[74] necessitate some attention to other fields.

Two Air Force developments are of particular relevance: one is the introduction of transports such as the giant AN-22. Together with the increasingly extensive utilization of helicopter strength,[75] this greatly increased the mobility of the airborne divisions. It furthermore entailed considerable consequences for the co-ordination of land and sea follow-ups to strategic (or non-strategic) missile strikes.[76] The other development related to the 1967 presentation of a VTOL (at the same Air Show which saw the Soviet variable geometry swing-wing jet first demonstrated[77]). The VTOL was clearly intended for service also on board the Navy's new 'mini-carriers'.

As concerns land developments, relevance may be assigned to operational tactics, again on the basis of the official stress on specialization and flexibility; the striving for independent unit survival capability complemented by easy insertability into joint operational endeavours. Like the naval marines, the land units were trained to operate under, and to utilize, nuclear conditions.[78]

The use of nuclear weaponry, either for take-out strikes or for high-altitude defence disruptive type explosions, is standard; ambitious land advances of 60 or more miles a day are planned for;[79] 'deep' helicopter/paratroop landings are envisaged, with co-ordinated thrusts by armoured units drilled in automatic and smooth transitions from marching to attack formations; no front and rear forces are delineated; rather, there are three consecutive 'echelons' with the ones behind pushing on or through immediately the front falters or slows down;[80] infrared equipment is standard, as is extensive amphibious water-fording equipment.[81]

And it may be proper to end by reverting to the aspect of specialization. It came to cause increasing awareness of the worth of the individual,[82] and a novel, if limited, emphasis on the need for subordinate commanders to display individual initiative.[83] The complexity of the weaponry and conceived combat conditions demanded high levels of troop education; inherent in the recognition thereof was a profound principal shift from earlier attitudes relating to combat personnel.

NOTES

1. This appears a fair assertion in spite e.g. of her important assistance to the Royal Navy (then paralized by mutiny) before the battle of Camperdown in 1797, in spite of her nuisance value during the 19th century (especially in the Mediterranean), and in spite of her (Baltic Fleet) round the world odyssey to disaster at Tsushima, 27 March, 1905.

2. Sokolovsky, V. D., Marshal, *'Voennaya Strategia'*, 3rd edition, Moscow, 1968, pg. 362–3, and see Cmdr. McGuire in *Brassey's Annual*, 1969, for a good exposition on the limited character of the Soviet Navy's tactical mobility at the time, and on its reliance on short-range shore-based air support.

3. Kouznetsov, N. G., Vice-Admiral, *'Nakanune'* (Memoirs) Voenizdat, Moscow, 1966: See discussions re Spanish Civil War and supply difficulties.

4. Djilas, Milovan, *'Conversations with Stalin'*, Pelican, 1969, p. 141 (Copyright by Harcourt, Brace & World, Inc., 1962).

One might interject that Stalin even before the War apparently considered it necessary ultimately to build aircraft carriers, heavy surface ships, destroyers, U-boats, supply ships, etc., so as to challenge the traditional seapowers. But as with Admiral Raeder's famous Z plan of 1936, the means for the plan's immediate or early realization were not available....

5. *Pravda*, 9th August, 1953.

6. *Pravda*, 15th January, 1960; See Chapters 1 and 2.

7. *Pravda*, 2nd February, 1962, and same 29th April, 1962.

8. For progress reviews of these efforts, see *International Affairs*, No. 11, November, 1963, p. 32, *Pravda*, 4th July, 1965, *Ogoniok*, No. 2, 1965; *Pravda* 19th November, 1966. See also Chapter 2.

9. Giese, Fritz, Lt. Cmdr. in *'Wehrkunde'* (FRG), October, 1959, reprinted as 'Behind the Scenes of the Red Admiralty', *Military Review*, Fort Leavenworth, May 1960, quotes Sokolovsky's comment (to Gorshkov) that the Navy was 'totally obsolete' for modern warfare. But these were the halcyon days of undaunted projections of the implications of missile procurements.

10. *Izvestia*, 19th May, 1963.

11. Sokolovsky, *op. cit.*, p. 340–1.

12. *Ibid.* p. 242–3, 246, 344 and 366.

13. *Ibid.* See also Fleet Admiral Kasatonov in *Kraznaya Zvezda*, 27th July, 1969, and *Tass*, 29th April, 1970.

14. Timofeev, K., 'The Role of Navies in Imperialist Policy', *New Times*, 28th November, 1969. Gun-boat diplomacy possibilities are herein treated in a serious vein and as of contemporary significance.

15. This delineation approximates to that presented by Capt. Raoust in 'L'Expansion Maritime de l'URSS', *Revue de Defence Nationale*, Paris, April 1969; – the article reported on a 8 December, 1968 Conference at the Institut des Hautes Etudes de Defence Nationale which reviewed our title topic in some detail. See *The Changing Strategic Naval Balance USSR* prepared for the Comm. on Armed Services, US. House of Rep.s, p. 13 and 26, for graphs depicting
(a) The rate of Soviet naval expansion, and
(b) The relative weight of old vs. new vessels in the respective navies.

16. See *Strategisk Bulletin*, April 1969, Utenrikspolitiska Institut, Stockholm; '*Shipping and Society*', 1969, Norwegian Shipping Federation, Oslo; and Carlson, V., 'The Soviet Maritime Threat', *US Naval Institute Proceedings*, May 1967, p. 44.

17. This author was himself temporarily employed on board such a vessel in 1965 (a Norwegian vessel working out of Vancouver).

18. See e.g. Wolfe, T., *Soviet Quest for More Globally Mobile Military Power*, RAND Memorandum RM 5554, p. 7, Santa Monica, Cal., December, 1967.

19. Raoust, *op. cit.*

20. *NATO, Facts and Figures*, p. 80, NATO, Brussels, 1969; and see also *Defence Policy*, p. 24, NATO Information Service, 1969.

21. *Krasnaya Zvezda*, 27 July, 1969.

22. Raoust, *op. cit.*

23. '*Defence Policy*', NATO Info. Service, 1969, *op. cit.*

24. In giving witness to the Armed Services Committee, transcript appearing in the *New York Times*, 15 June, 1969.

25. Petrov, V., 'Soviet Canals', *US Naval Institute Proceedings*, July 1967, p. 32–44.

26. The Alligator – about 5000 tons d.w.; The Polosny – about 900 tons d.w.

27. *NATO Letter* September, 1970, p. 20–22.

28. *Ogoniok*, 25 June, 1965, p. 47.

29. On 1967 Navy Day near Leningrad, – witnessed by a colleague of this author.

30. At the 1967 November 7th Moscow Parade: – numbers estimated as 8,000 by 1968, 12,000 by 1969 and 15,000 by 1970 ('*The Military Balance*' 1968–69, and 1970–71, ISS London). See also Norwegian Minister of Defence Grieg-Tidemand, *Parliamentary Debates*, Oslo, 29th October, 1968.

31. E.g.: *Krasnaya Zvezda*, 24 June, 1969, pictured landing craft nudging ashore, emitting amphibious tanks; *Krasnaya Zvezda*, 3rd August, 1969, carried pictures/ stories of amphibious operations; *Krasnaya Zvezda*, 2nd November, 1969, did same (Amphib. tanks and personnel carriers were on or reaching a beach with marines storming on; the mother ships lay 100 yards to a mile off shore; as did also *Tass*, 29 April, 1970 (Extensive report on Rubachi landing exercises, – as one aspect of the world-wide Okean exercise.

32. The Penguin, developed in Norway (with which this author became acquainted while working for Norway's Defence Research Establishment), and the Exocet, developed in France (see e.g. Le Monde, 31 May, 1969, and 31 July, 1969 for comment), are sea-to-sea missiles thus being developed.
And see *US Fiscal Year 1969 Navy Budget Posture St.*, p. 1 and 7, for description of the Sea Sparrow tentative anti-ship-to-ship missile.
See also Revue de la Defence Nationale, Paris, January, 1968, for further comments.

33. *The Changing Strategic Naval Balance*, p. 20 – prepared for the Comm. on Armed Services, US House of Rep.s., December, 1968.

34. US Ambassador Harland Cleveland in *NATO Letter*, November, 1967, Brussels.

35. *The Military Balance 1969–70* ISS, London, 1969.

36. Western European Union Report prepared by Mr. Griffiths, Rapporteur of the General Affairs Committee, surveyed in *NATO Letter*, June, 1969, p. 2–7.

37. This potential scenario was elaborated on by James Cable, of ISS, in discussion with the author on 4 February, 1970.

38. See also Timofeev, K., *op. cit.*

39. This classification matured and profited by the mentioned discussion with J. Cable, *op. cit.*

40. Minister of Defence Grieg-Tidemand in *Parliamentary Debates* 29 October, 1968, Oslo.

41. From the *Guardian's* Parliamentary Report of 20 November, 1970.

42. Bundeswehr's *Soldat und Technik*, No. 11, 1969, p. 626; and same, No. 4, 1970, p. 198–9.

43. *Ibid*, No. 10, 1970, p. 566–70; Concise article 'Neue und Modernisierte Kriegschifftypen der Sowjet-Flotte', with accompanying, detailed and confirming photographs. See also the Military Balance 1969–70, *op. cit.*, for lists of various vessel and missile types.
NOTE also the 3,500 ton gas-turbine rocket destroyer (NATO codenamed KRIVAK DDG) which 'appeared' in the spring of 1971, – embodying the new theories' total practical implementation. No equivalent vessel is either serving or (as yet) projected for service with any Western navy.

44. As suggested by Erickson, John, in 'Soviet Naval Presence in the Mediterranean', *Bulletin of Soviet and East Eur. Jewish Affairs*, No. 3, January, 1969, p. 9–15.

45. Soldat und Technik, *op. cit.*, No. 8, 1970, p. 428–31, and same No. 9, p. 500.

46. *Ibid.*, No. 7, 1969, p. 381 – see graph relating to capabilities of Soviet Sark, Serb and 3rd generation missiles (respective radii: 1,500, 2,000 and 3,000 plus km).

47. Two were commissioned during 1968–69. See the Military Balance 1968–69 and 1969–70, *op. cit.*

48. *Krasnaya Zvezda*, 28 May, 1969, carried a picture of the first helicopter carrier to be commissioned, the Moskva, with a caption defining it as an anti-U-boat cruiser.
See Sokolovsky, *op. cit.*, p. 363; hostile subs and aircraft carriers are defined as prime targets.

49. *Literaturnaya Rossia*, No. 30, 25 July, 1969.

50. *Izvestia*, 19 May, 1963.

51. *US News and World Report*, 9 September, 1969, asserted that the US Navy spent about 40 per cent of its funds in supporting its strike carrier program and activities.

52. Sokolovsky, *op. cit.*, p. 246, lists the coordination of the activities of missile-carrying vessels, missile subs and missile-carrying planes as the essential requisita for action against distant hostile bases and territories.

53. *Ibid*, p. 344. And see Krasnaya Zvezda, 27 July, 1969, *op. cit.* – This was obviously why 'some people, previously and at present continue to fight for the construction of aircraft-carriers'. – See Admiral Gorshkov in *Morskoi Sbornik*, February, 1967, p. 19.

54. At Domodjevo, 8–9 August, 1967; the VTOL showed similarities with the British Hawker Siddley Harrier, the only Western equivalent. A first prototype model, a plane-helicopter with motors on the wingtips and rotors placed above these, was demonstrated as early as 1961, at the (Soviet) Tushino Air Show, 9 July, 1961.

55. *Tass*, 29 April, 1970.

56. *Ibid.*

57. Air Marshal P. S. Kutakhov, in *Krasnaya Zvezda*, 17 May, 1969 (this author's stress). And see Admiral Kasatonov in *Krasnaya Zvezda*, 27th July, 1969, *op. cit.*

58. Sokolovsky, *op. cit.*, p. 340.

59. *NATO Letter* September, 1970 (pp. 6–11, for described charts).

60. See e.g. *Izvestia*, 3 September and 1 October, 1969; *Krasnaya Zvezda*, 13 May, 1969, which deals with the return of a fleet just completing a 7 months cruise of African and Asian ports; – or Admiral Gorshkov, in *Pravda*, 27 July, 1969: 'Units of the Pacific Fleet have just returned from a 6 months cruise in the Indian and Pacific Oceans, covering more than 30,000 miles and visiting 30 different nations'. And note their pro. temp. achievements in constructing floating docks and complex logistic and supply depots off sheltered coasts; See Murphy, F. M., 'The Soviet Navy in the Mediterranean', *US Naval Inst. Proceedings*, March, 1967.

61. In *'Starshina Serzhant'* No. 7, 1969.

62. See Kolosov, L., *in Izvestia*, 11 November, 1968.

63. See Admiral Gorshkov in *Ogoniok*, 3 February, 1968.

64. 'Soviet Mediterranean Squadron', – Declassified chart of which Soviet vessels visited the Mediterranean, and for what length of time, during 1968–69, the Ministry of Defence, London, January, 1970.
– And see evidence regarding rapid turnover in operational commands and short tours of duty, presented in the *Bulletin* of February, 1969, of the Munich Inst. for the Study of the USSR.

65. See e.g. *Pravda*, 14 and 16 and 20 April, 1970, or *Izvestia*, 14 and 17 April, 1970.
– For Western reports, see e.g. *The London Times*, 25 March and 24 April, 1970. *The Guardian*, 23 April, 1970, or the *Sunday Times*, 26 April, 1970 (for interesting radar photograph). For good synopsis, see *Soldat und Technik* No. 8, 1970, p. 428–31.

66. NATO Letter, September, 1970, *op. cit.*, (Testimony by the Supreme Allied Cmdr., Atlantic).

67. *Soldat und Technik*, No. 9, 1970, p. 500.

68. Cmdr. McGuire's *Guardian* feature of 26 August, 1970, perpetuates this now outmoded underestimation (although this may be explained by contemporary political considerations; the article discussed Soviet interests only as related to the UK South African Arms Debate). – Compare with SACEUR General Goodpaster's October 1970 interview; see e.g. *Aftenposten*, 29 October, 1970 Oslo.

69. See *New York Times*, 1 November, 1971.

70. Admiral McDonald, Chief of US Naval Operations, in '*Military Procurement Authorizations for Fiscal Year 1967*'. Hearings before the (US Senate) Committee on Armed Forces, p. 65, GPO, Washington, D.C., 1966.

71. Admiral Sir John Hamilton, Former Cmdr. in Chief of Allied Forces Mediterranean, in 'The Changing Strategic Naval Balance' (USSR vs. USA), *op. cit.*, p. 31–2.

72. *Krasnaya Zvezda*, 12 November, 1968. See also *Izvestia*, 11th November, 1968, *op. cit.*, and *Pravda*, 27 November, 1968 (art. by V. Yermakov).

73. See e.g. Col. Gen. Shtemenko, in *Nedelia* No. 6, 6 February, 1965; Sokolovsky, *op. cit.*, p. 340 and Minister of Defence Grechko in *Pravda* 23 February, 1970.

74. *Ibid.*; And e.g. *Krasnaya Zvezda* 17 May, 1969, *op. cit.*, and *Krasnaya Zvezda*, 27 July, 1969. See also Chapters 2 and 3.

75. See *Aviation Week and Space Technology* (US) 30 September, 1968; and Lt. Gen. Taranenko in *Krasnaya Zvezda*, 28 January, 1968, for comments re. air-lift capabilities, as tested in the Dnjepr manoeuvres of late 1967.

76. Sokolovsky, *op. cit.*

77. In mass production (about 12 a month) by 1970, according to *Newsweek's* 'Periscope', 21 September, 1970.

78. *The Military Balance 1969–70*.

79. See e.g. comment by Sir John Hackett, recently retired BOAR Commander, to *New York Times*, 29 November, 1969; A Soviet offensive might (then) be expected to reach the Rhine within 48 hours.

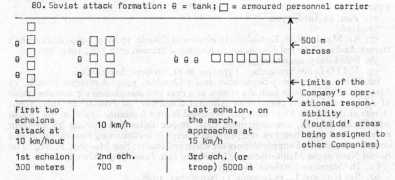

80. Soviet attack formation: θ = tank; □ = armoured personnel carrier

(The Company as a whole stretches 6 kilometers)

81. 'The Military Balance 1970–71', ISS, London, 1970, p. 8. – And see for example *Krasnaya Zvezda*, 8 October, 1969, for pictures.
82. Seen e.g. in articles like Army Gen. Belik's in *Krasnaya Zvezda*, 4 January, 1970, which dug out relevant Lenin quotes.
83. See e.g. Air Chief Marshal Vershinin, Pravda, 26 January, 1968 – and above references.

6

Geo-Political Determinants of Soviet Strategic Policy

No analysis of the extraordinary qualitative and quantitative improvement of the USSR's strategic capabilities can be complete without a consideration of geo-political factors. Certain areas have their political and security setting affected by their geographical location. There are areas that are so sensitive and vital to a nation's survival that the nation is propelled to demand control also over adjacent areas. Leningrad, and the historical Russian and Soviet insistence on control of the area north-east of that city provides one illustration. Another illustration is provided by the fact that the industrial and population basin of north western USSR (including Moscow) was the first to be protected by BMD deployments.[1]

By the late 1960's dynamic developments on the Kola Peninsula and in the southern far east singled these areas out as cores of equally decisive actual or potential strategic significance. They gained singular importance as the main naval base complexes, at a time when the navy's strategic strength was emerging as the most potent and reliable component of the Soviet Union's assured second strike capacities.[2] Their importance was further augmented by forward land missile deployments. This chapter concerns itself with the geographical factors which made these development and dispositions inevitable.

A survey of alternate naval bases illuminates the issue. With regard to the Black Sea and Baltic fleets a glance at a map suffices to ascertain that their strategic role is crucified by the nature of the straits that lead out of the two seas. The Dardanelles and Oresund straits are both so narrow that they can be closed with ease, either through action from hostile shores, or through aerial bombardment and mining. Improvements of the overland canal and water artery system between the two seas have facilitated inter-Fleet mobility, and they have affected dispositions.[3] But war time benefits would be minimal, if only because of the time factor involved in traversing the distance. The fact that the drenchings were not sufficient to permit the passage of large atomic submarines (which often exceed 10,000 tons d.w.)[4] reflects Soviet appreciation of the limitations. Smaller patrol vessels could be rotated, and the improved waterway was therefore of significance for defensive concepts and planning. But it did not obviate the implications of the geographical constraints; the Fleets were not of significant strategic concern.[5]

Freedom of access limitations led to a search for alternate bases. The facilities provided by Cuba, Algeria, Egypt, Sudan, Yemen and others[6] reflected this search. But the facilities appeared to be of 'depot and repair' rather than 'base' character.[7] And political considerations alone would in any case militate against Soviet acceptance of any decisive reliance on foreign facilities. Similar drawbacks affected the floating docks and the complex floating logistics and supply bases which the Soviet Union designed and constructed (off sheltered coasts).[8] They were useful auxiliaries, but they could not alone provide for the long term needs of a large navy.

The only realistic alternatives as major bases for the strategic fleet were therefore such as could be found along the northern and Pacific shores. But, as can be seen from the first two of the following maps,[9] the suitable stretches of shoreline are limited. Ice conditions effectively restrict the sections that may be utilized to part of the Murmansk coast, the tip of the Kamchatka Peninsula, and the Vladivostok area.

Before considering these areas one should note a climatic peculiarity: the maximum extension of the ice in the Far East regions occurs in February; in the Kola (Murmansk) region it occurs during March-April. The difference is caused by the fact that the rivers flowing north have their upper reaches melted before their lower. The pressures which build up as a result of this 'push' the ice out, while simultaneously 'screwing' it. It is the emergence of this type of ice which extends the hazardous period. The Far East, of course, has no rivers of similar characteristics.

THE KOLA CORE AREA

The area in question is presented in a close-up schematic form in the diagram which follows the maps. The diagram and the maps serve to focus on some of the geographical determinants which affect the construction of base facilities. At its maximum extension (see maps) the ice curves around at a mean distance of only 180 miles from the Kola coastline, until it turns southwest to meet the coast near Mys Svjatoi Nos.[10] The distance from the Norwegian border to the ice-limit is 240 nautical miles, not counting the fjord leading into Murmansk and the smaller bays. While a harsh winter may partly freeze even the fjord, the bays, and some of the surrounding waters,[11] this strip of the coast can be kept open at all times with the use of ice-breakers. The coast is steep, with granite cliffs and slopes which often reach heights of between 300 and 600 feet.[12]

With access assured, and land composition and formation conducive to the protection of installations, the area's development as a naval base was inevitable. Harbours could be blasted into the rock; the ice conditions were tolerable; and navigational depths were satisfactory. (The latter may be seen from a study of the third and fourth maps. See also footnote 10).

Three of the geo-political restrictions affecting the Kola base complexes stimulated post-war Western apprehension that the USSR might covet Northern Norwegian shores.[13] The restrictions which spawned the fear were: the limitations to the lengths of shore-line available for bases; the fact that the area also accommodated the Soviet merchant and fishing fleets of the Arctic and their facilities; and the fact that the Norwegian Cape sector lies nearly 300 nautical miles closer to the Atlantic. But one of the assumptions underlying the fear had always been wrong. And the developments of the 1960's did much to undermine the others. The apprehension of the 1940's and '50's was not relevant to the situation of the '60's and '70's. The reasons are relevant to this study.

The number of Soviet harbours in the area is classified. But a scrutiny of maps 3 and 4 invites the confident assertion that the geographical capacity for base expansions can not have been exhausted. The ice-free shoreline may be limited in length, but it is extraordinarily rich in harbour potentials. The rapid conversion of the strategic fleet to nuclear fuel during the 1960's furthermore decreased

USSR – Ice Limits

North Pole

Permanent Ice
Southern limit of ice
200' depth contour
1000' depth contour

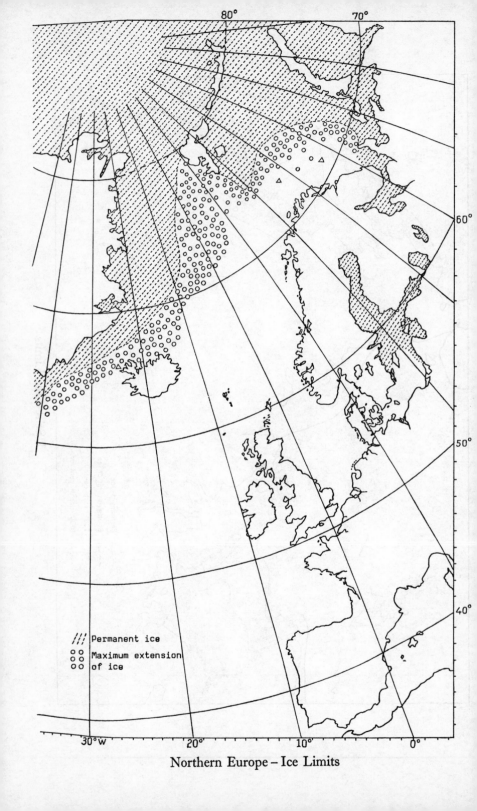

Northern Europe – Ice Limits

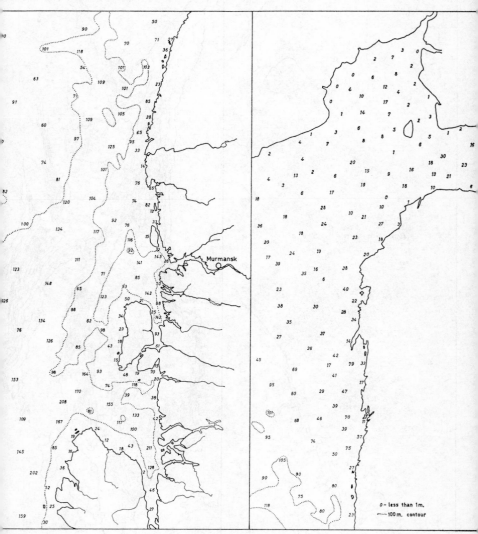

The Kola Coastline

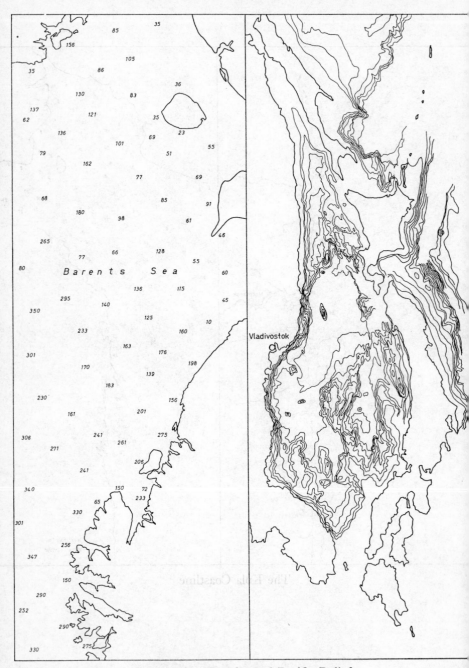

Barents Sea Depths and Pacific Reliefs

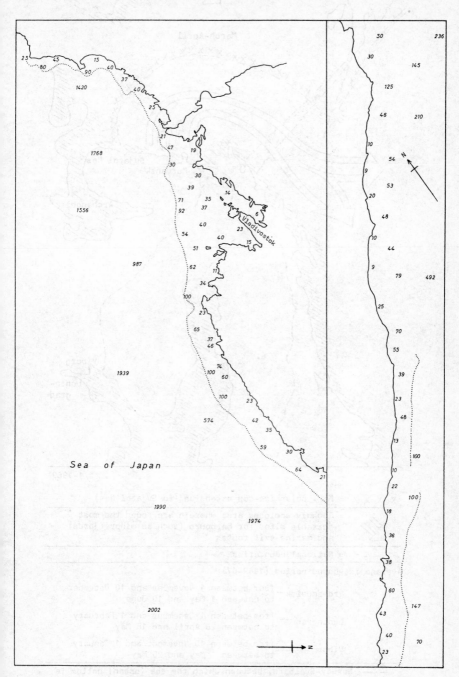

The Soviet Far East Coastline

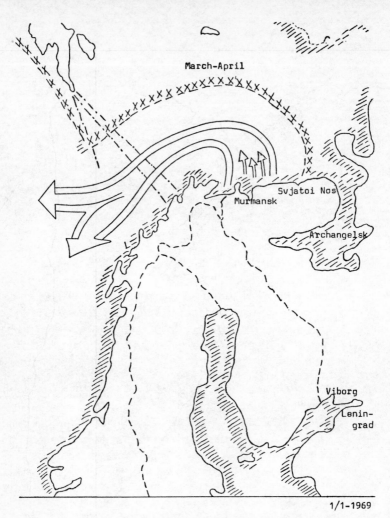

March-April

Svjatoi Nos
Murmansk

Archangelsk

Viborg
Lenin-
grad

1/1-1969

X X X X = Máx. polar ice-cap extension (to Svjatoi Nos)

 = Roughly encloses area wherein are found the most
suitable sites for harbours (such as minor fjords)
and marine exit routes

⌐ - - - ⌐ = National boundaries

Average ice-bound period (1949-67)

Archangelsk — from between 1 November and 10 December
to between 1 May and 10 June

Leningrad — from between 1 December and 1 February
to between 20 April and 15 May

Viborg — from between 10 November and 1 January
to between 1 May and 20 May

—·—· Norway-Svalbard, between which the sea (ocean) bottom is
reserved for Norwegian exploitation (pr. 1958 convention on the
continental shelf; see technological developments).
Compare Soviet need ('legitimate') for electronic surveillance
and early warning - and ballistic missile evolutions.

the navy's need for extensive base complexes. The Soviet navy did not need Norwegian territory.

And finally, the distance to the Atlantic had a positive corollary. Enemy action against the Kola complexes would be hampered by a loss in range and time equal to that which affected forward Soviet operations. Defensive benefits could be seen to offset the disadvantages. This is not to say that Soviet naval planners would not look with favour on access to the Norwegian coast. It is admirably situated as a location for 'mobile bases' (utilizing depot ships) and support facilities in the event of war.[15] But these could be moved in quickly; permanent facilities are not needed. The Norwegian coast would constitute a convenience, not a necessity. A war would probably see Soviet action to secure its benefits, but the peace-time need was not acute.

Towards the end of the Second World War, in a discussion with the then Norwegian Foreign Minister Trygve Lie, Molotov presented a succinct synopsis of the basic Soviet concern. Its presentation serves to indicate the enduring character of the Soviet considerations involved. The statement followed Norwegian refusal of a Soviet demand that she give up her sovereignty over Svalbard and Bear Island (the former was to be put under a joint Soviet-Norwegian administration which would act 'as a condominium'; the latter was to be transferred outright). It was frank and to the point:

' . . . the Dardanelles . . . here we are locked in . . . Oresund . . . here we are locked in. Only in the North is there an opening, but this war has shown that the supply-line to Northern Russia can be cut or interfered with. This shall not be repeated in the future. We have invested much in this part of the Soviet Union, and it is so important for the entire Union's existence that *we shall in future ensure that Northern Russia is permitted to live in security* and peace'.[16]

Molotov acknowledged that the Norwegians were friendly neighbours, but persisted: 'shall we settle this in a friendly manner, or shall there be a dispute?'[17] Admiral Golovko summed up: 'Without the Kola inlet the Northern Fleet cannot exist. . . . the Kola inlet is necessary to the state.'[18]

The dynamic post-war expansion of Kola base facilities and the introduction and build-up of strategic naval forces underlined the significance of the area. The basis for the abiding Soviet concern is clearly to be found in the field of security. Her acute sensitivity reflects strategic realities. Control over Kola *is* essential to her survival, and more so in the missile era than ever before. A brief survey of defensive and offensive strategic imperatives bears this out.

Considerations of defence will be treated first. The successful activation of ballistic missile defence and other defence systems is predicated on the prior completion of a complex of sequential events (radar contact and identification, information processing, the transmitting and execution of command decisions, etc.).[19] This condition entails two absolute needs. The first is that hostile offensive weaponry cannot be tolerated within a certain minimum distance. The second is that certain forward military facilities, especially radar, must be acquired in order to ensure tolerable, adequate reaction times.

Tacit Norwegian recognition of the first need, and its sensitivity, was implied by her refusal to permit the stationing of offensive missiles on her soil, and by her refusal to permit NATO exercises within about 300 km. of the Soviet border.[20] It was further implied by her insistence that she has not permitted and will not permit the peace-time utilization by Polaris submarines of Norwegian radar facilities.[21] The Norwegians clearly conduct some tactical electronic and other surveillance of Soviet developments. The fact that the Western coast of the Ribachi Peninsula is within visual, naked eye, surveillance distance from the border (as shown by maps 3 and 4) makes this inevitable. But this limited tactical surveillance can be tolerated by the USSR. It is surveillance integrated into hostile strategic offensive systems that could not be tolerated. Any act or tendency which promised such integration would clearly tread on very sensitive Soviet corns. (See footnote 19).

This is evidenced by articles such as that carried by Krasnaya Zvezda in the spring of 1969: it forcefully condemned *alleged radio and radar communications between Northern Norwegian installations and US nuclear submarines on patrol in Northern waters. . . .*[22] There appeared little reason to doubt the Norwegian assurances that the charge was mistaken. The Soviet Union must furthermore have known that it was inaccurate. She presumably has means of verification. The Soviet allegations did therefore not mirror a belief, but rather a fear regarding potential activities. They were best seen in the light of declaratory policy, as a definite warning of the unacceptable nature of such communications.

If the prime concern has been correctly identified, and if the Soviet statements have been correctly interpreted, then it would be logical to conclude that the referred-to type of intelligence integration would not only be theoretically unacceptable but would provoke countering actions. In other words: a Norwegian departure from the tacit concession to the demands inherent in the core area character of Kola *cannot* be initiated with a view to improving Norwegian (or NATO) bargaining positions. To the contrary, any such departure would constitute an invitation to 'a Cuba in reverse'; Kola security demands are so essential that the USSR would probably accept the risks associated with intervention.[23]

The need for forward military facilities, to ensure adequate warning time for the activation of defences, and to ease the process of verification and control of enemy activities, has been satisfied. The failure to acquire Svalbard and Bear Island facilities was compensated for by the establishment of military bases (and radar installations) on ice floes in the Barents and White Seas, and on Franz Josef Island.[24] These facilities, complemented by electronically equipped surface vessels, evidently satisfy the basic requirements.

With regard to considerations of offence, the obverse considerations are (potentially) involved. A hypothetical Polaris or Poseidon ABM capacity would, if it was synchronized with Norwegian radar capabilities, seriously detract from the effectiveness of ICBMs from the Northwestern USSR. It would make interception of an ICBM during the ascent phase of its trajectory, the period of its greatest vulnerability, a distinct possibility. This would inherently detract from calculated 'assured' offence capabilities, and would therefore seriously affect strategic missile considerations and deployments.

There is, finally, one further consideration of concern. Its implications have never been publicly (or officially) recognized in either the Soviet Union or Norway. Yet at least one Norwegian strategist (Col. Egge[25]) has indicated awareness of the situation, and Soviet awareness may be presumed.

As shown by the accompanying sketch, the ice-limit not only restricts the area where bases can be located, but furthermore forms what can be termed one shore of a narrow 'fjord' leading into the bases; the 'fjord's' mouth spans the area Svalbard-Norway's Cape. This has resulted in an environmentally determined constricted 'shipping lane'. One obvious consequence of this restriction is to dramatize the Soviet need for supervision and control.

A related consequence may be found in the dramatization of the implications which flow from the shallowness of the ocean floor at the mouth of the 'fjord' (see maps 3 and 4). The contemporary international law defines a nation's privileges off its coast to extend to a depth of 200 metres, or to such depth as to which exploitation of resources is feasible.[26] An astoundingly accelerated process in underwater exploratory techniques during the 1960's had, already by the time the treaty was ratified, promised the elimination of restrictions to 'exploitable depths'.[27] The treaty could therefore be interpreted to grant a coastal power exploitation rights over all waters inside the half-way mark between it and the coastal nation on the other side of the waterway, sea, or ocean.[28] With reference to our area of interest this would mean a form of Norwegian control over the entire ocean floor between Northern Norway and Svalbard. It could be interpreted to provide a legal rationale, however tenuous, for NATO 'base' type installations.

This interpretation of the Treaty was unacceptable to most observers, for political, economic and ecologic reasons; the Treaty's intent had clearly been overtaken by the unforeseen speed of technological progress, and there was an urgent need for revision.[29] But quite apart from this general unacceptability of the wording of the Treaty, it was clear that the USSR neither could nor would tolerate its military implications.[30] It was in fact clear by 1969 that both the US and the USSR were contravening the treaty's provisions, by establishing fait accompli ocean floor installations (with developments in the Barents-Norwegian Sea area dictated by Soviet determination to safe-guard her security prerequisites).[31]

Leaving the legal and technical possibilities aside, the above survey serves to highlight the geo-political considerations which affect Kola. It also indicates the limited and vital security policy options which are activated by these considerations.

A final observation must be made with regard to the Soviet Naval manoeuvres of the late 1960's. Repeated naval (and naval air-arm) manoeuvres and operational patterns in the North Sea and the Eastern Atlantic[32] suggested a Soviet attempt to establish an outer defence perimeter *west* of both Iceland and Great Britain. Two indisputable benefits would accrue from such an endeavour, if successful. It would guarantee access to Kola. And it would have the additional benefit of limiting the danger of enemy penetration to that other bottleneck, the Danish Straits. (It would, of course, also affect the strategic role assigned to the Baltic Fleet).

Operations such as the Sever 'pinch', and other amphibious forces manoeuvres around and outside Norway,[33] could be seen as evidence of, and symptomatic of, a Soviet intent to establish a regular presence in the area. A regular presence, which turned these seas into a Mare Sovieticum, could be seen to have the further consequence of facilitating contingency Soviet intervention plans. (NATO assistance would be more doubtful if it risked encountering major resistance en route[34]). But the operational patterns were more likely to make Norwegian territory even more superfluous, by placing it a considerable distance *behind* the Soviet front-lines[35] . . . .

THE FAR EAST

The three other important Soviet base complexes with 'direct' access to the sea are all located in the Far East. They are Petropavlovsk on the Kamchatka Peninsula (primarily a submarine base), the extensive Vladivostok installations, and Sovietskaya Gavan' (opposite Sakhalin and about 500 miles Northeast of Vladivostok). As with Kola, these locations have to some extent been defined by the ice conditions. The presently utilized sections can easily be kept open through ice breaker activity, but the areas available for extensions are limited.[36]

The relevant characteristics of these base complexes may be synopsized as follows:[37]

VLADIVOSTOK has about 85 days of fog and freezes for three months, as of December; it is kept open by ice-breakers. Its main disadvantage lies in the fact that all channels of access into the bay, except the shallow and frequently iced Tatar Strait, face Japan. Mobility in and out of Vladivostok is therefore subject to foreign surveillance. It could be fettered by problematic barrier operations in times of conflict.

SOVIETSKAYA GAVAN' incorporates a major submarine base and has dock facilities sufficient to accomodate any naval vessels. But the base is ice-bound from December to March. And it is excessively prone to fog (up to 22 foggy days have been noted in July alone!).

PETROPAVLOSK's sole *raison-d'être* is naval activities. Although it freezes in December and remains subject to freezing for three to four months, the ice is not severe, and can easily be removed by ice-breakers. It is protected from winds and fog by Kamchatka's volcanic mountain ranges. It is primarily a submarine base. It is presumably the base which is responsible for severing the East-West shipping route from the USA in the event of war (it lies 500 miles north of this route).

Core area definitions and considerations may be applied to all these complexes, singly or together. But proximity to operational theatres of consequence gives VLADIVOSTOK pride of place. Its geographical location and natural harbour ensures its position as the Pacific Fleet

Headquarters and as the home base for naval operations in the Japan, Yellow and China Seas, in the Southwestern Pacific and in the Indian Ocean. A consideration of the major missile base at its neighbour Khabarovsk[38] suggests a defining of the core area as based on the Khabarovsk-Vladivostok axis.

Its crucial significance, dictated by geo-political considerations, may be seen as emphasized by a 1957 Council of Ministers' Decree.[39] This designated Peter the Great Bay, within which Vladivostok and the naval bases are located, as part of the internal waterways of the USSR. The closing line or limit established for the bay was 108 miles in length, with the justifying priniciple evoked being that these waters constituted an 'historic bay'. (Soviet definitions of this designation see it as part of the internal waters of the coastal state, and as subject to this state's unlimited sovereignty.[40] The White Sea within the Sviatoi Nos-Kanin Nos Line, the Azov Sea and Riga Bay have been similarly classified; so also have the Kara, Laptev, East Siberian and Chukotsk Seas.[41])

As in the case of Kola, the Far East area's proximity to potentially hostile borders entails certain security imperatives. This is especially so with regard to the sensitive Khabarovsk-Vladivostok basin. Core area considerations (see above analysis of Kola) entail and demand a certain supervision of or over the adjacent Chinese territories. The frequent Chinese claims that the USSR has conducted such supervision (the allegations proliferated after the Czechoslovak intervention,)[42] may therefore probably be accepted at face value. They may be seen to confirm Soviet appreciation of the security prerogatives involved.

Overflights of Chinese territory near Vladivostok-Khabarovsk complies with a military need which is not of a nature such as might be affected by the state of political relations. While adverse political circumstances might lead to demands for more intensive supervision, favourable ones would *not* lessen the military need for continuous (adequate) supervision. This is reflected in military support for an uncompromising Soviet position vis à vis such Chinese aspirations as might be inferred from the 1969 Ussuri border battles. It may furthermore be presumed that the area's sensitivity pre-dispositions the military in favour of a more active forward stance in general, whether it be of initiating or responding character. The satisfaction of Soviet requirements in the area appears to be a military need that cannot be compromised.

A few comments specifically regarding the NORTHERN SEA

ROUTE may finally be desirable. This sea route, which is kept open for up to 150 days a year by ice-breakers (including the nuclear powered 'Lenin'), was on March 28, 1970, declared by the Soviet Union soon to be opened to commercial shipping of all states. It was furthermore announced that unspecified fees would be charged.[43] The commercial significance needs no elaboration. It is self-evident both for the Soviet Union itself, especially in view of the recently discovered major oil and gas deposits of Northern Siberia,[44] and for participants in the Japan/Far East-Europe trade. The distances that must be traversed by this trade would be significantly shortened.

But more important to our analysis are the military implications of the implicit Soviet confidence in her ability to keep the route open and navigable. Submarines had long been able to use the route, in winter as well as summer.[45] The new development meant that surface ships could make the transit with equal ease through a major part of the year. Two prime advantages accrued: one was the significant cutting down of transit time; the other was the security bonus, that hostile surveillance attempts were made far more problematic. The transit time, as well as the adverse geographical conditions, remained sufficiently awesome to discourage major peace-time redeployments along the route. But the development greatly facilitated war-time contingency planning.

CONCLUSION

Geographical factors clearly dictated – and delineated – the evolution of the Kola and Far East regions into vital and sensitive core areas. The importance of both regions was long recognized by Soviet planners. Some of the traditional considerations and consequences no longer apply (e.g. the need for more base space, which was made superfluous by the conversion to nuclear power). But these have been replaced by others of even greater sensitivity and further-reaching ramifications: strategic capabilities, concepts and technology have introduced new problems, new demands and new logic.

NOTES

1. '*The Military Balance 1968–69*', ISS, London 1968.
2. *Okean*, Voenizdat, Moscow, 1970. *The Military Balance* 1969–70, ISS, London, 1969. *Nato Facts and Figures*, p. 80, NATO, Bruxelles, 1969.
3. Petrov, 'Soviet Canals', *US Naval Institute Proceedings*, July, 1967.
4. *Est & Oust*, Association d'Etudes et d'Informations Politique Internationales, Paris, 20 November, 1967.
5. M. Edmonds and J. Skitt, in their otherwise competent 'Current Soviet Maritime Strategy and Nato', *International Affairs*, No. 1, Jan. 1969, make the mistake of confusing the traditional defensive requirements with those associated with strategic concepts and facilities.
6. Guy de Carmoy, 'France Algeria and the Soviet Penetration in the Mediterranean', *Military Review*' Fort Leavenworth, March, 1970. See also e.g. the *New York Times*, 16 July, 1968, and *Neue Zurcher Zeitung* 15 December, 1968.
7. See e.g. *Komsomolskaya Pravda* 28 May, 1971 for text of new Soviet-Egyptian Treaty: This might result in somewhat more extensive arrangements.
8. Murphy, F. M., 'The Soviet Navy in the Mediterranean', *US Naval Institute Proceedings*, March 1967.
9. The maps:
Map 1. USSR ice limits, from 'The World Atlas', Moscow, 1967, pp. 102–3.
Map 2. Northern Europe, ice limits, from 'Atlas der Eisverhaltnisse des . . . Ozeans', publisher unknown, Hamburg, 1960.
Map 3. The Kola coastline, from 'Nordkapp to Mys Kanin Nos including the White Sea', Admiralty, London, 1958.
Map. 4. Barents Sea depths from 'Carte General Bathymetrique des Oceans', Carleton University Geography Department Map Library, 9200, Acc. 1487; Pacific reliefs from 'Relef dna Tikhovo Okeana,' Carleton U. Geography Map Library, 9200, Acc. 1651.
Map 5. The Soviet Far East Coast, from 'The Kuril Islands from Honshu to Kamchatka', Admiralty, London, 1966.
Sketch. The mouth of the ice-constrained 'fjord' (see text).
10. *Ibid.* See also 'Sailing Directions for Northern USSR', Hydrographic Office publication No. 47, vol. 1, Government Printing Office, Washington, DC, 1954, and H. O. publication No. 550, GPO Washington, D.C., 1955.
11. *Ibid.*
12. *Ibid.*
13. The Swedish Deputy Minister of Defence has identified these as constituting one of the major Soviet objectives in Europe: '*Sveriges Sakerhetspolitik*', Stockholm 1955. See also Capt. Araldsen, 'The Soviet Union and the Arctic', *US Naval Institute Proceedings*, June, 1967, p. 49–57.
14. *Ibid.*; N. Orvik, 'Scandinavia, NATO and Norwegian Security', in *International Organization*, Summer 1966.
15. This view is presented by Torgil Wulff in '*Kungliga Krigsvetenskapsakademiens Landlingar ock tidsskrigt*', No. 9, The Royal Military Science Academy, Stockholm, November, 1968 . . . in a comment on Jan Klenberg's 'The Cap and the Straits', *Occasional Paper in International Affairs*, No. 17, Harvard Univ., February, 1968. (With evidence such as presented above Klenberg denied any Soviet 'need' for Norwegian bases.)
16. Molotov, as quoted by Trygve Lie in *Hjemover* (Homeward), Tiden Norsk Forlag, Oslo, 1958.
17. Trygve Lie, *Ibid.*
18. Golovko, Arseni, *With the Red Fleet. The War Memories of Admiral Golovko*, Pitman, London, 1965, p. 40 (First published Voenizdat, Moscow, 1960).
19. These concerns are referred to e.g. in *International Affairs*, No. 12, 1969

(Moscow). On p. 62 it quotes *NATO Letter*, September, 1969, p. 16, to the effect that 'from the point of view of NATO strategists the coast line of Northern Norway affords the best surveillance sites for controlling the exits of the Russian Arctic Fleet into the Atlantic Ocean'. It goes on to refer from the same source, p. 19, as showing that 'they (NATO strategists) persistently recommend increasing the co-operation between the United States, Britain and Norway, in reconnaissance operations in this area'.

20. Confirmed by Col. Hope (Senior Research Officer) of the Norwegian Defence Research Establishment, May, 1968. And verified by a perusal of public accounts of past manoeuvres, their general rationale and course (as always made available through the national press, TV, and broadcasting networks). And see J. Klenberg's 'The Cap and the Straits', *op. cit.*

21. See e.g. Norwegian Minister of Defence, G. Harlem, In *Parliamentary Debates* (Stortingsforhandlinger) 1964–65, Vol. 7, p. 2475: incl. ' . . . it is correct that the new very low frequency radio station which has been authorized for construction in Norway will not serve Polaris submarines'.

22. *Krasnaya Zvezda*, 30 March, 1969 – author's emphasis.

23. NATO-aligned communications and early warning systems, NATO manoeuvres as previously conducted and the preparation of bases to permit wartime reinforcement of men and equipment – described by Anne Sington in 'NATO defensive installations in Norway', *NATO Letter*, January, 1966 – certainly represent cause for Soviet anxiety. But such NATO activity can be (and has been) tolerated and accepted. It does not infringe on essential Kola security requirements in the way that the described potential radar utilization would.

24. T. J. Laforest, 'The Strategic Significance of the North Sea Route', *United States Naval Institute Proceedings*, December, 1967.

25. Col. Bjorn Egge, ex-military attache to Moscow and Senior Research Officer of the Ministry of Defence, Oslo, touched on this problem-complex in numerous informative and informal discussions during 1968–69, while this author was fortunate enough to work as his colleague.

26. 1958 (Geneva) Convention on the Continental Shelf – ratified in 1964.

27. Mr. Mellingen of Norway's Technical Natural Scientific Research Institute has pointed to the following development (in a discussion with the author on 28 January, 1969, at the Institute): Already by 1968 oil drilling and exploitation was conducted regularly at depths of 200 metres and experimentally at depths of 300 metres, (especially by the French), while exploitable depths of three times that were acknowledged by most experts as reachable within 5–10 years. Unwieldy bathyscopes had reached the deepest ocean floor 8 years previously (August Piccard). Now new manoeuvrable (and even nuclear) deep-submurgence vessels were being constructed.
See also Arvid Pardo, 'Who will control the Seabed?', *Foreign Affairs*, October, 1968.

28. Arvid Pardo, *Ibid.*

29. Arvid Pardo, *Ibid.*

30. Jens Evensen, Director of Legal Affairs, Norwegian Ministry of Foreign Affairs, *Present Military Uses of the Seabed: Foreseeable Developments*, Document presented to the symposium on the International Regime of the Sea-bed, Rome, 30 June–5 July, 1969.

31. Jens Evensen, *Ibid.*

32. One may, for example, point to the Soviet naval manoeuvres in the Atlantic of April 1969 and 1970. Non classified data on the manoeuvres can be obtained from the Ministry of Defence, London, or NATO Secretariat, Brussels. See also *NATO Letter* September, 1970, p. 6–11: art. on 'Soviet Naval Exercises 1960–70', documents and charts Soviet Naval exercises of the period, and demonstrates the increasing extension and outward thrust of the regular manoeuvre patterns: Baltic and Arctic Seas→North Sea→Iceland→Mid-Atlantic.

33. Norwegian Minister of Defence Grieg-Tidemand, *Parliamentary Debates*, for 29 October, 1968.

34. The *New York Times*, 1 November, 1971 quotes a senior US General as saying 'As things are today I doubt if the Navy could get the carriers through the Russian submarines to provide support for NATO in Europe, especially the northern flank'.

F

35. See also Col. B. Egge, *De Danske Streders betydning i Sikkerhetspolitisk perspektiv* (The Role of the Danish Straits in a Strategic Perspective), Copenhagen, 1970. He draws the conclusion following a similar exposition that the SU sees the Baltic, the Norwegian and the North Sea as belonging to the same functional strategic buffer terrain protecting the USSR's Western Flank as does the Barents Sea. They are to be similarly considered.

36. T. J. Laforest, *op. cit.* See also the first map.

37. S. A. Swartstrauber, 'Alaska and Siberia, A Strategic Analysis', *Naval Review 1965*, p. 159, US Naval Institute.

38. This should be noted as of primarily Asian import. Because as concerns the direct USSR-USA configuration even Western USA is within closer reach of missiles from Western USSR than from Khabarovsk.

39. *Izvestia*, 21 July, 1957. See Nicolaev, 'O Salive Petra Velikovo', *Mezhdunarodnaia Zhizn*, No. 2, 1958.

40. Art. 4, 1960, Statute of the (USSR) State Boundary.

41. Z. Meshera, *Morskoe Pravo: Pravovoi Rezhim Morskikh Putei* (Maritime Law: Legal Regime of Maritime Routes) p. 10, 1959, Moscow.

42. *NCNA* (the New China News Agency) 16 September, 1968, listed about 40 Soviet Air sorties into Heilungkiang province between 9 and 29 August, 1968. Their purpose was designated as 'reconnaissance, harassment and provocation'.

43. See treatment by Rochard Boyle, 'Arctic Passages of North America', *US Naval Institute Proceedings*, January, 1969, p. 52. The sea route is deemed Soviet territorial waters since passage must be made through the straits between Severnaya Zemlia and the mainland (Vilkitskovo) and between Novaya Zemlia and the mainland – both of which are less than 24 n. miles across (Soviet-specified territorial waters extend 12 n. miles from any coast line). Of interest is the 1967 refusal of passage through Vilkitskovo to the US Coast Guard vessels Edisto and Eastwind, which had attempted to pass north of Severnaya Zemlia, but been forced south by the ice. See also T. J. Laforest, 'Strategic Significance of the Northern Sea Route', *US Naval Institute proceedings*, December, 1969, p. 56–65.

And S. A. Swartstrauber, *op. cit.*, for description of secondary Soviet Naval bases in the area, and of fuel and depot bases for the Northern Sea Route.

44. *Ekonomicheskaya Gazeta*, No. 22, May, 1969, and R. Boyle, *op. cit.*, p. 52.

45. Lt. Cmdr. D. Luehring, 'The Never-never Sea', *US Naval Institute Proceedings*, August, 1969.

PART IV: COMMAND CHANGES AND
DOCTRINAL SHIFTS

7

The Changing Pattern of Soviet Military Leadership

Chapter 8 will present a detailed analysis of military-Party relations and the integration of the military into Soviet society. It will investigate the military's societal role, and will attempt to illuminate the inter-relationships and interdependencies which bind the military to other establishment hierarchies. The present chapter is intended as an introductory survey of recent military appointment trends, and of the emerging new military elite.

Marshal Malinovsky's death was followed by a rather extensive replacement, transferral and supplementing of leading cadres within the Armed Forces. His death is best seen as a co-incidental and not a causal factor. But it serves as a convenient point of departure.

At the centre, Marshal Grechko's 12th April, 1967, appointment as Minister of Defence was by the end of 1967 accompanied by: Marshal I. I. Yakubovsky's elevation to 1st Deputy Minister of Defence, and Warsaw Pact Supreme Commander; Army General S. L. Sokolov's transfer and promotion from Cmdr. of the Leningrad Military District to 1st Deputy Minister of Defence (and co-ordinating officer within the Ministry); Army General I. G. Pavlovsky's promotion from Cmdr. of the Far Eastern M.D. to Deputy Minister of Defence, and Commander in Chief of Soviet Land Forces[1]; and Naval Cmdr. Gorshkov's elevation to Admiral of the Fleet of the Soviet Union.

By the end of 1968 eleven of the 15 Military Districts had been given new Commanding Officers: Belo-Russian M.D. – Col. General Tretyak (June 1967); Carpathian M.D. – Col. General Bisyarin (October 1967); Far Eastern M.D. – Col. General Losik (May 1967); Kiev M.D. – Col. General Kulikov (July 1967); Leningrad M.D. – Col. General Shavrov (June 1967); Moscow M.D. – Col. General Ivanovsky (June 1968); North Caucasus M.D. – Col. General Altunin (October 1968); Odessa M.D. – Col. General Shurupov (May 1968); Siberian M.D. – Col. General Tolubko (June 1968); Trans-Caucasian M.D. – Col. General Kurkotkin (May 1968); Volga M.D. – Col. General Parshikov (May 1968). And preparations were made for the creation of a new Military District, the Central Asian M.D., carved out of the old Turkestan M.D. in response to increasing Chinese border tensions (it was officially constituted in November 1969). It became responsible for all areas bordering on Sinkiang, was headquartered in Amla Ata, and put under the command of Army General Lyashchenko.

Five Military Academies received new Commanding Officers[2]: The Gagarin Air Force Academy – Air Force Marshal Rudenko (October 1968); The General Staff Academy – Army General Ivanov (October 1968); the Frunze Academy – Army General Stuchenko (November 1968); The Military Armoured Corps – Col. General Babadzhanyan (October 1967); The Military Commanders' Academy, Air Defence Forces – Col. General Zimin (December 1967).

Other notable changes of this period were: General Shtemenko, Deputy Chief of the General Staff became also Chief of Staff, Combined Armed Forces of the Warsaw Pact[3]; Air Force General Kutakhov emerged to become 1st Deputy Commander in Chief of the Air Force,[4] and was promoted to Marshal in anticipation of an imminent succession to ageing K. A. Vershinen as Commander in Chief[5]; Army General Maryakhin succeeded the 71 year old Bagramyan as Deputy Minister of Defence and Commander of the Main Directorate for the Rear Forces[6]; Col. General Malykhin was appointed Maryakhin's 1st Deputy[7]; Col. General Grigoriev became 1st Deputy Commander of the Strategic Rocket Defence[8]; Col. General Ogarkov was promoted from Cmdr. of the Volga M.D. to 1st Deputy Chief of the General Staff[9] (Presumed to be in charge of Operations); Lt. General Mayorov became Commander of the new Central Forces Group[10] (Czechoslovakia); and Lt. General Sozinov became Chief of Staff of the Air Defence System.[11]

1969–70 saw a continuation of this high rate of transfers and replacements, the chief of which were: Col. General Tolubko was transferred to Commander of the Far Eastern M.D.,[12] while his predecessor there, Col. General Losik, became Commandant of the Tank Academy in Moscow;[13] Lt. General Ivanov replaced Col. General K. Provalov as Commander of Southern Forces[14] (Hungary); Col. General Khomulo was transferred from 1st Deputy Cmdr. in Chief of Soviet Forces in the DDR to Commander of the Siberian M.D.[15]; his former Commander, Marshal Koshevoi, was soon thereafter replaced by Col. General Kulikov[16]; Lt. General Salmanov took up duties as the new Commander of the Kiev Military District[17]; Col. General Dankevich was confirmed as Deputy Commander of the Strategic Rocket Defence[18]; Marshal Kutakhov's promotion to Commander of the Air Force was similarly confirmed (see note 5); while PVO (Static Air Defence) Commander Batitsky was promoted.[19] Col. General Silant'yev was made Chief of the Main Air Staff, while Lt. General of the Tank Corps Obaturov was made Commander of the Carpathian M.D.

In 1971, the 50 year old Army General Kulikov was appointed to the post of Chief of the General Staff, in succession to the ailing 73 year old Marshal Zakharov.[20] Zakharov's health had been deteriorating for some time, and it had been evident since the summer that Kulikov was being groomed for the succession.[21] Col. General Kurkotkin (Transcaucasion M.D. Cmdr.) was appointed to succeed Kulikov as Cmdr. of the Soviet forces in Germany.[22] Both could expect imminent promotions to ranks commensurate with their new prominence. Kulikov's appointment and the 1972 promotion of Tolubko (see below) rounded off, at least temporarily, an extraordinary infusion of younger blood into the top military leadership. Subsequent promotions, such as that of Col. General Govorov to head the Moscow Military District, and Lt. General Tyenischev to Commander in Czechoslovakia, served only to highlight the continuing nature of the process of rejuvenation. A generation shift had occurred. The old hierarchy was disappearing.

Within the Navy the same period saw the appointment of Rear Admiral Ya. N. Globa as 1st Deputy Commander of the Baltic Fleet.[23] But of greater importance was the appointment of Admiral Smirnov, ex. Commander of the Fleet's Operations Department,[24] to Pacific Fleet Commander. His predecessor, Admiral Amelko, was transferred on 1 April, 1969, to Deputy Commander in Chief of the Soviet Navy.

Shortly thereafter the incumbent 1st Deputy CINC of the Navy,

Kasatonov, was promoted to Fleet Admiral.[25] This was followed by the promotions to Fleet Admirals also of Sergeyev, the Chief of the Admiralty Staff,[26] and of Lobov, the Commander of the Northern Fleet.[27]

The most important naval leadership was thus to look as follows: Commander in Chief – Admiral of the Fleet of the Soviet Union[28] Gorshkov; 1st Deputy Commander in Chief – Fleet Admiral Kasatonov; Deputy Commander in Chief – Admiral Amelko; Chief of Admiralty Staff – Fleet Admiral Sergeyev; Commander of the Northern Fleet – Fleet Admiral Lobov; Commander of the Pacific Fleet – Admiral Smirnov.

In attempting to draw relevant implications from these changes, the first comment ought perhaps to be that they brought a new generation of commanders into prominence. The amorphous 'Stalingrad group' retained its hold on policy-influencing positions, as indicated for example in memberships of the Central Committee. But younger cadres were being promoted at a rate not generally appreciated in the west (see below).

Special importance was attached to certain positions and areas, especially the Kola and Far East Command areas (The geo-political reasons for this were analysed in Chapter 6). This fact was not novel. Its long standing relevance is reflected in a list of some of the previous commanders: Zakharov, Krylov, Eremenko, Pavlovsky and Malinovsky in the east; Stuchenko, Zakharov, Krylov, Bagramyan, Kazakov and Sokolov in the northwest.

Previous distinction appeared to be a pre-requisite for commands in these areas, as seen for example in the cases of Tolubko, promoted to Army General in May, 1970,[29] and Admiral Smirnov. And a successful execution of command seemed to lead to positions of high central military authority, as seen in the cases of Generals Pavlovsky[30] and Sokolov, and Admiral Amelko.

The importance of these areas is further testified to by the fact that the Pacific Fleet and the Far East M.D. Commanders are Candidate Members of the select CPSU Central Committee, as is the Northern Fleet Commander; the Leningrad M.D. Commander is a full Member (as are the former M.D. Commanders Pavlovsky and Sokolov).[31] But it is necessary to note that the prominence attested primarily to the positions, not to the incumbents. Admiral Amelko had to give up his

Candidate standing upon leaving the Pacific command, in spite of his promotion. This reflects on the exclusive character of the Central Committee (Gorshkov himself, a full Member, is the only other naval representative),[32] and it reflects on the vital nature of the above-mentioned commands.

Some commentators saw Tolubko's transfer as epitomising a new policy, according to which prior experience with both conventional and non-conventional weaponry brought priority consideration for any promotions of consequence. This was based on the fact that he had been a tank officer prior to being transferred to the Strategic Rocket forces (where he served as 1st Deputy Commander, before being given the Siberian M.D.). Khomulo has also been seen as exemplifying this perceived trend, in consideration of the nuclear-conventional integration of his former command, Soviet Forces in the DDR.[33]

Yet this appears to be incorrect. The integration of nuclear weaponry within the Armed Forces clearly placed a premium on corresponding training and experience. But the real trend was towards greater specialization, not towards generalized acquaintance.

This is supported by the following assertion by Col. General Grigoriev, 1st Deputy Commander in Chief of the Strategic Rocket Forces (in a review of the role and capabilities of his command)[34]: '. . . Our troops are composed of mature and highly educated cadres. It is enough to mention that more than 95 per cent of the missile officers have a higher and secondary education. The officer corps possesses outstanding command skills and organizational abilities. The percentage of engineering and technical personnel in our units is growing constantly. At present these personnel account for 80 per cent of the entire officer corps. The commander who is at the same time an engineer has become a central figure'.

Or, as stated by Marshal Krylov[35]: '. . . A missile soldier has no right to be a specialist of only average competence; he must be a true master of his profession'. Similar assertions became increasingly prominent also with regard to other Service branches, the Navy in particular.[36]

Tolubko's promotion therefore encouraged a concentration on his earlier tank commands, and the inference that his transfer reflected a return to the non-strategic command ladder and hierarchy (albeit to a post in which his years associated with the rocket troops would have definite psychological benefits). Khomulo's promotion appeared to be similarly motivated. His reputation as an expert on combat training made it probable that his recall was connected with the reorganization of combat training practices and concepts which was being implemented.

Tolubko's promotion, however, soon proved to warrant a different explanation. His previous prominence as 1st Deputy Commander of the Rocket Troops jarred with interpretations which denigrated his strategic expertise. And his 1972 promotion to Commander of the Rocket Troops vindicated the doubters.[38] His Siberian and Far East commands had in fact reflected the acrimonious relations with China and the build-up of Soviet missile capabilities in these areas; they represented the final grooming of the chosen successor to the ageing incumbent commander of the rocket troops.

This primary emphasis on the requirements of the position rather than on the character of the incumbent invites also a focusing on Maryakhin. His appointment as Commander of the Main Directorate for the Rear was made important by the crucial nature of logistics within Soviet tactical concepts. (See Chapters 1, 2, 3 and especially the end of Chapter 5). With the achieving of strategic parity, and the emergence of interventionary and general purpose forces, the question of logistics necessarily commanded increasing attention and priority.

But it is nevertheless time to survey also the character of the new incumbents. The first point must refer to their relative youth. There remained a number of older officers still serving in prominent positions, such as Marshal Zakharov until sidelined by illness in 1971 (he was born in 1898), Marshal Krylov until his death in 1972 (he was born in 1903) and Chief Air Marshal Vershinen (born in 1900). This reflected partly the fact that Marshals and Admirals of the Soviet Union do not have to retire: they are exempt from the 60 year retirement age which applies to all officers through 4-star rank. It also reflected on their capabilities. And it reflected, finally, on a reported shortage of higher officers(!) – presumably arising out of the cumulative effects of the Czechoslovak intervention and continuing tension along the Chinese border.[39] The service of these elder officers should not, however, be allowed to obscure the trend towards the promotion of youth.[40]

A large percentage of prominent incumbents in 1972 were under 60, a considerable number were in the 50–55 year bracket, and some were still in their forties. They generally made their name originally as lower and middle rank officers during the 2nd world war, achieving the first rank of General only in the 1950's. Army General Maryakhin's career pattern is a typical example, as is also that of the new Chief of the General Staff.

Many of them did not choose or feel obliged to join the CPSU until comparatively late in their careers. Typical are Navy Commander in Chief Gorshkov, who only joined the Party in 1942 (a year after becoming, at 31, the youngest Admiral of the Soviet Navy); Admiral Amelko, who joined the Party at 30 years of age, in 1944; and General Ogarkov, who joined the Party in 1945, when he was 28.

Yet they subsequently gained access to the highest policy councils, excepting only the Politburo itself. An analysis of the 100-odd top marshals, generals and admirals (including CPSU Central Committee Members and Candidates, Supreme Soviet representatives, and the remaining 4-star rank and above personnel of the Armed Forces), points to two conclusions[41]: The first confirms the conclusion regarding relative youth. The second relates to the fact that well over half occupy seats in the Supreme Soviet. It is not untypical for them to hold '. . . high Government posts (outside the Military). Yet only a few are Political officers, as opposed to regular staff officers and line officers'.[42]

This last point reinforces the evidence of a greater stress on professionalism within the Armed Forces. Military competence was accorded somewhat greater priority vis-à-vis 'political' considerations than had been the case in the past. This does not mean that political considerations, in the form either of fine ideological variations or of personal contact with politicians, may not remain a factor of concern. In fact, rumours that such are responsible for this or that promotion can often be picked up in Moscow. But such rumours usually prove to be misleading; even when they are not contradicted by subsequent events, they cannot be verified. The evidence presented in the following chapter clearly suggests a basic and mutually recognized compatibility of Party and military aspirations. And it suggests that this compatibility is of an order to allow the Party confidently to delegate most problems of military concern to the councils of military professionals.

NOTES

1. Armed forces appointments and transfers in general emerge only through a scrutiny of the Soviet press, – typically through the printing of an article by the affected officer, with the new title or position noted beneath the officer's name at the end of the article. A variation of this practice was exemplified by Pavlovsky's promotion. This was first noted when a *Krasnaya Zvezda* report on a speech he gave to military journalists (24 December, 1967) ascribed the said title to him.
2. Rudenko's and Ivanov's promotions emerged from '*Voenno-Istorichesky Zhurnal*', No. 10, 1968; Stuchenko's, Babadzhanyan's and Zimin's appeared in *Krasnaya Zvezda*, 6 December, 1968, 27 October, and 31 December, 1967; Babadzhanyan was later promoted to Marshal of the Tank Forces (*Izvestia*, 29 October, 1967).
3. *Krasnaya Zvezda* 6 August, 1968, (A comeback towards the authority he enjoyed as Chief of Staff under Stalin).
4. *Izvestia* 18 August, 1968, and *Krasnaya Zvezda* 22 February, 1969.
5. Duly confirmed by *Krasnaya Zvezda* on 19 March, 1969 – following also his elevation to USSR Deputy Minister of Defence, (*Krasnaya Zvezda* 26 April, 1969).
6. *Krasnaya Zvezda* 16 June, 1968, and 28 June, 1968; – he died late spring 1972.
7. *Krasnaya Zvezda* 14 August, 1968.
8. *Krasnaya Zvezda* 15 November, 1968.
9. *Krasnaya Zvezda* 16 August, 1968.
10. *Krasnaya Zvezda* 29 December, 1968.
11. *Krasnaya Zvezda* 4 December, 1968.
12. *Krasnaya Zvezda* 6 August, 1969.
13. *Krasnaya Zvezda* 8 August, 1969.
14. *Krasnaya Zvezda* 7 November, 1969.
15. *Krasnaya Zvezda* 31 July, 1969 – Khomulo's successor in the DDR was Lt. General Govorov; as re. his Siberian fief, a new Chief of Staff, Maj. General Pashuk, had been assigned just prior to Khomulo's transfer. See *Krasnaya Zvezda* 24 May, 1969.
16. *Krasnaya Zvezda* 17 November, 1969, and *Izvestia* 1 May, 1970 (For his promotion to General of the Army).
17. *Krasnaya Zvezda* 10 December, 1969.
18. *Krasnaya Zvezda* 5 August, 1969. He may have assumed the post as early as 1966; he was pictured with the other Deputies by *50 Let Sovetskikh Vooruzhiennikh Sil*, Voenizdat, Moscow, 1967. He was certainly a member of SRT's military council by that time.
19. *Krasnaya Zvezda* 15 April, 1969.
20. *Radio Moscow*, 23 September, 1971.
21. *Muenchener Merkur*, 26 July, 1971. See also *Radio Liberty Dispatch*, 23 September, 1971.
22. *ADN*, 23 September, 1971.
23. *Mors. Oboron* No. 4, 1969.
24. During which time he served as Cmdr. of the Fleet in the Mediterranean and wrote a lengthy article on its activities; his transfer was first noted in *Izvestia*, 20 May, 1969.
25. *Krasnaya Zvezda*, 11 October, 1969.
26. *Pravda*, 1 May, 1970.
27. Supr. Soviet decree of 28 July, 1970.
28. *Izvestia*, 29 October, 1967.
29. *Izvestia* 1 May, 1970.
30. Brought to Moscow in June, 1967 after (according to Moscow Army sources) having 'revolutionized' Far East defences while Commander of the Far Eastern

M.D., – to perform the same on a national scale. One of his minor but interesting Far East innovations is thought to be the introduction of helicopter inspection of the Mongolian-Chinese border by joint Soviet-Mongolian crews.

31. *Pravda*, 10 April, 1971.
32. *Ibid*. CC elections resulted in three representatives from the Navy, three from the Air Defence, two from the Strategic Rocket Troops, two from the Air Force, one from the Rear Services, three from the Political Administration, and two from the Ground Forces. Military District Commanders are not included in this enumeration. See Chapter 8 for further details.
33. See e.g. Peter Kruzhin, in the *Bulletin* of the Inst. for the Study of the USSR, Munich, Vol. XVI, No. 10.
34. 'Powerful Strike Force', in *Izvestia* 20 November, 1969.
35. 'Strategic Missile Troops', in *Pravda* 19 November, 1969.
36. See e.g. Kasatonov, in *Krasnaya Zvezda* 27 July, 1969.
37. A. A. Grechko, *Na Strazhe Mira . . .* , *op. cit.*, Chapter 3, Section 4.
38. First specifically mentioned in *Programma Televidenia i Radioveshchanie Mai 8–14*, 1972, p. 5, but indicated by his front row position in the *Krasnaya Zvezda* 26 April, 1972 picture from the military-party 'summit meeting' of the previous day.
39. The existence of a deficit in the number of higher officers was 'revealed' by Colonel Losik, then Military Attache (ex-Cmdr. of the Moscow garrison, and with Siberian experience), to a colleague in 1968. The deficit is startling when compared to what has been considered the reverse situation in the West during the post-war years, and the inference above therefore appears warranted.
40. It is proper here to comment on Western speculations regarding Soviet military senility and/or purges, such as were occasioned by the 23 April to 10 May, 1969, *Krasnaya Zvezda* announcements of the death of 12 Generals. On that occasion 6 of the deceased were over 65 years of age. And a wider reading revealed that the 12 deaths brought the number announced so far that year to only 33; the number who died during the same period the year before was 37. The deaths may therefore be seen merely as confirming the suggested demand for experienced officers to remain in active service.
41. See Harriet Fast Scott, The Soviet High Command-Age Analysis, in '*Soviet Military Doctrine, Its Formulation and Dissemination*', SRI Paper, April, 1971. The treated CPSU CC is that elected in 1966; the Supreme Soviet that elected in 1970. The CPSU CC-elections of 1971 confirm her conclusions, – as evidenced in her revised manuscript, also for S.R.I. (this author has seen draft sections, but is not is not in possession of the full text). See also the following Chapter 8; section on Military Representation on Party and Government bodies.
42. *Ibid*.

8

Military – Civilian Integration in the USSR

Soviet theory on the integration of the military into Party-led society will first be presented. It will be contrasted with western theories of perceived disintegrative factors. The consequent analysis will be followed by an investigation into military participation in formal Party and state organs. The final section will treat the military's actual involvement in the planning, administration, and execution of societal programs.

SOVIET THEORY ON THE MILITARY'S ROLE IN SOCIETY

Peaceful co-existence 'serves as a basis for the peaceful competition between socialism and capitalism on an international stage and constitutes a specific form of the class struggle between them. As they consistently pursue the policy of peaceful co-existence, the Socialist countries are steadily strengthening the positions of the world socialist system in its competition with capitalism. Peaceful co-existence affords more favourable opportunities for the struggle of the working class in the capitalist countries and facilitates the struggle of the peoples of the colonial and dependent countries for their liberation.'[1]

'Politics is the guiding force, and war is only the tool.'[2]

The military is a tool of society, but it serves peacetime as well as wartime functions. Some of the peacetime functions relate only indirectly to the preparing of the nation for war; they have considerable economic, social, and psychological implications, both with regard to policy promulgation and to policy implementation. This will be returned to below.

The military's role emerges from the following definitions: Military science is defined as the absolute base, 'a unified system of knowledge about the preparation and waging of armed struggle' in general.[3] Military doctrine is the specific 'unified guiding view accepted by the Soviet state concerning the nature and aims of a possible war, concerning the fundamental problems of preparing the country and the entire people.' . . . 'It is based on the conclusions of Soviet military science . . . (and) is a synthesis of (its) knowledge.'[4]

Military science cannot 'decline to analyse new phenomena,' as it must look to the future and consider all possibilities and hypotheses.[5] Military doctrine, however, consists of that which is appropriate to the contemporary period and is therefore inherently correct and non-flexible. Any challenge to it would therefore cause 'a serious fissure in the entire military structure.'[6] It would consequently be unthinkable.

Military doctrine is 'the officially approved system of concepts on the fundamental problems of war;' – 'the general political line of the (every) state's ruling social class determines military doctrine.'[7] Another source explains: '(one elaborates) a single statewide system of views on the character and purpose of war in the given historical conditions, the principles of military construction and the art of war, and (prepares) the country and the armed forces for war. Such a system . . . has been arbitrarily called military doctrine.'[8]

Then there is military strategy, which 'proceeds from these general positions, develops and studies concrete problems bearing on the nature of the war.' It encompasses the study of 'the conditions and factors that determine, at any given historical moment, the nature of a future war, the distribution of military and political forces, the quality and quantity of weapons, the military and economic potential, the probable composition and strength of the opposing coalitions and their geographical distributions.' It should 'develop the means for its (the future war's) conduct.'[9] The distinction between strategy and doctrine corresponds to that between war and politics.

The Party therefore has absolute authority as the sole definer of military doctrine, or dogma, at any one time. The military leadership's authority is absolutely limited as within the frame of the definitions.

It has, as quoted, to 'proceed from these general positions,' and can develop and study only 'concrete problems'. It can put the theory into practice, and it can develop the theory's implications, but it cannot alter the theory.

It can control and manipulate the material and tasks accorded to it by the theory. But even this is limited as regards 'modern weapons', since these 'are such that the political leadership cannot let them escape its control'.[10] In other words, they and their potential use have political implications which inherently categorize them as falling within military doctrine.

The military does influence the formulation of military doctrine, but then as part of the party. The practical aspects of this are treated below. Some of the theoretical implications were pursued in a lengthy 1957 investigation by Colonel A. Lagovskii. It was entitled 'Strategy and Economy,' with the subtitle 'A sketch of their mutual inter-connection and influence.'[11]

The first chapters gave a historical summary of the increasingly close connection between strategy and economy, of strategy's increasing dependence on the conflicting parties' levels of technical and economic development, and of its dependence on their economic potential. A nation's economic, moral and military potentials were accepted as inherently inter-related.

The central third and fourth chapters presented a systematic survey of the economy's determining effect on strategy. It was noted that military dispersal considerations might dictate the building of smaller, but more numerous, factories or plants, even when considerations of optimality favoured greater concentrations. The necessity to co-ordinate the economy in peacetime with potential military requirements was taken for granted, and part of the analysis concentrated on evolving the most efficient method for such co-ordination: 'The strategic leadership is . . . duty-bound to act as consultant in numerous questions concerning the state's economic life, which in one way or another may influence the nation's defensive capabilities.'

'Under modern conditions a demand has arisen for officers who are specialists in military economy. Let us call them (analogous to military engineers) military economists. Such specialists must be added to higher military staffs, but also to the planning organs and the economic organs within the state administration.'

'One must not believe that the military under modern conditions shall concern itself only with purely military concerns, and the economists with economic concerns.'

The book also contains an analysis of the effects on strategy of an enemy's economy. The author treats the United States' and Western Europe's dependence on overseas resources (a table showing 'strategic raw materials' and their locations is provided) and on sea transport. Naval strategies and technical innovations which affect such transport are dealt with in some detail.[12] But the quintessence lay within the scope of the above quotes. And it clearly commands the same acceptance today as it did then.[13]

This quintessence may be related to the above-quoted definition of peaceful co-existence. Peaceful co-existence has restricted relevance; it is pursued only as long as it is the policy alternative most likely to facilitate the 'struggle of the working class in the capitalist countries,' and the struggle of other non-liberated peoples, 'through the strengthening of the position of the world socialist system'.

The Soviet appreciation of the inter-relation between economic, military and political factors, and the appreciation that economic criteria on occasion both must and can be subordinated to the other criteria, has domestic relevance. It also has clear foreign political and trade relevance. Willingness to consider unfavourable economic returns as compensated by political or other rewards represents a potent weapon.[14]

There remains, of course, a 'grey area' as regards the limits to the authority that has been delegated to the armed forces. A more precise general delineation of responsibilities was the one ascertainable change in Party-military relations after the fall of Khrushchev.[15] But later events, such as related for example to 'modern weapons', demonstrated remaining uncertainties. SALT provided one case: *Pravda* published positive reviews of the talks, stressed the potentials for improved US-Soviet relations, and extolled on the hoped-for benefits of 'slowing the strategic arms race, the limitations and then reduction of such weapons'[16]; the military press chose largely to disregard the talks, and instead made pointed reminders regarding the need to be vigilant, and not jeopardize Soviet might.[17]

WESTERN THEORIES OF PERCEIVED DISINTEGRATIVE FACTORS

These have usually been developed around or from apparent anomalies of the type referred to above. But one must be careful. The most belligerent of the 'military' spokesmen, and those most often cited by commentators convinced of the existence of acute military-Party tension – namely Colonels Rybkin and Bondarenko[18] – are in fact political officers. Both are instructors at the Lenin Military-Political Academy, and therefore speak for the Party; their most un-compromising articles in 'Communist of the Armed Forces' have been accompanied by small-print announcements that they form part of special Party lecture series.[19]

The referred-to Pravda converges of SALT developments provide another example. Their favourable inclination should not be allowed to obscure their unwavering support for a high relative state of Soviet readiness; agreement is favoured, but not if it endangers Soviet security.[20] This appreciation encourages a more complex conception of Party aims and endeavours than commonly accepted in the west. Differing tenor and superficial contradictions as between articles are often explained by a consideration of different readerships, – and/or contemporary domestic or external politics. There is after all censor-ship; real editorial independence does not exist. Articles in the military press have been cleared by Party censorship organs.

One must finally consider Western conceptions of 'factions', and factional differences. The most readily accepted concerns 'the Stalingrad group', of officers associated with Krushchev on the Stalingrad front, officers whose rise to prominence paralleled Khrushchev's. The relevant data was assembled by R. Kolkowicz.[21] But his treatment's questionable assertions regarding immediate post-war group allegiances and factional preferences invite scepticism, as do the unanswered questions which arise from his inferences regarding the 1950's and 1960's. One may furthermore query the basis for his group identification.

Common war experiences certainly acted as a cementing agent. But the identified group members had bonds of even greater age: most of them studied together, at the Frunze Academy, or at the General Staff Academy.[22] The early contacts and interactions between not only contemporary military leaders, but between them and contemporary Party officials, will be returned to below. Suffice it here to urge caution in the assigning of prefixes.

MILITARY REPRESENTATION ON PARTY AND STATE BODIES

It is clearly often too easy to infer military-Party friction; apparent discrepancies are usually misleading. There is a considerable degree of integration of the military within the Party.

On the one hand Party membership is more widespread in the Armed Forces than in any other profession of any scale. By 1965

Marshal Malinovsky, then Minister of Defence, could assert that 'almost 90 per cent of our officers, Generals and Admirals are Communists or Young Communists.'[23] Just over a year later, on 3 April, 1966, he revised the figures as follows: 93 per cent of officers were then declared to be Party or Komsomol members, as were 80 per cent of total Armed Forces personnel. There remained some variations as to relative Service percentages. For example, 'nine-tenths of all sailors are Communists or Young Communists.'[24] But in no service was the percentage very significantly below average.

On the other hand, there was considerable military representation on the higher elected organs of both Party and State. The latter will be considered first.

The over-all scale of representation is indicated by the late 1965 announcement that '10,760 fighting men have been elected to the (1966) USSR Supreme Soviet, the Union and Autonomous Republic Soviets, and to the local Soviets.'[25] A similar number was elected in 1969; of these 58 marshals, generals and admirals were elected to the Supreme Soviet which convened in June 1970.[26]

They included all the Military District commanders, all the Fleet Commanders, both PVO (air defence) commanders, and all the commanders of Soviet military groups abroad.

Turning to military representation on Party bodies, it was in 1966 announced that the 23rd CPSU Congress was attended by 352 military delegates representing 890,000 Party members and candidates.[27] T. H. Rigby considered it appropriate to correlate Border Guard representation – and concluded that a disproportionate 7 per cent of the total Party membership belonged to the Armed Forces or the Border Guards.[28]

But it is more appropriate to analyse the Central Committee elected by the Congress. The analysis will be based on the C.C. elected by the 24th Congress in 1971,[29] as providing the latest data. There were few changes from the 1966 C.C. Thirteen military members were re-elected (Bagramyan, Batitsky, Gorshkov, Grechko, Dement'yev/Ustinov[30], Yepishev, Zakharov, Konev, Krylov, Moskalenko, Sokolov, Chuikov, and Yakubovsky); three ex-candidates became full members (Lyashchenko, Maryakhin and Ogarkov)[31]; six new members were elected (Bugayev, Ivanovsky, Kulikov, Kutakhov, Pavlovsky and Shavrov). Five candidates were retained (Budenny, Getman, Grushevoi, Lobov and Psurtsev); nine new ones were elected (Gorchakov, Koldunov, Kurkotkin, Mayorov, Okunev, Salmanov, Smirnov, Tolubko and Tretyak) – their distinguishing feature being youth, with the 'old man out' 56, the youngest 47 years old. It ought to be noted that the size of the turnover is deceptive: a large number of the 1966 members or candidates who did not retain their seats in 1971 had died.

The smaller number of candidates elected in 1971 entailed a decrease in total military representation, from 10 to 9 per cent. But the net addition of six full members[32] meant that the military voting strength increased from 8·2 to 8·7 per cent (thus even more disproportionate than their share of total Party membership).

Service-wise the 1971 C.C. looked as follows: the Navy had three, the Air Defence three, the Strategic Rocket Troops two, the Air Force two, the Rear Services one, the Political Administration three (no change), and the Ground Forces two representatives (not counting Military District commanders).

Only the most critical Military Districts, Groups abroad and Fleets gained representation on the Central Committee, Changes are therefore noteworthy. In 1971 they reflected first of all the Chinese border tension: 1966 had produced candidate memberships for the Pacific Fleet and the Turkestan Military District commanders, and Audit Commission membership for the Far East M.D. Commander; 1971 produced candidate stature for the Pacific Fleet and the Far East M.D. commanders, Audit Commission membership for the Trans-Baikal M.D. commander, and full Member stature for the commander of the new Central Asian M.D. which was carved out of the Turkestan Military District. In the West: the commander of Soviet Forces in Germany was raised from Candidate to full Member; the commander of the Central Group of Forces (Czechoslovakia), which was constituted following the 1968 intervention, was appointed a Candidate member.

These bodies are, however, too unwieldy in size (the 1971 C.C. contained 396), and meet too infrequently, to serve as effective policy deliberators. One must therefore turn elsewhere for the decision-making agencies concerned with such matters as military doctrine or strategy.

THE MILITARY'S PRACTICAL INVOLVEMENT IN POLICY
PROMULGATION AND EXECUTION

POLICY PROMULGATION

The 1950's and 1960's efforts towards the establishment of better-qualified strategic research and decision-making councils provide a suitable point of departure. Initial developments lay within the context of such exhortations as: 'Political leaders must know the potentialities of strategy in order to set tasks before it skilfully (at each historical stage)'[33]; of assertions that even economic developments entailed such strategic implications as made military participation within the relevant planning organs both desirable and necessary[34]; and of pointed reminders regarding the implications of specific strategic realities.[35]

The inherent anxieties and the logical conclusions were spelt out in the period following Krushchev's removal. There was the major article by Marshal Grechko, '25 years ago,' of 25 May 1966: a review of past experiences led to the unambivalent assertion that political leaders could in theory make mistakes when dealing with military matters. And Grechko himself followed this up the following year, again on the basis of a review of the 2nd World War, and of the mistakes and hesitations which preceded it, by emphasizing the fact that 'correct and timely evaluation of the situation prior to war, and the reaching of initial decisions' took on increased importance and urgency in 'the nuclear age.'[36] Other articles in a similar vein also appeared.[37]

As to conclusions, these were first explicitly pursued by Marshal Sokolovsky and Maj. General Cherednichenko in a 1966 article.[38] Its theme expressly concerned the need for greater flexibility – and improved quality – of military doctrine in particular and strategic thinking in general. Their main argument related to the Soviet need to match the combat readiness and deployment spread with which NATO was credited. NATO's asserted peacetime deployment of forces in the right places, numbers and proportions for the achievement 'of its main war tasks in a short period' was held up for emulation. And the implied NATO sophistication was utilized to support the recommendation that either one established research institutions such as the RAND Corporation of the USA, or else one encouraged more extensive discussions at General Staff levels than had hitherto been possible.

These aspirations clearly won establishment appreciation of the need for significant military expertise access to defence policy decision-making councils.[39] There even emerged informal admissions of the need for a new 'supreme military-political organ,' – through which information might more easily be procured, and decisions more easily disseminated.[40]

No announcement about the establishment of such an organ or institution was forthcoming. In order to gain an approximate appreciation of the current status it becomes necessary to delve briefly into the historical evolution of the military command apparatus.[41]

March 1918 saw the establishment of a Higher (Vysshiy) Military Council, composed of 'the military leader and two Political Commissars', and responsible for 'leadership of all military operations of the Red Army'. 'Subsequently the composition and tasks of the Higher Military Council were significantly broadened.' And 'from April 1918 the People's Commissar for War and Naval Affairs, members of the Collegia of the People's Commissariat for Military Affairs and also specialists on military and naval affairs were on the Higher Military Council'.[42]

But it failed to cope satisfactorily with wartime demands, and was re-organized: 'On the 2nd of September 1918, by special edict of the VTsIK, the country was declared a military camp, and the Revolutionary Military Council of the republic was formed as the highest organ of direction of the Red Army'.[43]

The Revolutionary Military Council continued to function throughout the Civil War and until 1934, when it was replaced by the Military Council, attached to the People's Commissariat of Defence.

This was again re-organized, in March 1938, when it became the Main (Glavny) Military Council of the Red Army: 'It was attached to the People's Commissariat of Defence. It examined basic questions on the organizing of the Red Army and on the strengthening of the defence capability of the country.' 'At the same time the Main Military Council of the Navy was formed.'[44]

On the second day of the war the Stavka of the High Command was formed, taking over responsibility from the Main Military Councils. Peace saw the Stavka replaced by the Higher Military Council.

'In February 1946, the Higher (Vysshiy) Military Council, which was attached to the Ministry, was formed.' . . .[45]

'In March 1950, subsequent to the division of the Ministry of the Armed Forces, the Higher (Vysshiy) Military Council was created. It was attached to the Council of Ministers of the USSR. Main (Glavny) Military Councils were formed which were attached to the War and Naval Ministries.'[46]

The pre-war terminological confusion was evidently resolved by naming the highest organ, at Council of Ministers' level, the Higher Military Council, and the Service Ministry organ or organs as Main. . . .[47]

Evidence suggests that this practice was continued after the 1953 re-uniting of the Service ministries into the Ministry of Defence, with one Main Military Council being attached to the Ministry.[48] ' . . . The most important questions of military policy are discussed and decided collectively at Congresses of the Party and Plenums of the Central Committee. Organs of collective leadership are also found directly in the Armed Forces in the Main (Glavny) Military Council, and in the military councils of the services of the Armed Forces, military districts and fleets. Military councils collectively examine and decide all important questions in the daily life and activity of the troops.'

This author could find no exact reference to the work of the supreme Higher Military Council during the early and mid-1960's. Marshal Sokolovsky (quoted above) referred to the Stavka. But the reference was unclear and highly ambiguous; it produced the impression that while the Stavka did not then exist, it would be created at times of war.

By the late 1960's, however, evidence emerged that the Stavka was synonymous with the Higher Military Council, or at least that the bodies enjoying either title had been so similar in function and composition as to encourage inter-changeability of designation.[49]

And by 1971 came evidence that a Stavka DID exist: 'In correspondence with . . . (respective) . . . tasks each Service of the Armed Forces is designated for waging military actions primarily in one sphere – on the ground, at sea, or in the air – and accomplishes the fulfillment of tasks under the leadership of the commander-in-chief of this Service of the Armed Forces, or directly of the Stavka of the Supreme Commander.'[50]

Sokolovsky's obfuscation may have been intentional, and motivated by political or security considerations. Or one might presume the Marshal's intimation to have been correct at the time, and infer that Stavka remained a war-associated term for the body otherwise known as the Higher Military Council. But it appears more correct to correlate the ambiguity of his wording with the book's publication date (it was prepared in 1967), and to see it as reflecting on the then remaining uncertainty. The later existence of a Stavka may then relate to the representations described in the introduction to this section. It may in fact be the new 'supreme military-political organ' that was called for.

The hierarchy established by the early 1970's, may in conclusion be delineated as follows:

(i) The Stavka, cum Higher Military Council, attached to the Council of Ministers. One can procure no information with regard to its size. But 'reliable sources' (1971) named Kosygin as chairman, with a Colonel General of the General Staff as Secretary, and with Marshal Zakharov enjoying a pivotal role (a role presumably transferred, as of late 1971, to his successor as Chief of the General Staff, V. G. Kulikov).[51] There are indications that the Minister of Defence and his 1st Deputy and Deputy Ministers are members. And one might perhaps further presume access as concerns CPSU General Secretary Brezhnev and the Secretariat's 'strategic overseer' Ustinov (if that is indeed his role).[52]

(ii) The Main Military Council, attached to the Ministry of Defence. Its composition is unknown. But representatives from each Service may be presumed to be members, together with the Minister and his Deputies.

(iii) The Military Councils attached to individual service branches and Military Districts. These were in 1958 (on the occasion of Khrushchev's re-emphasizing of the Party's directing role), expanded to include the military commander, his 1st deputy commander, and his chief of staff, plus his 'political' military colleague, the Secretary of the local Party committee, and 'leading workers'.[53]

Apropos of military-Party integration and mutual sympathy: among the local Party Secretaries then included were K. T. Mazurov, V. P. Mzhavanadze, N. V. Podgorny, and A. P. Kirilenko.[54] The first, third and fourth are today full Members of the Politburo, the second is a Candidate member . . . all with a number of years of close contact with the commanders of their areas' Military Districts behind them. Many of the latter have meanwhile become leading members of the Ministry of Defence and the Defence Establishment.

The exact importance, function or responsibility of the different Councils is unknown. There are, as shown, indications that the Stavka/Higher Military Council may for some years have been in abeyance as a formal body, only to be resuscitated following the acceptance of the need for more sophisticated research and policy-coordinating facilities. But it is difficult to gauge to what extent practices have been altered by the formal re-constituting of the Stavka and the appointment of a civilian supreme commander.

One presumes that the Supreme Commander is governed in his

decisions by professional military opinion, as represented by the Chief of the General Staff and the Stavka Secretary, also of the General Staff (viz. above).[55] There remains the question as to whether the Stavka has acquired independent facilities. It may be that its actual operational mode remains akin to the British pattern. That is, with most policy-deliberation and decision-making conducted not in quorum, but through informal ties between the political leadership and some of the more prominent military professionals. As for strategic research it appears plausible to view it as still basically fragmented between the various headquarters and commands. But a certain amount is presumably coordinated, either through direct commission from the supreme body or one or more of its members, or through research facilities attached to the General Staff.

MILITARY INVOLVEMENT IN POLICY IMPLEMENTATION –
THE ECONOMY

At the 24th CPSU Congress in 1971, Brezhnev acknowledged that ' . . . 42 per cent of its (the defence industry's) output is used for civilian purposes'.[56] The figure reflects on the privileged position of Soviet defence industries as regards the recruiting of scientific manpower; it reflects on the productive capacity of the defence industries, and it reflects on the state of military-civilian integration. An understanding of the size and implications of the defence budget therefore becomes a necessary ingredient of any analysis of military-Party relations.

If one looks for example at the 1967 budget[57] one finds that defence allocations officially constituted 13·2 per cent of the total. But unofficial reports then circulating in Moscow credited Brezhnev with admitting that 18 per cent was a more realistic figure, when taking into account military value-endeavours incorporated in other budget posts.[58] Western strategists in Moscow at the time tended to increase this, again, to 20–22 per cent.[59] Reports of Academician Aganbegyan's 'secret speech' of 1965, which indicated that defence industries accounted for about a third of the national total, supported exaggeration of the military's economic role and position.

Or one might choose another example, such as the 1969 budget. This was presented to the Supreme Soviet by Finance Minister Garbuzov on 10th December, 1968, and allocated 17·7 billion roubles to defence. Western reactions were epitomized in the *Economist's* estimation, that the realistic figure was between one-fifth and one-third above the official allocation. In other words, the realistic budget was estimated to be of an order of 21–24 billion roubles.[60] Estimates along these lines received support also from information provided by US Secretary of Defence Laird.[61]

There are two basic problems involved. One concerns the size of 'hidden' budgetary allocations, and the other concerns the rouble-value question. Estimates of either are at best educated speculation, since the essential primary data are unobtainable. But a survey of some such speculation will be presented below, since it does help one acquire a more composite picture. It is thought to convey as accurate an impression as may be gathered at this time.

One of the analyses of interest is that completed by Emile Benoit in 1968: 'Economics of Arms Control and Disarmament, the Monetary and Real Costs of National Defence'.[62] Weighing 'real procurement costs', 'opportunity costs of defence', and other similar data, as well as the difficulties surrounding the establishment of their value, he hazarded the following estimates of 'Purchasing Power Equivalents' (PPE), as between US and USSR Defence costs at the time:

	Real Costs Million $ PPE	Real Cost Per Capita PPE $	Monetary Cost (National Unit Currency, Millions)	Monetary Cost as % of CNP
USA	63,283	322	63,283	9·1%
USSR	44,500	191	—	—

Most experts consider sizeable military-oriented funds, for example as pertains to research and development, to be 'hidden' under other budgetary headings.[63] One ought to be sceptical regarding the over-rating of the extent of these practices. But if the 1967–69 data presented above were correct, in estimating that 'real' Soviet defence expenditures represent an increase of, say, 25–30 per cent of the official figure, then this would tend to produce respective PPE's of near comparable order (see below).

This appears to be supported by R. W. Davies' and R. Amann's calculation of 1969[64]: '. . . the USSR operates a research and development establishment comparable in size to that of the US. The differences between the two are getting fewer'.

Abraham S. Becker of the Rand Corporation offered a subtly different analysis leading to a similar conclusion[65]: He declared that while US and USSR defence expenditures appeared to be comparable in cost effectiveness (or PPE) terms, this did not necessarily entail that the Soviet monetary burden was twice that of the US (with reference to the fact that the US GNP was then considered to be twice as large as that of the USSR). He estimated that the respective burdens, or percentages, were in fact similar: as regards finance allocated to the military, and military hardware costs, there was reason to believe that the USSR received in excess of US \$2·00 worth per rouble (vs. official rate of \$1·11 = 1 rouble).[66] The USSR furthermore enjoyed favourable manpower costs. For these reasons Soviet military expenditures could be declared equivalent to those of the US, in spite of the fact that the percentage she allocated to defence was similar to that allocated by the USA out of a far larger budget/GNP.

Becker cautioned against the overrating of 'hidden' expenditures. He was plainly aware of, and wary of the consequences of the common ignorance of price behaviour in the military sphere. But the conclusions he hazarded do support the judgment that the effective military value procured through the respective budgets was comparable – as was the respective strain on the economies.[67]

Two peripheral points are relevant. One concerns the 1969 US Arms Control and Disarmament Agency survey of World Military expenditures.[68] This established the fact of rapid world-wide increases in armaments, as also the fact that the relevant graph is going up at a faster rate than the World GNP graph. It documented that military expenditures constitute an ever-increasing drain on resources; it expanded by noting that these expenditures already, with only a few exceptions (these exceptions not including the US and the USSR), significantly exceeded the nations' expenditures on education and health. Other authorities have documented the increasing economic drains of military procurement. One of the more prominent was the Stockholm International Peace Institute[69]; its 1969 report received the following acknowledgement from Pravda[70]: 'The compendium documents the yearly spiralling of the arms race that continually increases the danger to international peace and the burden of expenditures to support it.'

The second, related, point concerns military over-spending and unreliance. It is clear that US military allocations have been wasteful, with ultimate weapons system costs spiralling far above the original estimates on which their approval was based, and with achieved weapon efficiency far too often proving greatly inferior to the prognostications which had justified their budgetary allocations (See footnote 66). Soviet industry's structural kinship to the monopoly situation of US Defence industries encourages the inference that similar developments occurred in the USSR, though perhaps not on quite the same scale. The waste resulting from monopoly and bureaucracy is probably comparable, but the financial waste of the immense profits in the US industry is presumably greater than that possible under Soviet conditions (?).

A further aspect to this military unreliance must be considered. This is that inherent in the 1969 testimony by Jonathan B. Bingham (US Congress Representative, and Member of US UN delegation),[71] and which he himself called 'illustrative' of 'the present trend:' 'In a presentation with regard to relative Soviet and US strength in submarines, the Navy deducted from effective US strength x per cent for those vessels that would have to be in home port at any given time. When asked what percentage had been deducted from the Soviet strength figure for the same reason, the answer was that no deduction had been made; the incredible excuse was that "we don't know what percentage their lay-up is"(!)'

The problem is the same as that referred to elsewhere,[72] with relation to the military's propensity to maximize degradation factors (factors detracting from efficiency expectations; – expected percentages of malfunction) associated with its own weapons, and to minimize those of the antagonist.

The Soviet Union is not immune to the guns vs. butter quandary and to the related real and psychological problem complexes.[73] But it is clear, that neither economic (or uneconomic) considerations, nor otherwise induced stringency, will alone force curtailment of military procurements thought necessary by the (integrated) decision-making authorities. Referring to projected Arms Control/Disarmament talks with the USA, a prominent Soviet Diplomat is reported to have emphasized the following in the Spring of 1969[74]: Soviet authorities considered an arms agreement as desirable and necessary, but as no more pressing on economic grounds for the USSR than the USA. He declared a firm belief that 'the 1941 complex' was still vivid enough, to ensure that the Soviet populace would endure the financial hardships necessary to guarantee that defence requirements were met, while he doubted that the same was true of the Americans.

The assertion had a certain propaganda value, but the belief is nonetheless one widely held. The Soviet Union appeared to be confident regarding her capability to sustain whatever military expenditures she considered to be necessary.[75]

CIVIL DEFENCE AND THE MILITARY TRAINING OF THE
CIVILIAN POPULACE

Related endeavours of noteable scale have long been a fixture of
Soviet society and policy. During the late 1960's their scope was
expanded considerably. They have definite military value and
implications. But their sponsorship by the Party points to a further
aspect: the political – and economic – utility of a more disciplined
populace. . . . A survey of these endeavours must therefore be included in any compendium analysis of military-Party integration.

Civil Defence was in 1966 defined as 'a system of state-wide defence
measures being carried out throughout the country for protecting
the populace and the national economy from the weapons of mass
destruction, and also for rescue work in the zone of a possible strike'.[76]
'Every city and inhabited point' was to be given protection.[77] Prime
shelter-building efforts were to be directed towards ensuring 'the
uninterrupted operation of units of the national economy if nuclear
war should break out.'[78] As for the population, cost and technical
difficulties precluded any encompassing shelter-building program.
But 'planned and systematic' training would be given to 'workers,
employees and the general public'; 'attention is being focused on the
preparation of the entire populace, on the ability to help oneself and
to help one's neighbour.'[79] Evacuation and self-help became adopted
concepts (with the implicit corollary that a nuclear era declaration of
war was not likely to be immediately followed by the initiation of
hostilities affecting super-power 'home areas'!)[80]

It appears propitious first to present a tentative summary of the
basic Economy-oriented efforts: shelters were constructed at or for
important enterprises and institutions,[81] and around the production
equipment of industries which must continue functioning.[82] They
were built to withstand (unspecified) blast pressures, heat, radiation,
and potential chemical and bacteriological attacks.[83] And they were
built for long-term occupancy, with a space allotment of 2–2.55
metres per person.[84] Civil Defence personnel involved were organized
along existing territorial-administrative structure lines, and subject
to the authority of the relevant administrative director (e.g. Soviet or
Sovkhoz chairman). Their work has been part-time but obligatory
with the men undergoing a minimum of 35 hours of instruction, and
their civilian superiors a minimum of 70 hours.[85] Full-time military
personnel have throughout been assigned to guide and direct each

'task force'. The total number of active participants was claimed to have reached 20 million under Khrushchev.[86]

Wider-ranging efforts – program extensions: these efforts together with the para-military cum sport like voluntary training long provided by DOSAAF, were as mentioned to be considerably supplemented. The first portents were soon evident, viz. the following 1965 statements:

Party and public organizations were directed to be 'more concerned with the military-patriotic up-bringing of school children'.[87] And it was noted that 'The YCL (Komsomol) committees are obliged to carry out more actively the work of military and patriotic education of Soviet youth and preparing them for service in the Armed Forces.'[88]

It was announced that there was to be established 'patronage over military units by workers, collective farmers and cultural figures', officially to 'help strengthen and expand the army's ties with the people'.[89] The scope and perspectives were further indicated in testimony by Pavlov, then YCL First Secretary.

'Following the example of the Pacific Fleet, entire Youth flotillas have been set up in the Black Sea, the Baltic and the North Sea. . . . In all corners of the Soviet Union this summer tents were pegged out for the 'Sons of the Regiment' camps where juveniles learned about military technology and studied the heroic history of the USSR Armed Forces.'[90]

The 1967 law cutting the length of military service added a decisive spur (as well as a part rationale) to the developments. On the first of January 1968 existing voluntary programs were extended to take in all youths down to grade 9. They were at the same time put on an obligatory basis. Then in November their scope was again extended, to incorporate also the training of pioneers. A lengthy September 1969 Izvestia progress report on the implementation of the decrees serves to provide an illustrative resume.[91]

It confirmed that *all* establishments, schools, institutes, factories, and farms were now obliged to provide training facilities. But while some areas (Moscow and Leningrad were among those named) had done so fully, others had not yet provided the necessary facilities. Certain enterprise and collective farm executives were furthermore said to have paid only superficial attention to the required military instruction. This could be interpreted as indicating that exam papers and results had not been made obligatory. Or it could be seen to mean that satisfactory marks were handed out no matter the level of achievement, by managers whose concern or need for their men's productive capacities led them to discourage the time-consuming and non-productive military training.

Yet such deviations were to be ensured against, according to the article. It stressed that *all* youths had to receive preconscription military training. They must study the service regulations and the servicemen's oath, and classes must be held to ensure mastery of drill and the firing of small-calibre weapons. Military instructors were to be chosen from reserve sergeants and first sergeants. The Komsomol should aid DOSAAF in the organization of the training, and public education agencies and military commissariats should aid both in ensuring supervision and verification of procedures and results. As a further security and benefit, the review recommended that every school and other training centre be adopted by some military unit or warship.

Five months later, in March 1970, another progress report appeared.[92] This stressed that the Party and Komsomol organizations do of course retain ultimate responsibility for insuring the universal implementation of the program (the scope of the responsibility delegated to the military being restricted to questions of curricula and modes of instruction). It was asserted that the military-patriotic theme must as a consequence 'never' be absent from the pages of provincial Komsomol newspapers.

It acknowledged that there still remained areas in which the programs were not carried out sufficiently. Some areas of Central Asia and the Maritimes were singled out for criticism. In the former there were, revealingly, declared to be cases of managers taking 'the wrong attitude' to the organization of mass defence work (see reasons, as analyzed above). In the Maritime territory there was said to exist 'no clear notion . . . of the number of persons acquiring military-technical specialities, their distribution, or the technical centres involved.'

The report stressed that this lagging must be rectified, and Kursk province (and the city of Saratov) was held up as the standard which must be emulated. There the Komsomol had organized the young people of 'every district' to work on Sundays so as to earn money for the construction of shooting ranges, clubs, and 'method centres' for military and patriotic training. Military reservists were utilized in the actual instruction, and participants were taught military history and theory as well as the handling of guns, rifles, and other equipment. Military sports were furthermore engaged in, to secure the desired physical standards.

There did not emerge any new formal programme specifically oriented towards increased shelter-construction or similar endeavours. But educationary efforts were evidently being given increased priority by the late 1960's.

Not only were there such as might be presumed to be encompassed within the scope of the above described programmes. There furthermore appeared a spate of surprisingly frank books for the general public, which expanded on nuclear potentials, stressed the need for relevant knowledge and suitable preparation, and provided detailed explanatory diagrams.

A typical example[93] began by discussing various contemporary nuclear missile weapon systems and concepts. It then dwelt on strike blast, heat and radio-active effects, and provided illustrative charts and diagrams. There finally followed a comparatively lengthy treatment of Civil Defence theory and practice, again accompanied by relevant charts, sketches and diagrams (on the effects encountered at varying radii from a strike centre, on the potentials of various protective measures, on simplified air-filter construction techniques, etc.).

It was indicative that even Moscow University, that most privileged and duty-exempt of institutions, became involved. Exhortatory posters were prominently displayed: 'Comrades! Master the knowledge of national defence!'; '*Every* citizen must learn how to protect himself from the effects of nuclear attacks, and how to protect his comrades!'[94] And students were called in for short-term training and refresher courses.[95]

By 1970–71, if not before, it had become impossible for anybody not to have acquired at least some knowledge. And it was clear that a large majority had received or was receiving at least some active training or instruction.

Conclusion: one may distinguish between three inter-relating military strands: the endeavours' effect on mobilization calculations; their effects on general survival prospects; and their implications vis-à-vis 'Home Guard' and 'People's War' potentials.

Mobilization Calculations: The 1968 intervention in Czechoslovakia and the spring and summer 1969 Ussuri border battles afforded illustrative glimpses. The former witnessed efficiently camouflaged selective mobilizations (with reference to 1968 one might interject that the utilization of Aeroflot capacity, evident at Prague airport, testified to yet another aspect of military-civil coordination). The 1969 events were accompanied by similar mobilizations, and a progression of divisional up-gradings. Some divisions previously classified as grade 3 (30 per cent manned) were brought up to grade 2 (about 60 per cent manned) standards, while some grade 2 divisions were re-inforced to grade one requirements (80–90 per cent manned).[96]

Two factors deserve comment: (1) Concerns the technical aspects of acquaintance with weaponry and the utilization thereof, and the complementary abstract that the resultant knowledge must increase confidence, and hence morale. Familiarity with one's weaponry induces confidence in one's ability to utilize its capabilities;[97] (2) Concerns the greater ease and speed with which trained civilians may supplement reservists, and be incorporated into divisional structures so as to affect their upgrading and combat readiness. This must facilitate military policy calculations and increase military options. An action such as the Czechoslovak intervention might for example otherwise have demanded a slower and more easily detected mobilization process, and might, therefore, have met or meet better prepared counter-measures.

General Survival Prospects: 'Familiarity' and its implications are again of paramount importance. A universal common minimum of knowledge of the theory and implementation of protective techniques, actions and devices must inherently decrease the likelihood or scope of panic, and increase survival prospects. The precise effects do not allow of calculations since they depend on too great a variety of unknowns (e.g. warning-time given) and abstracts (e.g. psychological factors). They will not suffice to negate US second-strike potentials, and will therefore not affect the 'axioms' of the present era of mutual assured second-strike capabilities (it is no longer logical to expect local wars, even if nuclear, to escalate to encompass the home-areas of the two super-powers; since mutual second-strike forces entail self-destruction for the initiator of a first strike, such becomes logically inconceivable; excepting and until the procurement by one of means negating the other's second-strike, both will explicitly or tacitly accept locale restrictions throughout the course of a future war).

But Civil Defence measures and knowledge will significantly improve prospects vis-à-vis the smaller and 'cruder' nuclear powers, which remain theoretically susceptible to the crisis-temptation of initiating a first strike due to the extremely vulnerable non-second-strike nature of their missiles. When added to the more important super-power BMD endeavours, the effecting of universal comprehensive Civil Defence training may be seen as resulting in practical immunity as concerns nuclear eventualities of this type.

Home Guard – People's War Potentials: post war USSR never established a Home Guard or territorial army. She appeared satisfied with the regular Army, supplemented by special border guard units. The practice of sending personnel to serve in other than their home provinces exacerbated the defensive gap as far as potential guerilla or partisan activities in the face of invading forces were concerned. The deficiency was presumably considered insignificant in view of the post-war stress on offensive operations, and the emerging confidence that a future war would not be fought on Soviet territory. A territorial militia was considered in conjunction with the troop cutting designs of the early 1960's, but was shelved.[98] Defence planners may have been inclined to consider it irrelevant in an era in which nuclear capacities would be used against an invader.

But the emerging problem-complex of the mid and late 1960's, of acute Sino-Soviet tension over a militarily highly problematic border, resurrected fears of hostile incursions, and stimulated a desire for supplementary capabilities. The above described training of civilians had as its implicit corollary the improvement and extension of Home Guard potentials. The emphasis of the above-quoted Pravda article on laxness in the Maritime Territory, and on the need to eliminate this, may be correlated with the fact that this area was obviously that for which a Home Guard appeared most important at the time.

This is supported by a Pravda article of May 1970.[99] After first lauding the border guards (they are 'mobile, motorized and technically equipped and possess crack cadres, modern arms and a high degree of combat readiness ... and (are) capable ... of repelling ... armed provocations on both the dry land and maritime sections of the border ... '), it proceeds to concern itself with 'the working people of the borderlands': 'The local Party and Soviet agencies hold a leading position in the organization of military – patriotic work and of mass mobilization for the rendering of assistance to the border-troops in the safeguarding of the frontier'.

One may finally consider the USSR's persistent refusal to acknowledge the Geneva convention according to which civil defence forces are prohibited from performing combat duties. Her 'grazhdanskye oboroni' have throughout been accepted as an integral part of her Armed Forces.

And it becomes logical to conclude that the USSR has in practice if not in theory effected a substantial 'Home Guard' equivalent.

AN OFFICIAL EXPOSITION: 'THE POLITICAL SIDE TO SOVIET
MILITARY DOCTRINE'

Towards the end of 1968, Colonel Candidate Milit. Larionov, (now
retired, and working with the Academy of Science's 'Institute,
USA'), then on the General Staff, wrote the above named article. It
constitutes one of the most comprehensive presentations of contemporary thinking.[100] Excerpts from it may therefore be quoted as a
valuable supplement to our discussion, as well as an interesting yardstick for comparisons.

'Within Soviet military doctrine it has been agreed to distinguish
two facets – one political and one military-technical. This is a
haphazard differentiation, since our military doctrine emerges as a
united harmonious system of the Party's and State's ideas and
decisions. . . . Thus Soviet military doctrine emerges as a concrete
expression of the Communist Party's military policy. . . . The
Communist Party and its views regarding questions of war and peace
in the present epoch retain the leading role in the formulation of
Soviet military doctrine . . . (wars') objective existing origin (is)
imperialism. Realistically viewing the possibility of new imperialist
agression, *the Party finds it necessary with all means to strengthen the*
economic and military might.
' . . . the CPSU 23rd Congress directives on the new Five Year
Plan state that we *must always show concern that our Armed Forces have*
the most modern types of military equipment at their disposal.[101] The
growth of Soviet defensive might is a necessary prerequisite to peace
and people's security.' ' . . . four-fifths of the industrial growth (in the
USA) since 1910 occurred during the two World Wars and the
Korean War . . . monopolies have broken through State borders . . .
super-concerns are formed . . . (and) military coalitions hostile to the
socialist conutries are built. . . . In the USA the military personnel
occupy many leading State positions, and they are often appointed
as diplomatic representatives, especially to countries where the USA
conducts armed interference in local conflicts . . . ' ' . . . the charac-
teristics/classifications (of war) can in our opinion be divided thus:
according to a war's political character; according to the class
structures of the warring nations; according to the extent of the
military conflict; according to the type of weaponry which is
utilized. . . . V. I. Lenin divided wars into just and unjust . . . just
wars are those conducted to liberate the subjugated from capitalism's

G

slavery, wars to protect freedoms won, and to achieve and assure national independence. . . . A decision as to a war's justness or unjustness is inextricably tied to its classification into types determined by the main lines in the social struggle. Such lines are: struggle between opposite social systems – socialism and capitalism; the proletariat's revolutionary attack on the bourgeoisie; the human masses' joint struggle against monopolistic amalgamations; peoples' national liberation wars against colonialists; battles between capitalist nations to strengthen the positions of monopoly capital. From these characteristics one may divide wars of our time into the following four categories: *wars between states with opposite social systems; civil wars; national liberation wars; wars between bourgeois states.*'

'The most bitter character belongs to wars between states with opposite social systems, *wars in defence of a socialist fatherland* against imperialist agression. *Such wars know no compromise and are conducted with a maximum utilization of all forces and means at the States' disposal.* Soviet military doctrine views such wars by socialist states as the most just of all wars history has known.'

' . . . The Communist Party and the Soviet State take full cognizance of the international situation which has emerged, the balance of forces on the world arena, the qualitative advances seen in the military field, and the capabilities of our probable enemies and the socialist brother nations. But at the same time our *doctrine rests on the superiority of the Soviet Armed Forces over the strongest capitalist armies, not only in a technical-military sense, but also, and this is especially important, in the sense of military preparedness and morale.*'

'To another category belong national liberation wars. . . . The uniting of different anti-imperialist forces often occurs on a national basis, and this often gives such wars a *nationalist* character. This must be taken into account. . . . Imperialist forces often interfere in genuine civil wars under cover of 'activity for peace', ostensibly to protect democratic liberties and with reference made to a request for help from the 'legitimate' government . . . (the existence of) the socialist camp, of course, limits and restrains the possibilities for imperialist intervention . . . but . . . *one cannot exclude the possibility that it can become necessary to provide the most determined opposition to interference into such countries from outside.* Therefore . . . the Soviet military doctrine reflects the thesis of active support to the proletariat's armed struggle in civil wars and readiness to cut off foreign interference with other nations' internal affairs.'

'In wars between bourgeois states, which are conducted to satisfy the interests of the exploiting classes, . . . various political compromises are permissible . . . enormous calamity for the people. . . . Leaders of the proletariat have always condemned the wars, while encouraging the people to unite in a revolutionary war . . . to turn a mutually destructive war of conquest into a civil war.'

' . . . Wars of our time may be world-wide or local. . . . A world war may cover a great part of our globe, including all continents and oceans, and space adjacent to the earth. Such a war will from the beginning have the character of a class war . . . (the parties) will set themselves determined political aims . . . the Soviet Union will (then) be forced to employ all its material and moral forces and possibilities so as to crush aggressors and once and for all smash capitalism as a system. In full accordance with this . . . *the Soviet military doctrine directs its main/prime attention towards the preparing of the nation and the Armed Forces for a world-wide thermonuclear war.*'

'On the basis of means for the conducting of conflicts, wars of our time may be divided into nuclear and non-nuclear . . . the Soviet Union's conduct is based on humane considerations. . . .'

'Within the State's activity to ensure the nation's defence capacity, its economic organizational policies play a major role. One cannot escape a mutual interlocking of tasks concerning the development of the USSR's defensive might. *An interlocking of considerations towards developing of the national economy and towards strengthening the nation's defence in peacetime make it possible to ensure that the Armed Forces correspond to today's demands.*'

'In wartime one achieves *interlocking of . . . internal domestic and external political functions through a near complete subordination of all to the achieving of the tasks of the nation's military defence.*'

'Soviet military doctrine determines the political principles for the military build-up. . . . Lenin formulated the political principles for the building up of an army of the new type. He placed the party's leading role in the forefront . . . certain population groups were (in the beginning) deprived of the right to serve in the army . . . the army's composition of several nationalities, due to the particular domestic circumstances of our State, serves as a clear expression of the *principle of internationalism* in the build up of the Soviet Military.'

'A most important principle . . . is the *single man leadership* . . . (it) ensures the necessary centralization of directions under conditions with very mobile and dynamic operations . . . the personnel is organized and disciplined.'

' . . . (the necessity) to keep a regular cadre army built on the basis of general conscription . . . (we must) at any/every moment be prepared to beat back an attack and inflict defeat on the enemy.'

'The principles of a harmonious development of the branches of the Armed Forces . . . do not entail that one keeps all forces and weapons-types on the same level, but that one seeks to have a rational ratio between them corresponding to . . . combat possibilities and tasks at any one time.'

' . . . the Party stresses . . . the increasing role of the personnel of the Army and the Fleet, and its morale. It correctly sees *the moral-political* and *psychological education of the troops as one of the decisive factors towards achieving victory in a modern war.* . . . A good result is based on humans equipped with modern material, who are fully conversant with such, who are ideologically steadfast and convinced that their cause . . . is just.'

'Important are . . . the principles of adherence to the demands of military science and the art of war, of combining of theory and practice in education, of taking account of technical developments in our nation and abroad, and of uniting a centralized leadership of the troops with initiative from the commanding cadres, and securing constant combat preparedness. . . . '

Comment seems unnecessary, except to note the stress on the troop morale factor, and to note the discrepancy between the generalities attached to the last three categories of war and the commitments attached to the first category – the only one which includes the USSR, by definition.

CONCLUSION

The Armed Forces are thus expressly stated to constitute one of the instruments at the disposition of a political leadership in the pursuit of its goals and aspirations. But the instrument should not be a dormant factor which is only to be activated in times of war. It has to be used actively in the battle for advantage also in the period of tension, of no peace – no war, in which the contemporary world lives.

And although the Armed Forces constitute only one of the policy-effecting instruments of the political leadership, the Armed Forces establishment is integrated into this political leadership to an extent which entails considerable influence on the choice of instruments. However, this does not necessarily constitute a stimulant to militarism or aggression in the usually understood sense. The degree of sophistication should not be under-estimated; furthermore: long-term military and Party aspirations appear to be similar and/or complementary. The 1960's has seen the achievement of two basic Soviet policy aims. The first was the development of 'flexible response' and interventionary-type forces of a scale and with a range to permit political (and, in a last resort, military) initiatives that would otherwise have been non-credible.[102] The other was the campaign to improve the civilian sector's capacity to support non-civilian policy initiatives, through the requisite programs of education and training – programs of psychological as well as practical nature, and, as mentioned, with domestic as well as military implications.

NOTES

1. *Program of the CPSU*, as adopted by the 22nd Congress, Foreign Languages Publishing House, Moscow, 1961.
2. Lenin, V. I., *Leninskii Sbornik*, XII, Moscow, 1931, p. 34.
3. *Krasnaya Zvezda* 11 May, 1962 (Col. Sidelnikov: 'Concerning Military Doctrine').
4. *Ibid.*
5. *Kommunist Vooruzhiennikh Sil*, No. 5, March, 1964, pp. 9–15 (Maj. Gen. Kozlov: 'Military Doctrine and Military Science').
6. *Ibid.*
7. Sokolovsky, V. D., Marshal, *Military Strategy* ('*Voennaya Strategia*'), revised English edition, Praeger, New York, 1963.
8. *Nedelia*, No. 6, 31 January–6 February, 1965 (Col. Gen Shtemenko).
9. Sokolovsky, *op. cit.*
10. *Krasnaya Zvezda*, 5 January, 1967 (Maj. Gen. Zemskov); see also *Krasnaya Zvezda*, 15 January, 1970, for yet another assertion of undiluted Party authority over military doctrine, and for a defining of strategic problem complexes as lying within the Party's domain.
11. Published by Voenizdat, Moscow, 1957.
12. For a contemporary analysis, see Jacobsen, C. G., in the *US Naval War College Review*, March, 1972, Annapolis, USA.
13. See e.g. such articles as Col. General Shtemenko's in *Nedelia* No. 6, 31 January–6 February, 1965: ' . . . The national economy will not have much time to re-organize during the course of military action . . . everything needed for work in wartime conditions must be prepared in advance.'
    And see A. A. Grechko, *Na Strazhe Mira . . .*, *op. cit.*, 1971, Chapter 2, Section 1.
14. Related speculation has concentrated on three rapidly expanding industries. One is shipping. *Strategisk Bulletin*, April 1969, Utrikespolitiska Institut, Stockholm, illustrated the Soviet merchant fleet's growth: about 3 million br. tons in 1950; 4·3 million in 1955; 5·5 million in 1960; 10·5 million in 1965; 12 million in 1968; 15 million (then projected) in 1970; and 20 million plus (projected) in 1980. The Norwegian Shipowners' Association's *Shipping Review* of 1971 put the Soviet Fleet at 15·5 million br. tons, or 6·3 per cent of world tonnage. See also Lloyd's Register, London. 80 per cent of the fleet is new; there is an emphasis on 'specialist ships'; its future growth is estimated at one million br. tons per year (see Merchant Marine Minister Bakayev in *Krasnaya Zvezda*, 13 March, 1966, and in February, 1969

APN – Novosti – Interview). Then there are the dynamically expanding oil and gas industries: see e.g. *Pravda* 19 October, 1967; *Planovoye Khosyaistvo*, No. 1, 1969, *Ekonomicheskaya Gazeta* No. 22, May, 1969; *Pravda* 16 February, 1970. Among other sources: *Kazakhstanskaya Pravda* 8 July, 1965; *Soviet News*, 28 January, 1969 (USSR Embassy, London); *Moscow Radio*, 16 September, 1969.
Dumping practices have occasionally been engaged in (see e.g. V. Carlson, in *US Naval Institute proceedings*, May, 1967, *and Foreign Report*, 11 March, 1969, London, with regard to oil; *The Times* of London, 21 January, 1969, with regard to shipping.

But it appeared that dumping was only engaged in so as to break Western monopolies and achieve a level of activity commensurate with Soviet needs, actual and projected (*Petroleum Press Service*, May, 1969 re oil; author's conversations with Norwegian Ship Owners' Association officials, May 1969, re. shipping).

15. Contrast the wording of e.g. *Pravda* 6 July, 1962 and *Pravda* 4 July, 1965.

16. See e.g. *Pravda* 19 November, 1969.

17. *Kommunist Vooruzhiennikh Sil*, Nos. 7 and 8, April, 1969; the articles by Cols. Rybkin and Bondarenko may be seen as early forerunners.

18. *Kommunist Vooruzhiennikh Sil*, – see especially No. 17, September, 1966, No. 24, December, 1968, and Nos. 7 and 8, April, 1969. NOTE: Bondarenko's old thesis was titled ('Sovremennaya nauchno-tekhicheskaya revoliutsia i dialektika rasvitia boevovo oruzhia') 'The contemporary scientific-technical revolution and the dialectics of arms developments'; this partly explains his preoccupation.

19. *Ibid.*

20. See e.g. V. Shestov's long analysis in *Pravda*, 3 February, 1971. NOTE: V. Shestov is suspected of being a pseudonom for V. S. Semionov, Head of the Soviet delegation to SALT.

21. Kolkowicz, R., *The Soviet Military and the Communist Party*, Princeton University Press, 1967, pp. 224–55, 279 and 281.

22. See e.g. Kazakov, M. I., *Nad Kartoi Bylykh Srazhenii*, 2nd ed., Voenizdat, Moscow, 1971.

23. *Pravda*, 23 February, 1965.

24. *Pravda*, 24 July, 1965.

25. *Izvestia*, 16 November, 1965.

26. See *Deputati Verkhovnovo Soveta SSSR, Sedmoi Sosiv*, Moscow, 1966, and *Deputati Verkhovnovo Soveta SSSR, Vosmoi Sosiv*, Moscow, 1970.

27. *XXIII s'ezd Kommunisticheskoi Parti Sovetskovo Soiuza 29 Marta-8 Aprelia 1966 Goda: Stenograficheskii Otchiot*, Vol. 1, pp. 283, Moscow, 1966.

28. Rigby, T. H., *'Communist Party Membership in the USSR 1917–1967'*, Princeton University Press, 1968. For a good historical resume of evolving Party membership patterns in the Armed Forces, see chapters 7 and 10.

29. *Pravda* 10 April, 1971.

30. Together they may perhaps count as one 'military' member; both are primarily civilian managers of defence industries and policy.

31. The fact that Col. General Ogarkov, the Soviet military representative at SALT, was raised to full Membership while V. S. Semionov, the senior Soviet representative at SALT, remained a Candidate, does not reflect so much on SALT relationships as on Ogarkov's position as 1st Deputy Chief of the General Staff; his predecessor here had been elected a Member by the 23rd Congress.

32. Counting cosmonaut Nikolayeva-Tereshkova (new member) as among the 'military'; the four 1966 members not re-elected were Beloborodov, Vershinen, and the deceased Malinovsky and Voroshilov.

33. *Voennaya Mysl*, editorial, March, 1956.

34. Lagovsky, *Strategia i Ekonomika*, Voenizdat, Moscow, 1957, *op. cit.*

35. Emelin, *Sovremennaya Voennaya Tekhnika*, p. 131, Voenizdat, Moscow, 1956 (referring to the inferiority-induced necessity at the time to strike first if the limited capabilities available were to be effectively utilized.)

36. Grechko, *Voenno-lstorichesky Zhurnal*; No. 6, 1966.

37. E.g. Zemskov, in *Krasnaya Zvezda*, 5 January, 1967, *op. cit.*

38. *Kommunist Vooruzhiennikh Sil*, No. 7, April, 1966.

39. *Krasnaya Zvezda*, 30–31 March, 1967 (Lt. Gen. Zav'yalov).

40. Zemskov, *op. cit.*

41. For much of the below I am indebted to the impressive detective-work and

translating of Harriet Fast Scott; see her 1971 SRI Paper on '*Soviet Military Doctrine, Its Formulation and Dissemination*', pp. 60–4.
42. Sokolovsky, V. D., *Military Strategy (Voennaya Strategia)*, 3rd ed., p. 417, Voenizdat, Moscow, 1968.
43. *Ibid.*
44. *Fifty years of the Armed Forces of the USSR*, p. 199, Voenizdat, Moscow, 1968.
45. *Ibid.*, p. 256.
46. *Ibid.*, p. 478.
47. Lagovsky, S. S., *Army of the Soviets*, p. 403, Politizdat, Moscow, 1969.
48. Zheltov, A. S., *V. I. Lenin and the Soviet Armed Forces*, p. 148, Voenizdat, Moscow, 1967.
49. Petrov, Yu. P., *The Structure of Political Organs of the Party and Komsomol Organs of the Army and Navy,* p. 391, Voenizdat, Moscow, 1968.
50. Kozlov, S. N., *Officers' Handbook (Spravochnik Ofitsera)*, p. 127, Voenizdat, Moscow, 1971.
51. *Radio Moscow*, 23 September, 1971; *Munchener Merkur* 26 July, 1971; See also Radio Free Europe *Research Bulletin* No. 1136, 23 September, 1971, and Radio Liberty *Dispatch*, 23 September, 1971.
52. The designation is inferred from (a) his long association with and supervision of defence industries, combined with (b) his Secretariat status. It is supported by his protocol ranking above the Minister of Defence (See e.g. *Krasnaya Zvezda*, 9 July, 1969).
53. Petrov, Yu. P., *op. cit.*, p. 444.
54. *Ibid.*
55. See e.g. Erickson, J., *Soviet Military Power*, RUSI, Whitehall, London, 1971, pp. 26–7 for interesting comment (though relating to the situation during the late 1960's, and now outdated . . . in view of later evidence, as presented above).
56. From his *Report to the Central Committee*, The 24th CPSU Congress, 1917, p. 77 of the Novosti edition, Moscow, 1971.
57. It appears conceptually advantageous to present a chart of the last years' military budgets, and the percentages these have formed of the total Soviet budgets:

Year	Defence Budget In Billion Roubles	Defence Budget as Per cent of Total Budget
1958	9·4	14·6
1959	9·4	13·3
1960	9·3	12·7
1961	11·6	15·2
1962	12·6	13·9
1963	13·9	15·9
1964	13·3	14.4
1965	12·8	12·6
1966	13·4	12·7
1967	14·5	13·2
1968	16·7	13·5
1969	17·7	13·2
1970	17·9	12·4
1971	17·9	11·1

Sources: Basic list taken from the *New York Times*, 11 December, 1968; the last figures taken from Finance Minister Garbuzov's '*O gosudarstvennom biodzhete SSSR na 1971 god i ob ispolneni gosudarstvennovo biodzheta SSSR za 1969 god*' Politizdat, Moscow, 1970.
58. Information received by author in Moscow, May, 1969.
59. Information received by author in Moscow, May, 1969.
60. *Keesing's Contemporary Archives 1969–70*, pp. 233–7.
61. US Secretary of Defence, Laird, National televised interview, Washington, D.C., 9 February, 1969.
62. In the *American Economic Review*, May 1968, pp. 398–416.
63. For comparison's sake: Research and development funds spent by private US firms competing unsuccessfully for government defence contracts might be

judged to constitute 'hidden' defence expenditures; but the basic research and development commitments of the chosen firm(s) are covered by the terms of the contract(s).

64. 'Science Policy in the USSR', *Scientific American*, June, 1969, pp. 19–29. This is also borne out by Dr. John S. Foster's 17 February, 1972 Congressional testimony (quoted in the *New York Times* of 18 February, 1972): he asserted that the level of Soviet research and technological sophistication was comparable to that of the US, and that it did in certain fields surpass that of the US.

65. *'Soviet Growth, Resource Allocation and Military outlays'*, St. to the Sub-Committee on Economy in Government of the Joint Economic Committee of the US Congress, June, 1969.

66. *US News and World Report* 13 April, 1970, p. 34 presented an extract from a list of US weapon systems being developed, prepared for the Senate Armed Services Committee by the State Department. The figures concerned 22 weapon programs: Total original estimates – \$39,750 million; total current estimates – \$54,873 million. *Note* also the 1969 Pentagon report, which concluded, following an analysis of previous weapon developments, that achieved operational efficiency was consistently far inferior to theoretical or planned-for efficiency.

67. As yet unpublished 1969–70 research by Professor Ariki at the Institute of Soviet Studies, Glasgow, demonstrates the adverse effects on the economic growth rate of military bugetary allocations.

68. *'World Military Expenditures, 1966–67'*, The Economics Bureau of the US Arms Control and Disarmament Agency, 1969. A synopsis is available by A. Alexander, 'The Cost of World Armaments', *Scientific American*, October, 1969, pp. 21–7. The analysis, in practice, accepts relative US-USSR PPE estimates akin to those by Benoit presented above.

69. *'Yearbook of World Armaments and Disarmament Problems'*, Stockholm International Peace Institute, Stockholm, 1969.

70. *Pravda*, 19 November, 1969.

71. Bingham, J. B., 'Can Military Spending be Controlled?' *Foreign Affairs*, October, 1969, pp. 51–66.

72. See Chapter 4.

73. *Pravda*, 15 February, 1964; Sokolovsky, *Military Strategy*, *op. cit.*, 2nd ed., p. 410.

74. Vorontsov, of the USSR Embassy in Washington was the Diplomat; the comments were made to a colleague.

75. Brezhnev's *Report to the Central Committee*, Moscow, 1971, *op. cit.* See also *Pravda*, 7 November, 1970.

76. Marshal Chuikov, Cmdr. of CD, in *Pravda Ukrainii*, 28 October, 1966.

77. *Krasnaya Zvezda*, 22 November, 1966.

78. *Ibid.*

79. *Pravda Ukrainii*, 28 October, 1966, *op. cit.*

80. *Ibid.* And see e.g. Pavly and Isivelev. 'The evacuation of Urban populations', in *'Sposob Zashchitii ot Yadernovo Oruzhia'*, Moscow, 1965. See also Text below. – Or see e.g. *Kommunist Tadzhikstana*, October, 27 1971; it provides detailed evacuation plans for that region.

81. A. Kharkevich, 'Shelters', in *Voennie Znanie*, No. 11, 1968, p. 20.

82. Marshal Chuikov, *'Grazhdanskaya Oborona v Raketnoyadernoi Voine'*, p. 16, Atomizdat, Moscow, 1968.

83. A. Kharkevich, *op. cit.*

84. *Ibid.* To the extent possible, and presumably for reasons both of convenience and cost, population shelter designs are incorporated into peacetime civilian activities and needs; this author 'inspected' the Arbat Metro station's protective door (to shut passage way and isolate shelter) in 1969, and others since.

85. A. Kharpichev, *Voennie Znanie*, No. 8, 1967, p. 20.

86. Leon Goure (of the Rand Corp.) in *'NATO's Fifteen Nations'*, June–July, 1969, p. 31. See also his outdated but still relevant and interesting *'Civil Defence in the Soviet Union'*, University of California Press, Berkeley, 1962.

87. Yefimov, in *Izvestia*, 16 November, 1965.

88. *Komsomolskaya Pravda*, 15 June, 1965.

89. *Izvestia*, 16 November, 1965, *op. cit.*

90. *Pravda*, 27 June, 1965.

91. *Izvestia*, 13 September, 1969, art. by I. Potapov and V. Sysoyev on 'A Matter of State – The Law on Universal Military Obligation is in effect' (The Decree in question: 'New USSR Law on Universal Military Service on the training of young men of pre-conscription age').

92. *Pravda*, 8 March, 1970.

93. A. Yvanov, I. Naumenko, M. Pavlov, '*Raketnoyadernoe Oruzhie i evo Porozhaioshchee Deistvie*', Voenizdat-Nauchno-Populyarnaya Biblioteka, Moscow, 1971. For shorter articles specifically re. related shelter developments, see e.g. I. Kraznov in *Voennoie Znanie* No. 1, 1967, or Lt. Gen. Shuvyrin in same, No. 10, 1968.

94. This author spent the academic year 1970–71 in Moscow, on the British academic exchange program.

95. *Ibid*; primarily first-aid oriented as far as the girls were concerned.

96. Information received by author in Moscow, August 1969; The three degrees of readiness are also referred to e.g. in '*The Military Balance 1969–70*', ISS, London.

97. USN Capt. G. Grkovic (Naval Attache to Moscow 1965–68) in 'Soviet Universal Military Service', *US Nav. Inst. Proceedings*, April 1, 1969, pp. 55–63, provides supplementary evidence before arriving at a complementary conclusion re. high morale and service pride among Soviet Armed Forces personnel.

98. Khrushchev, *Pravda*, 15 January, 1960; Malinovsky, Bditelnoe . . . , *op. cit.*

99. *Pravda*, 28 May, 1970.

100. Colonel Larionov, *Kommunist Vooruzhiennikh Sil*, No. 22, November, 1968. The quotes are as translated by this author, who is also responsible for the emphases occasionally added.

101. *Materials from the CPSU's 23rd Congress*, p. 233.

102. This process, which may be said to have been begun in 1961 under Khrushchev, was largely completed by the end of the 1960's. See Chapters 1, 2, 3, 4 and 5.

9

Super-Power Implications

SUPER-POWER STATUS: REFLECTIONS

Henry Kissinger is the best known exponent of the 'military bipolarity, but diplomatic multipolarity' concept, as that best describing the situation of the later 1960's. He considered this to have evolved once the mutual destruction capability of the super-powers became assured. With mutual destruction capability assured, one could no longer envisage a raison d'être for either to initiate a nuclear exchange; he concluded that the very strength of the super-powers' nuclear arsenals in fact provided greater security for lesser powers. It gave them greater freedom to pursue independent national interests.[1]

His conclusion may be correct. But its validity is contingent on a very different logic: his argument appears to be at fault. Assured mutual destruction and second-strike capability did evolve. But this does not in itself preclude the use of nuclear weapons in some capacity in local military conflicts, interventions or initiatives. It could to the contrary merely ensure that local conflicts, whether nuclear or not, would not escalate to the stage of involving either super-power's 'home area'. Military bipolarity might in fact not militate against either's involvement in local conflict-areas (through fear of escalation and destruction), but rather encourage involvement, since its inherent corrollary would inhibit the other from escalating beyond the local confines.

It might be expressed somewhat differently: excepting the real possibility of significant changes, through the development of unknown or new weapon systems, present developments leave little room between 'breakthrough' level and 'elimination' level. What is referred to, of course, is the anomaly whereby the super-powers have not only reached some kind of equilibrium in their technological and weapon systems development, but have achieved or can achieve invulnerability to all but major assaults by the other.[2] Two conclusions follow: (a) There no longer exists a plausible basis for expecting either super-power to intervene against the other's national area or sphere, no matter the cause or circumstance (always remembering the above reservation); and (b) vital inhibitions on potential inclinations to engage in fringe interventions may thereby be removed. This could lead to an escalating scramble to secure the adherence of non-committed states to either's sphere, a scramble which could see 'preventive interventions' – based on the logical conviction that the other will not interfere against the presence of one's own forces.

Herein lies a basic potential for instability, as well as for super-power confrontations. The crucial point which follows from (a) is that such confrontations would be local, or at least remain in areas outside the two's immediate spheres, whether the confrontations are nuclear or not. *The limitations are restricted to locale, not to the scale of the conflict.*

As regards the possible removal of inhibitions affecting interventionary designs, this may have consequences not immediately obvious. Concerning West Europe some strategists concluded by the late 1960's that any expectation of US retaliation against Soviet agression had become utopian, and/or irrational, with the advent of an assured Soviet capacity to strike against the US homeland.[3] They proceeded from this conclusion to urge acceptance of the thesis that the installation of a US BMD did not reflect or entail US isolationism. By providing some credible defence capability, it to the contrary reintroduced the otherwise defunct possibility that the US might intervene in defence of West Europe.[4]

The argument is correct, but insufficient. The credibility of US assured destruction capabilities did together with the credibility of her activating and utilizing this, act as a deterrent to any Soviet designs that might be envisaged. But the emerging credibility of the Soviet countering capabilities, acted as an equally powerful deterrent against US reactions (or actions). If our suggestion, that the development of mutual capabilities had reached the stage wherein any direct action by either against the other's home area was inconceivable, then a very different alternate conclusion emerges.

This would see the elimination of the deterrence on both action and reaction, by either super-power, as regards non-direct confrontations. The possibility or likelihood of local conflicts, even on the European continent, would be increased at least as long as mutually acceptable agreements were not arrived at (e.g., through a European Security Conference of some type).

There remained the possibility that a cycle of super-power interventions leading to localized super-power confrontations might nevertheless lead further, to mutual declarations of war. But our analysis of nuclear stalemate, resting on secure second-strike capacities, leads one to query the effects of any such declarations. They would most likely reflect psychological considerations; they would not reflect immediate intent. Mutual all-out hostilities would remain implausible, or illogical. The result would probably be a shadow war of some years, with both super-powers concentrating on all-out civil defence constructions, plus energetic BMD research and deployment efforts, – in the hope of achieving survival capability.[5] The most likely conclusion would be a truce based on the results of the localized fighting, without any all-out exchange ever being initiated (-in lieu, of course, of potentially decisive new weapon systems developments, or plain irrationality).

In this context it is relevant to challenge also the commonplace belief that the distinction between conventional and nuclear conflicts is of necessity clear-cut. One might (as has, e.g., Professor Erickson)[6] imagine a hypothetical status quo testing Soviet attack into West Germany, an attack utilizing nuclear weapons only at high altitudes, for defence-disruptive purposes, and which is halted at the Rhine. In response to this scenario West Germany would probably herself veto allied use of nuclear weaponry to dislodge the intruder. But, of greater consequences: since no actual ground or human destruction explosion had been effected, – could one really consider the 'nuclear threshhold' to have been crossed?

Whether because of logical or practical reasons, the old nuclear-conventional distinction had clearly become obsolete by the late 1960's. The distinction held potential value only as long as one feared escalatory war, leading inevitably to all-out exchanges. The inhibition associated with passing the threshold was diluted, and possibly eliminated, when it became unrealistic to expect that local nuclear exchanges would entail the ultimate involvement of the super-powers' 'home areas'.

This analysis received indirect support from the new NATO policy of December, 1969, which permitted the initiating use of tactical nuclear arms against Warsaw Pact aggression in Europe.[7] But (on US insistence) such a utilization of nuclear arms was authorized only against possible East European (forward) bases, and *not* against USSR (rear) bases . . . ![8] The policy decision was supported by deployment decisions, whereby only missiles incapable of reaching the Soviet heartland were stationed in West Europe.[9]

Further indirect support of the above analysis may be seen in Soviet practice. The integrating of nuclear capabilities in all branches of the Soviet armed forces implies (a) that she no longer conceives of non-nuclear wars of consequence; and (b) that she conceives of the possibility of total war, but not as resulting from escalation caused by the use of tactical nuclear weapons. (In view of Soviet capabilities and concepts, non-nuclear scenarios such as related for example to the Czechoslovak intervention of 1968, are as previously indicated best viewed as 'police operations').

But attention must be reverted, to the new balance, and to the above-treated lessening of associated inhibitions. The emerging situation was also one of increased potentials for the political utilization of strategic strength. For example: what would or could Sweden answer if the USSR approached her, stating that present technological and reaction time considerations demanded Soviet ABM (atomic war-head) interception of US ICBMs over Swedish territory? The USSR might declare that this was in order to secure the safety of Soviet territories, the priority consideration of Soviet defence calculations. – 'We presume the consequent but unavoidable fall-out to be undesirable for Sweden. But in order to make earlier interceptions possible we need radar facilities and installations on Swedish territory. May we . . . ?'

A Swedish analysis similar to ours might logically see the danger as tolerable, since any such nuclear exchange would be considered to be highly unlikely. Yet one must always allow for uncertainty factors, so . . . ? And there remained, of course, the corollary that if the analysis was correct, and if Soviet 'aggressive' designs were a fact, then refusal might precipitate the physical advances which were made more conceivable by the analysis. . . . On the other hand, there was the further corollary that the US would also be less inhibited. . . .

Another sequence possible as a 1970's scenario involves hypothetical Soviet action against Northern Norway. This would be unlikely to be motivated purely by a desire to test or alter the status quo; and the decreasing need for bases (associated with the Soviet fleet's conversion to nuclear propulsion) lessens the importance of the fjords in the area. The area's strategically dangerous proximity to the 'core area' of the Kola peninsula, could, however, tempt intervention, if the USSR feared a hostile utilization of its capabilities (e.g. close radar supervision and detection which affected missile interception or exchange potentials – see Chapter 6). The strategic balance could be interpreted to imply considerable impunity as regards action, and considerable leverage as regards political pressures based on credible action alternatives or needs.

It is relevant to pose a reminder. While local conflicts with super-power engagement can now occur without Armageddon implications, the range of political, military and economic factors involved in any decision to intervene remains substantial – even if the prime immediate deterrent will be political, and the prime long-term deterrent the attrition costs of unfriendly occupation. The deterrence value of non-super power armies has become of secondary value to both perspectives.

The lesser powers' military capacity to deter has rightly met with scepticism. Two developments concerning the defensive options of lesser powers are of interest:

In Norway tanks and other heavy equipment have been assigned to the limited conscription forces available (– forces entrusted with the task of hindering the establishment of hostile forces in Northern Norway, until the expected NATO aid). This orientation of military procurement is being questioned by some Norwegian experts. They consider heavy conventional army units to be vulnerable, and believe that the distance between their bases in any case makes immediate action against certain enemy initiatives difficult. They fear, for example, that a naval landing might enjoy the benefit of surprise, if a peace-time pattern of naval manoeuvres off the coast had evolved during the preceding period. A beach-head, as well as more far-reaching objectives (e.g., an airfield), may well be secured by an enemy before native forces had time to engage

Within such a scenario immediate if small-scale engagement prior to an enemy's establishment could cause relatively far greater damage than consequent counter-attacks by conventional units. This 'school of thought' therefore seeks an expansion of the existing home guard, with armed depots scattered sufficiently to always ensure immediate access. The resultant posture is expected to represent a more viable deterrent. The Swiss pattern, of peace-time weapon distributions to citizens, causes interest.

In France early 1969 saw the emergence of a related debate, through numerous articles published in *Le Monde*. Among the more notable was an article by J. Georges-Picot, 'Apres l'universite, L'Armee'.[10] He defined the present 'trilogie' of forces dissuading enemy action as (a) the nuclear force; (b) the regular army; and (c) the operational territorial defence (now practically non-existent).

He suggested that the regular army be disbanded, as he considered that it was no longer capable of serving any function commensurate with its cost. He thought that the nuclear force (concentrated e.g., in Polaris-type vessels) should be kept, since it expanded the concept of deterrence to encompass also retaliatory capability (however dubious the extent of this might appear).

The article then referred to the wars of France (1942–44), Indo-China, Vietnam and Biafra. These were seen to have demonstrated the relative efficacy of a 'territorial defence equivalent'. The third factor of the 'trilogie' should, therefore, be that relied on. The present barrack system, with its inherent time-wasting, was declared to be conducive only to instilling distaste – especially when its futility was recognized. The aim of reform must be to involve everybody, not least the intellectual and moral elite. Decentralization of authority, even down to communes, and the incorporation of natural student leaders into responsible positions, were seen as necessary complements to a training which must be truly universal, and short-term but frequently repeated ('refreshed'). The 'regular army' would then be composed of only the needed number of instructors and the like. (Similar features were incorporated into the 1969 Yugoslav national defence law; it emphasized decentralized small-unit independent capabilities, and 'total mobilization'[11]).

Yugoslav and Norwegian experience during the Second World War, the Asian wars of the 1950's and '60's, and even the Palestinian 'resistance' following the Arab defeat by Israel in 1967, supports the thesis that a 'people's war' (guerilla movement), which enjoys popular support, has greater durability, and attrition possibilities, than more traditional forces. This certainly appears true when these forces are restricted to the levels within reach of lesser or medium powers.

A related line of thought indicates that such a policy might not only prove a better deterrent. It might conversely be that best used against the super-powers themselves, – through encouragement or aid to their dissident ethnic or other minorities. The 1965 Watts Negro riots in Los Angeles, the spectacle of the 1968 Chicago Democratic convention, and similar events, may be seen as evidence of US vulnerability. The most vocal Soviet supporters of the Czechoslovak invasion were party leaders from the areas most exposed to the reception of ideas from Czechoslovakia (the Ukraine and especially Zakarpatskaja oblast).[12] This could be taken to indicate Soviet unease about potential Soviet vulnerability.

The suggestion inherent in the above, is, of course, that as the super-powers have increased their military capabilities to the extent of securing near military immunity, this has not affected their vulnerability vis-à-vis internal unrest. This vulnerability has furthermore been exacerbated through the greater dissemination of people's war and guerilla type theories, which occurred during the '50's and the '60's as a result of Chinese and Vietnamese experiences.

In 1954 the Vietnamese victory at Dien Bien Phu destroyed only a small section of the French army, which remained militarily superior, but it crystalized a moral defeat and weariness which brought about the French withdrawal from South-east Asia. Equally instructive (although questionable) is Professor Galtung's theory of the chances of success if the Czechoslovak reaction to the 1968 intervention had been 'friendly disapproval'.[13] Galtung noted the historic incidents of Red Army soldiers refusing to fire on fraternal workers in East Germany in 1953 and in Hungary in 1956. He suggested that while despairing of the efficacy of armed opposition, the Czechoslovaks ought not, as they did, have chosen a mixture of moral condemnation and passive obstruction (e.g., refusal to provide food and lodgings). They ought instead to have 'invited them in'. Instead of severed contact, this would have resulted in far more extensive Red Army personnel awareness of the issues. This awareness would then have had a better chance of seeping eastward, where the decisive changes would have to come from. (One must comment that the far-sighted discipline implicitly demanded of the Czechs may not be within human reach. . . .)

Both the actual events, and the hypothetical event, indicate the potential strength of otherwise inferior population groups – when united. The necessary degree of unity would in most cases remain ephemeral. But while a universal knowledge of guerilla techniques is of no consequence when there is no unity or will, small conventional armies are of no consequence even when there is unity and will.

H

DOMESTIC CONSIDERATIONS

The previous section indicated that the following situation had emerged by the late 1960's: (1) the Soviet Union had increased its strategic capabilities so as to achieve a guaranteed second-strike capacity; this breaking of the earlier US monopoly of such capacity produced a logically secure guarantee that neither nation would escalate any local conflict to the point where it might affect the other's 'home area'; (2) Soviet non-strategic capabilities were furthermore such as to overwhelm those of any but its fellow super-power. The Soviet Union had achieved full security vis-à-vis any exterior military threat. The question that emerges from an acceptance of this correlation, is whether her security can be challenged by internal threats.

This section will therefore investigate the possible existence, nature and viability of internal threats to societal stability in the USSR. Two venues will be pursued; first, instability within the leadership or establishment,[14] and thereafter instability external to it. Information with regard to both became more accessible after the ousting of Khrushchev, and especially following the Czechoslovak intervention of 1968. These years will therefore be those concentrated on.

The years saw a multitude of rumours of shifting Politburo personnel alliances and conflicts. There were rumours of policy disagreements, of coup attempts, and of purges. The unexplained absence of any Politburo member would immediately fuel speculation; the fact that the absence most often proved to have been caused by genuine illness, or something equally mundane, never affected the reaction to subsequent absences. A new spate of rumours was always ready to step into the breach.[15]

Much of the speculation focused on Shelepin. He was young, and he imparted an image of dynamism, intelligence and competence. He emerged from the departure of Khrushchev with Politburo, Secretariat and Council of Ministers membership, as well as with the chairmanship of the Party-State Control Commission. He was touted as the main challenger to Brezhnev, and the rumours that he had attempted to replace Brezhnev as 1st Secretary in October of 1965 did not appear ludicrous. They gained credence from the subsequent demotion of officials thought to have been associated with Shelepin.[16] And they were further encouraged when Shelepin gave up his Secretariat and Council of Ministers posts, and when his Control Commission was abolished.

Although Shelepin later added the chairmanship of the National Trades Union Congress to his Politburo membership (in July, 1967), the sequence of events was by most observers taken to reflect a relative demotion. But the following years saw the re-appearance and re-emergence of most of the demoted officials.[17] And the Trades Union Congress' hitherto innocuous newspaper, Trud, soon emerged as a paper of major import and influence; it began to carry policy-affecting articles of the type which previously appeared only in Pravda and Izvestia.[18] By 1970 Shelepin was again singled out by rumours as the instigator of a coup attempt.[19]

Another focus for speculation was provided by Suslov. He was reported to have been offered the 1st Secretaryship after the ousting of Khrushchev, but to have declined due to ill health; the subsequent nomination of Brezhnev was seen as the logical post-script. Suslov's long tenure as trouble-shooter and 'eminence grise', and as the political apex of the Party's ideological cadres (spearheaded today by Ponomariov), encouraged the acceptance of the report. The report also gained credibility from the fact that Suslov enjoyed a unique respect (and, maybe surprisingly, affection) among large sections of the populace, both Party and non-Party.[20] When he recovered from his illness sufficiently to reassume his ideological responsibility, most observers concluded that he had also assumed or reassumed a position of considerable background influence.

Interest in Suslov was further stimulated by his apparent conversion from a 'dogmatist' propounder of the Party line to a 'moderate' supporter of greater flexibility and imagination. The image of doctrinaire rigidity probably always represented an oversimplification. But it served to encourage a reaction of surprise to 1968 reports of Suslov's 'moderate' position on Czechoslovakia.[21]

The 'new' Suslov was equally distinct the following year. In defiance of the then current trend towards a partial rehabilitation of Stalin, and towards a whitewashing of the deprivations endured under Stalin,[22] he castigated the 'consequences of the cult of Stalin'.[23] At the Moscow Comecon meeting of 24 March, 1969, he pointedly ignored Ulbricht's emphatic and traditional definition of Social Democracy as the 'main' historical enemy of the Communist movement. In a 'Kommunist' article he proceeded to acknowledge that it was no longer proper to speak of 'a leading centre of the communist move-ment'.[24] Some of Suslov's assertions and actions, or non-actions, could be said to reflect peculiarities of the contemporary international situation (the new Soviet detente approach to the FRG,[25] and the on-going efforts to convene a world Communist Parties summit in Moscow). But they appear stronger than dictated by tactical necessities. The composite picture strongly suggested that Suslov's influence was now being asserted in favour of greater flexibility. It is not without interest that rumours associated him with Shelepin in the purported coup design of 1970.[26]

Other Politburo members were also implicated by rumours and speculation. In the early post-Khrushchev days Podgorny was thought to be over-eager to placate consumer demands before military needs were satisfied.[27] He incurred a rebuke from Suslov,[28] and there followed what Michael Tatu saw as a purge of Podgorny supporters.[29] In 1967 there were rumours that Poliyansky was uneasy about the tardy implementation of the agricultural investment programs.[30] And, finally, one might point to Mazurov's involvement, with Poliyansky, in the oppositional rumours of 1970 (see footnote 26).

But the apparent evolution of the Politburo towards a split between 'moderates' and 'dogmatists' is misleading. Podgorny is in later years reputed to have allied himself with the hard-liners on a number of issues. The unadventurous Brezhnev, on the other hand, appeared to spearhead early '70's moderate opinion on rapprochement with the FRG, and on the question of arms agreements.[31]

The moderate-dogmatist labels were misleading because they had limited relevance, and were usually issue-oriented. The Trades Union Congress' (Shelepin's) *Trud* exhibited this in its editorial policy: it was clearly 'moderate' in its coverage of West Germany;[32] it was among the most 'dogmatist' in its coverage of China.[33] Another good example is provided by the evolution of Suslov's pronouncements. His early hard-line attitude, and his rebuke of Podgorny, should be related to his obvious dissatisfaction with Soviet military capabilities. His conversion to a 'moderate' stance may then be related to his growing satisfaction during the late '60's that military needs had been and were being met.[34] The moderate label is best replaced by characterizations like sophisticated or flexible, while dogmatist might be replaced by unimaginative or over-cautious.

There were clearly differences within the Politburo. This is no surprise, if only because some of its members must, surely, have supported Krushchev. The evidence presented above allows of little doubt that a number of issues during the '60's occasioned sharp disagreement, at least on the question of relative priorities and policy implementations. The issues of 'Political Diary' (this previously unknown journal will be returned to below) which reached the West in the early 1970's provided conclusive evidence of disagreements also over some questions of policy.[35] And if one believes in the adage that there is seldom smoke without fire, then the tenacious rumours of coup designs and minor purges take on added importance.

But the crucial point is that unsuccessful challengers within the Politburo were never successfully removed, and the victors never managed to utilize the situation to establish their own hegemony. The relative oscillations affected minor officials; the principals remained to fight another day. While allegiances and policies might shift they never did so to an extent which permitted the definite ascendancy of any one power group or concentration.

This could partly be explained by the fact that the basic 'Weltanschaungs' and policy conceptions were similar or complementary. It could partly be explained as reflecting Politburo acceptance of the principles of Lenin's theory of democratic centralism: democracy during the policy-debating stages, but centralism and unity following the policy-making decision and the evolution of a definite majority view. But it may be best explained by the related concept of collective leadership. The experience of the previous decades had led to a strong aversion to the abberation of one-man leadership and personality cults, and to the scope for personal quirks and general insecurity which these entailed.

This was evidenced by pointed press references to the dangers of one-man rule and managements. One-man and committee decisions arrived at without prior consultations with relevant organs and assemblies were derided;[36] there was trouble in store whenever a leader 'starts to become dizzy with success, if he abuses his official position, if he gets puffed up and thinks he is infallible, if he stops consulting people and fails to show them concern and consideration.'[37]

Brezhnev's position is illustrative. His tenure as Party 1st Secretary, and later as General Secretary (the 23rd Congress decided to revert to the pre-Khrushchev designation), obviously tended to make him 'first among equals'. There were often rumours that he was trying to manoeuvre towards true ascendency (late 1971 provided a spate of these rumours). But the qualification of 'among equals' remained.

This is illustrated and emphasized by the obvious acceptability of an unusual display observed in the Black Sea tourist resort of Sukhumi in 1971.[38] The popular base for boat and aquatic equipment rentals boasted a prominent pictorial display of four historical personages. They were Marx, Engels, Lenin, and Kosygin(!).

'Political Diary', the limited edition and unofficial inner-Party journal which first became known in the West in 1971, documents that the range of Party opinions on any one issue is very considerable indeed (attitudes to the Middle East provide one example[39]). This is not surprising, but the freedom to express it – even if only in a restricted forum – is surprising. The relatively increased tolerance which this mirrors is also reflected in the national press. Journals like Ekonomicheskaya Gazeta and Krasnaya Zvezda displayed a considerable latitude during the '60's in their discussions of policy implementations, policy implications, and even policy alternatives. With a few others, like Trud, they appeared to acquire greater freedom to print policy-affecting articles and editorials.

The freedom was of course limited. Censorship remained. The journals mirrored the Party line. Pronouncements which affected basic policy directions reflected Party decisions, and not the other way around. The latitude and tolerance which their development during the '60's displayed is perhaps best described as reflecting the inner-Party devolution of authority entailed in nearly a decade of collective leadership.

There was increased scope for flexibility, but it remained generally restricted to questions of administrative and implementative concerns, and to questions which were not vital to the basic policies of concensus. The situation is also reflected in the Party's ambivalent attitude to the intelligentsia opposition. There can be little doubt that some traditionalists desire a clamp-down on the illegal press, Samizdat, and on, for example, Solzhenytsin. And there can be even less doubt that such could be effected. The survival of Samizdat, and Solzhenytsin's relative security, can only be explained by support from within the Party. One might hypothesize that his support is motivated by a desire to retain a safety valve which can dilute oppositional bitterness, or it might be motivated by a more positive appreciation of outside influences. . . . The fact that some protection can be provided reflects on the determination to short-circuit any possibility of return to one-man rule. . . .

Samizdat and like phenomena are treated further below, in the discussion of domestic pressures external to the establishment. Before turning to this aspect, it is necessary to present a judgement of the evidence relating to stability within the leadership. The trend appeared to entail a considerable measure of stability. Uncertainty surrounded the still unresolved problem of leadership succession procedures. But the problem no longer appeared as acute as in earlier decades. Pressures towards stability and cohesion appeared stronger than the pressures towards disarray.

With regard to pressures external to the establishment, these may be perceived primarily through the mirror of establishment reactions. Evidence of the stern official attitudes prevalent at least in some authoritative quarters during 1968–70 are to be found in quotes like the following:

There were numerous fears expressed concerning apathy and lack of consciousness. In December 1968 Sovetskaya Rossiya attacked a youth's claim that his generation was developing 'immunity against ideological demagogy'.[40] This was pursued by complaints against 'apolitical attitudes' and 'non-class interpretations of such concepts as democracy, personal freedom and humanism'.[41]

There evidently existed a widespread view according to which ideology was seen merely as another 'emotion'.[42] To some extent this was acknowledged as a result of a generation-gap which appeared to have developed also in the Soviet Union.[43] But it was furthermore seen as reflecting a more general malaise, of attitudes such as adopted, for example, by Academician Sakharov; he denied any positive value to any ideology, and took refuge in traditional liberal humanism.[44]

The malaise was clearly considered to reflect dangerous hostile subversive influences and bourgeois propaganda, some of which emanated from or through East European sources.[45] This was seen as all the more odious for accompanying nationalist and separatist propaganda.[46]

There therefore ensued strong demands for 'vigilance' over writers, artists, the communication media, and what was termed 'purveyors of alien views' in Soviet life.[47] Pravda attacked 'certain authors of scientific and literary works' who 'sometimes depart from class criteria', and castigated 'certain workers in publishing houses, press organs and television' for 'insufficient steadfastness'.[48]

In a similar if cruder vain, Piotr Shelest was reported, at a Kiev rally of 18 February, 1969, to have attacked 'some young people, including students' who were 'spreading various rumours and fables from the dirty wave of foreign radio broadcasts'. They were declared to employ a 'dissolute manner' and 'dirty tricks', 'insulting their elders' and 'falling prey to the erosive bourgeois culture'.

Less emotive were a number of stern warnings concerning the permissable limits of criticism, as well as reminders that the Party retained the power to silence those who continued to criticise action policies, or who attempted to develop factions within the Party.[49] It was made clear that such warnings would be acted on if necessary. The reported trials of recalcitrants, such as that of Chernyshevsky in Kiev in early 1968 (which followed his persistent challenging of the legality of previous closed trials involving Ukrainian intellectuals),[50] testified to Party determination.

The dissidents and 'civil rights' champions were not stifled, and they continued to express themselves in illegal Samizdat printings.[51] But it remained highly questionable whether such had much import outside their own groups. There was reason to believe that the groups were basically isolated, and that the major population groups were, if not hostile to them, at least indifferent.[52]

In conclusion: the Party remained acutely aware of the danger of internal opposition and threats, as to some extent it had always been. But there was reason to believe that the vigour of the public concern of some of its leaders reflected anxious over-reaction to limited, if persistent, circles of critics, rather than the true extent of these critics' disruption potentials. There was no evidence that opposition might be either widespread enough, or sufficiently organized, to represent any real threat to the establishment's power apparatus.

There was in fact evidence that some sections of the Party condoned and supported at least some of the oppositional forces: some Party officials apparently viewed limited tolerance as a necessary safety valve; others appreciated the rejuvenating potentials of unofficial debates (see above). There was full agreement that no serious challenge to the Party's societal role could be permitted. But even some segments of the Party appeared to have concluded that the opposition did not constitute a serious challenge, and that the fear was inappropriate or irrelevant.

NOTES

1. Kissinger, 'Central Issues of American Foreign Policy', in Brookings Institute's '*Agenda for the Nation*', 1968.
2. Viz., the cost-exchange ratios revealed by the US Dept. of Defence's 'Posture Papers' of 1967 and 1968, *op. cit.*; the assertion refers, of course, to the technological possibility of BMDs of great effect. See previous presentations and discussions.
3. Herman Kahn presented this view forcefully at the 1969 Oslo Conference, *op. cit.*
4. *Ibid.*, ' . . . no-one should or can expect the USA necessarily to intervene in

aid of friends if she herself is not attacked and if her intervention may mean self-destruction!' That is: in a last resort self-preservation considerations would outweigh moral commitments.

5. This hypothesis was tentatively discussed at the same Conference, *Ibid.*
6. Conversation with author, 17 January, 1969.
7. *BBC News*, 3 December, 1969, 10:30 p.m.
8. *The Times*, 2 December, 1969, written by Defence correspondent Charles Douglas-Home.
9. Major-General Hansteen, *Protocol for Norwegian Disarmament Committee Meeting 1 December, 1969* (released by Norwegian Foreign Office), p. 9 – re. discussion as to which weapons systems might be considered comparable within the context of Strategic Arms Limitation Talks.
10. *Le Monde*, 1 January, 1969, ('It took the May revolution to reform the university; will it take Soviet tanks in . . . , to reform the army?').
11. *Le Monde*, 26 February, 1969, Paul Yankovitch.
12. See e.g. *Partinaya Zhizn*, 6 January, 1969 (or *Pravda*, 13 February, 1969, for parallel evidence re Tadzhik nationalism).
13. In '*Tsjekkoslovakia Haertatt*', Minerva, Oslo, 1968.
14. This was pursued further in: Jacobsen, C. G., '*The Party Leadership*', an unpublished 1969 analysis prepared at the Inst. of Soviet and East European Studies, Glasgow.
15. *Newsweek*, 20 April, 1970.
16. Such as KGB Chairman Semichastny, Moscow Party Chief Nikolai Yegorichev, and Head of Tass Dimitry Goryunov.
17. Semichastny, for example, who had not been heard from since his May 1967 demotion, was by November–December, 1968 again referred to in public as functioning in his position as 1st Deputy Premier of the Ukraine; Pavlov, who had been demoted to chairman of the Central Council of Sport Societies and Organizations, had his new responsibility upgraded to a Union-Republic committee in November, 1968.
18. E.g. *Trud*, 11 February, 1969 (on the then imminent West German presidential election) and *Trud*, 4 and 5 March, 1969 (on China's 'bandit attack' on the Ussuri).
19. *Newsweek*, 13 April and 20 April, 1970.
20. Information received by the author in Moscow in January 1965, and reinforced by information and impressions gathered by the author while in Moscow on the British Academic Exchange Program, 1970–71.
21. These rumours are collated in: Jacobsen, C. G., *Soviet Decision-making During and After the Czechoslovak Intervention*, NUPI, Oslo, May, 1969.
22. See for example the article by D. Chesnokov in *Voprosi Filosofi*, December, 1968: it also provided justification for the continued use of coercion, societal discipline, and political controls, even after the material conditions for a better life had been created; or see, for example, the reviews by Ye. Boltin, in *Kommunist*, February, 1969. Some derogatory references to Stalin were published, in Anna Klyueva's summer 1968 booklet on the 20th Party Congress, and elsewhere. But they were authored by minor officials, and generally in obscure publications March 1969 was the first time since the 23rd Party Congress that a major Party figure had attacked Stalin.
23. He was joined by Panomariov (see text above), who asserted that the personality cult had entailed a 'retreat from Leninist norms'. See *New York Times*, 26 March, 1969, translation from '*Problems of Peace and Socialism*'.
24. *Kommunist*, No. 5, March, 1969.
25. The fact that Ulbricht was not received by either Kosygin or Brezhnev, and the breaking of protocol upon his departure (only Pelshe of the Politburo and Katushev of the Secretariat saw him off), suggests that the non-communication with Suslov reflected further-ranging policy differences. Ulbricht's later retirement may not have been completely co-incidental.
26. *Newsweek* 13 April and 20 April, 1970, and major Western newspapers of the preceding weeks. The younger Politburo members D. Poliyanski and K. Mazurov were reported as supporting the Suslov-Shelepin 'opposition'.
27. *Pravda*, 22 May, 1965.
28. *Pravda*, 5 July, 1965.

29. 'The Kharkov group'; see analysis in Michel Tatu's *'Le Pouvoir en L'URSS'* Bernard Grasset, Paris 1969.

30. One might find evidence in his speech reported in *Kommunist*, No. 15, October, 1967.

31. In his March 30, 1971 *Report to the 24th CPSU Congress* (re his six-point 'peace-program'), and in his May 14, 1971 Tbilisi speech (concerning the reduction of armed forces and armaments).

32. *Trud*, 11 February, 1969.

33. *Trud*, 4 and 5 March, 1969.

34. See e.g. *Pravda*, 7 November, 1970.

35. See excellent analysis, with excerpts, (probably prepared by Per Egil Hegge) in *Aftenposten*, Oslo, 21 August, 1971.

36. See e.g. *Partinaya Zhizn*, 4 February, 1969.

37. *Trud*, 9 February, 1969, (article on 'The authority of a Leader').

38. Seen by British Exchange academics, this author included, who visited the resort at that time.

39. *Aftenposten*, *op. cit.*

40. *Sovetskaya Rossiya*, 12 December, 1968.

41. *Sovetskaya Rossiya*, 21 February, 1969.

42. *Sovetskaya Rossiya*, 27 December, 1969.

43. *Literaturnaya Gazeta*, 2 July, 1969.

44. Sakharov, *'A Cry for Liberty'*, published by the Norwegian Committee in Support of Smog (a movement of young Soviet intellectuals).

45. *Kommunist Ukrainy*, No. 1, 1969 (see reported speech by Yuri Ilnitsky, 1st Secretary of the Transcarpathian oblast).

46. See e.g. *Partinaya Zhizn*, 6 January, 1969, and *Pravda* 13 February, 1969, re Tadzhik and Central Asian developments. And *Pravda*, 19 February, 1969, re 'tenacious' and 'dangerous' national sentiments in Lithuania. See also *Kommunist*, No. 1, 1969, – which demanded more cultural uniformity; and *Literaturnaya Ukrainy*, 9 December, 1969.

47. *Pravda*, 14 February, 1969.

48. *Ibid.*

49. E.g. *Kommunist*, No. 16, 1968.

50. Hill, Christopher R., ed., *'Rights and Wrongs'*, Penguin, 1969, (especially chapter by Peter Reddeway, LSE Lecturer).

51. *Ibid.*

52. See also Chapter 8, re Civilian Training, for related establishment efforts.

10

Perimeter Defence

THE WARSAW PACT – MILITARY INTEGRATION INTO SOVIET
COMMAND STRUCTURE

THE WARSAW PACT – MILITARY INTEGRATION INTO SOVIET COMMAND STRUCTURE

In a comment on this subject-topic, NATO Secretary General Brosio declared in late 1967: 'A veil is drawn over the fact that the Soviet Union has already concluded a network of bilateral pacts with its allies, such as to render the Warsaw Pact superfluous, and make the dependence of the Eastern countries upon the Soviet Union even more entire'.[1] As concerned military relations, the first point was true even at the time of the Warsaw Pact's founding,[2] and has remained so since.[3] This fact gives credence to interpretations of the Warsaw Pact as a super-structure created primarily for political and psychological reasons.[4] It is the intention of this chapter to indicate the extent of the military integration within the Warsaw Pact, and to clarify the extent to which East European military events must be viewed as concerning or influencing Soviet military decisions, and vice versa.

It was only in 1961 that joint military manoeuvres became acknowledged. Since then such manoeuvres have become regularized, with between two and seven every year,[5] a frequency which in itself suggests close integration. Military Staffs and Defence Ministers' meetings or conferences became more frequent, especially after 1965.

The same years witnessed a trend for most of the manoeuvres (and talks) to be organized in, and to involve primarily, 'northern tier' countries.[6] The development could be seen as partly motivated by strategic considerata, which were far more involved where the northern countries were concerned. This interpretation explained the fact that Bulgaria, while certainly one of the staunchest supporters of unity, nevertheless often participates on a lower level than the other active members. There could conversely be little doubt that political differences, or scepticism regarding utility, was a factor in the case of Roumania. She did not participate in any manoeuvres between September, 1964 and August, 1967,[7] and did thereafter again refrain from participation until March-April, 1969,[8] – and even then only to a limited extent.

But, with the probable exception of Rumania, there were indications that military integration between Warsaw Pact nations increased further during the late 1960's. That integration was the operative word, rather than mere co-ordination, was made clear by the then Warsaw Pact Chief of Staff, Army General M. I. Kazakov, in 1967. He 'made it abundantly plain that the basic organization of the air defence forces of the Warsaw partners was 'different from former times' in that it formed part of a unified system which included the air defence system of the USSR. This arrangement, he was careful to stress, gave the PVO forces of the Warsaw Pact the capability "of striking at air targets far from the installations to be safeguarded".'[9]

On March 17, 1969, in Budapest, came the first Warsaw Pact meeting after the five-nation intervention in Czechoslovakia. The two-hour meeting, presided over by Alexander Dubcek, produced two published documents;[10] the one referred somewhat vaguely to new command structures; the other was a moderately worded call for a European Security Conference. Western speculation concluded that the very vagueness of the first meant defeat for a hypothetical attempt to streamline the Pact according to the requirements of Soviet control.[11] And Dubcek's elaboration upon his return to Prague,[12] – that the meeting had established a Committee of Defence Ministers, and had promulgated a 'Statute on the Combined Armed Forces and Combined Command', and that the Conference's main purpose had in fact been the improving of the 'organization' of the combined command of the Pact's forces, – was interpreted to mean that the USSR had agreed to Roumanian-Czech demands for a greater sharing of command and policy authority. Subsequent rumours, that consideration had been given to the idea of a joint staff, in which the participation of members would be in proportion to their contribution to the alliance (a la NATO . . .),[13] were similarly interpreted. Later evidence, however, indicated that, while the Pact meeting had achieved or at least presaged a greater unification of Pact command procedures, this was not of a kind to diminish Soviet authority. . . .

The first evidence appeared in April. Unification of command over the Pact's air defence forces was reaffirmed and emphasized when Marshal B. F. Batitsky, Commander in Chief of Soviet PVO forces, was appointed to act also as Commander of the PVO forces of the Warsaw Pact as a whole.[14] (Retro-actively the appointment of Cmdr. of Soviet Land Forces Army General Pavlovsky, to act as Cmdr. in Chief of the Warsaw Pact Forces engaged in the intervention in Czechoslovakia, might also be seen to reflect on command unification endeavours).

Command unification, under the relevant Soviet Commander, may be intended to be activated or enforced only for the more vital manoeuvres or events. But the import is of great importance. It should be related to indications that the Soviet military presence, at least as concerned the northern tier of the Pact, was increasingly regarded as permanent rather than temporary.

This assertion rests especially on two 1968 events. There was first of all the Czechoslovak intervention and the resulting Soviet-Czechoslovak Treaty. This clearly indicated such permanency. Then came the DDR, 7 November, 1968, celebrations, at which Marshal Koshevoi was addressed as 'The Supreme Commander of the Soviet Armed Forces stationed in the DDR'.[15] The titulation contrasted with previous practice: 'temporary' (zutweilig) had always been inserted before 'stationed'.

In January 1970 came apparent confirmation that the indicated unified command pattern had been instituted on a wider basis than that of just individual or specialized services or tasks (in an editorial by Army General Shtemenko,[16] which referred specifically to the 1969 Warsaw Pact meeting). It remained for Western analysts to draw the conclusion that, if instituted to any extent, then such a unification of command must be presumed to encompass only 'northern tier' countries, and perhaps Bulgaria, with only a symbolic contingent from Roumania.[17]

It may, however, be proper to view Shtemenko's article not as reflecting an innovation, but rather as confirming previously developed and known practice.[18]

This expands on the fact that Warsaw Pact territory, and especially that of the Northern tier, is considered per definition to constitute the forward defence area of the USSR (which necessarily represents the

core of the Pact and its defence).[19] This, again, reconfirms and aug-
ments the tenet that a prime concern of the Pact's forces is to ensure
that '(Soviet) . . . installations . . . be safeguarded'.[20] Regular training
and administrative procedures to this end appeared to have been
instituted. . . .

The data reflects on the previously presented evidence, with regard
to Soviet strategic and tactical concepts, and with regard to American
recognition of these. It also provides desirable emphasis to a factor
and degree of military concern in Eastern Europe which necessarily
entails a 'military influence' on inter-state policies. It points to the
need for analysts of East European developments to consider military
requirements.

The developments may be synopsized by the following quotes:

1963: 'Operational units of the armed forces of different socialist
states *can be created* to conduct joint operations in military theatres.
The command of these units *can be assigned* to the Supreme High
Command of the Soviet Armed Forces'.[21]

1970: 'Until recently Warsaw Pact Forces (of USSR, Poland and
GDR) operating in the Baltic were separate but similarly equipped
entities. This is no longer true, as intensive training has made them
capable of being *integrated under a single command team*'.[22] Grechko
elaborated: 'To better co-ordinate co-operation each Armed Forces
has allotted staffs and formations from the Army, Air Force, PVO and
Navy. *There exists a Military Council for the united forces*; the statutes
for the committee of Warsaw Pact Ministers of Defence have been
sanctioned (ratified)'.[23]

And *Pravda* weighed in with the following doctrinal (and conceptual) promulgation: 'The boundaries of the Soviet Union and other
socialist states are boundaries of a new type. . . . These brothers-in-
arms see that their international duty lies in the reliable safe-guarding
of their states' frontiers as *component parts of the whole socialist* camp's
boundaries. . . . The idea of *fellow-ship in arms runs like a red thread*
through all these treaties'.[24] (The referred-to treaties were those
recently signed with Hungary, Poland, Roumania and Czechoslovakia).

– One may juxtapose this with the contemporary definition of the
main 'duty' of the Soviet armed forces: – To *defend* the Socialist
Fatherland and socialism's and communism's victories, and to *halt the
spread of counter-revolution*.[25]

The Warsaw Pact (1971)

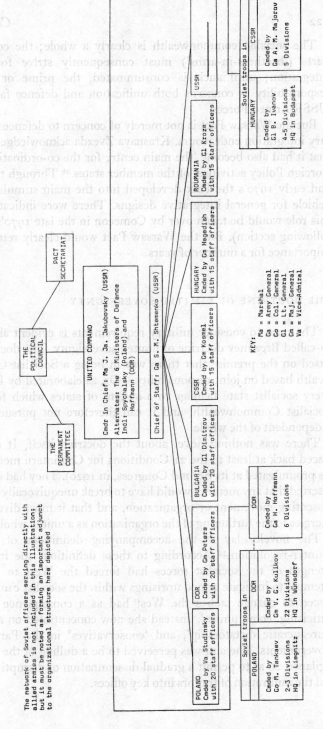

The network of Soviet officers serving directly with allied armies is not included in this illustration; but it must be noted as forming an important adjunct to the organizational structure here depicted

The socialist commonwealth is clearly a whole; the component parts ('brothers-in-arms') must consequently strive for greater integration; until such is consummated, the prime or ultimate responsibility as concerns both unification and defence falls to the USSR Armed Forces.

But the Warsaw Pact is not merely of concern to defence and military integration endeavours. Krasnaya Zvezda acknowledged in 1972 that it had also become 'the main centre for the co-ordination of the Foreign Policy activities' of the member states.[26] Through the 1960's and early 1970's the Pact developed into the main stimulus to and vehicle for general integrative designs. There were indications that this role would be taken over by Comecon in the late 1970's (see the following section). But the Warsaw Pact would clearly retain major importance for a number of years.

THE DOCTRINE OF LIMITED SOVEREIGNTY

The need to consider military requirements is evident also in the so-called Brezhnev doctrine of limited sovereignty. The doctrine was based on the premise that there was in being a Socialist Commonwealth based on joint responsibility.[27] Or, as elaborated by Pravda[28]: every socialist state belongs to a system of states which forms the Socialist Commonwealth, and it can therefore not pursue policies independent of the whole.

There was nothing novel about the doctrine itself. It could be traced back at least to the 21 Conditions for Comintern membership (as promulgated at its Second Congress, in 1920). They had explicitly asserted that any member would have to break unequivocally with any dissenting movement or organization, and that it must divert all its energies to the furthering of the organization as a united whole.[29]

The novelty lay in the accompanying definitions of peaceful counter-revolution.[30] According to these definitions the increasing strength of the socialist forces had forced the West to abandon attempts to instigate armed uprisings within the socialist camp. Thus forced to change tactics the West had as a consequence stopped criticizing 'communism'. Instead she now concentrated on attacking 'bureaucratic dictatorship', and 'conservatives' in the Parties and Governments. The aim was perceived to be a dulling of the people's vigilance, so as to permit a gradual dissemination of disruptive ideas, and the infiltration of traitors into key offices.

This defining of peaceful counter-revolution is novel in that it entails an easing of the conditions in response to which the Socialist Commonwealth majority would consider intervention against an errant member to be necessary and justified. The kernel of the peaceful counter-revolution concept might also be considered to have been inherent in the 21 Conditions, but this had not then been elaborated explicitly.

The two concepts were after 1968 re-emphasized and elaborated on until no one could doubt their relevance to contemporary affairs.

The Parties which remained faithful to Leninist ideals were declared per definition to 'avoid actions which could contradict the tasks of the general struggle of all communist parties against imperialism'.[31] As regards the determining of these tasks, it was pointed out that 'the experience of the construction of a socialist society in the Soviet Union . . . has been adopted by the communist and workers' parties as the basic model of socialism'.[32] Other models which had been constructed *a priori* (i.e. the Czechoslovak Dubcek model), were declared to have 'contradicted the experience of the Soviet Union and the whole international communist movement'.[33]

Notwithstanding Suslov's 1969 acknowledgement that one could no longer speak of 'a leading centre for the communist movement',[34] it was made clear that the USSR still considered her experience to entitle her to priority influence in the directing of the communist movement, – certainly as long as imperialist designs were seen to make united action necessary. It was made clear that the Stalinist concept of intensified class struggle as a nation approached communism retained validity.[35]

The imperative need for unity was elaborated as the basic premise. Anyone who supported a 'theory of relying only on their own forces', must be affected by 'adventurous, hegemonistic tendencies': such a theory could only be based on a rejection of 'the internationalist principle of the defence of the socialist fatherland'.[36]

The intervention in Czechoslovakia was a 'confirmation of loyalty to the principles of internationalism (by) the five fraternal countries'.[37] One was left in no doubt that similar aid would be extended to defend the 'socialist achievements' of any future member considered by the Commonwealth to be unable to secure this alone.[38]

Soviet conceptions, of the need for unity and for co-ordinated action, were reflected equally in the economic field: economic considerations complemented those of a political, ideological and military nature.

The economic integration was, as yet, far from fruition. The 1969 meeting in East Berlin[39] of the Comecon Council and its Executive Committee (21–23 and 23–27 January) had for example not succeeded in significantly furthering integration endeavours. It had produced only vague references to the co-ordination of 1971–75 plans, and to the need for recommendations regarding production specialization, currency and foreign trade problems; it had stressed the need to strengthen existing links between 'interested partners', and had noted that the Engineering Commission was authorized to program further intra-Comecon (including Yugoslavia) specialization of machinery and like equipment.

But by the time of the 1970 Conference (in Warsaw) it was claimed that considerable progress had been achieved on an agreed program of integration.[40] This conference approved a draft project for an international bank, to co-ordinate investments, and to provide credit for ventures under the program of international socialist division of labour (a program of production specialization as between the members). And in August, 1971, in Bucharest, it was finally agreed to introduce a 'collective currency', based on a convertible, or at least transferable, rouble (further specification, or time-table, was not provided); a far-reaching 15–20 year program for East European economic integration was approved at the same conference.[41]

How far or fast the integration of the respective economies would proceed remained in question (especially in consideration of the lack of enthusiasm by Roumania, regarding the theory and its implications,[42] and by others, with regard to detail[43]). But since the 'hegemonistic tendencies' inherent in departing from co-ordination with the whole of the Socialist Commonwealth were accepted as potential justification for fraternal 'aid',[44] it remained probable that closer integration would be pursued and implemented. Some leeway might be conceded to Roumania, but, as concerned the Northern tier countries at least, it was clear that integration was and would remain a priority policy aim.

The priority concern for political and economic integration, and the putting into effect of measures to this end, supports a 'realpolitik' view of Eastern Europe as an integral part of Soviet home area. To put it somewhat differently: the strategic defence of the perimeter was considered as inseparable from the strategic defence of the home area; the two were in a very real sense considered parts of the same whole. The Soviet conception received, or commanded, the adherence of East Europe (excepting possibly the ambiguous

Roumania). And its importance in Soviet eyes was clearly such that she would do *all* in her power to ensure that this adherence be permanent.

Yet one must be cautious in drawing inferences. The Soviet Union certainly saw the perpetuation of friendly regimes in Eastern Europe, or at least in the northern tier, to be vital to her basic security interests. And she would clearly intervene against any development which threatened the ultimate viability of these interests. But the Soviet Union of the early 1970's could not be compared to the bull in the china shop. All the evidence of the previous chapters pointed to a relatively high degree of sophistication. She was likely to be appreciative of all the diverse factors which might relate to an intervention, including both short and long term psychological repercussions.

The 1968 intervention in Czechoslovakia therefore entails a 'why'?; on what basis did the USSR decide that intervention was necessary? There was clearly a wide spectrum of reasons, economic, strategic, political and ideological.[45] But Hungary has instituted more far-reaching economic reforms than Czechoslovakia ever did, and the USSR has herself discussed possible reforms with equinamity and interest.[46] Rumania has pursued a more adventurous foreign policy than Prague, and even East Germany has on occasion pursued policies which could be seen as more assertive than those followed by Czechoslovakia.

All of these cases are complex, and not amenable to simple classification schemes. But they do encourage the assertion that the one peculiarity which more than any other differentiated and isolated the Czechoslovak experience was the apparent dilution of Party control which it entailed. *Formal* explicitly non-Party organisations were established; they could all too easily be seen as the foetuses of new parties, and therefore as exemplifying the erosion of Party control.

The USSR insisted on the preservation of the role of the Communist Parties. And she clearly saw a high degree of integration in general, between herself and the nations of East Europe, as a most desirable and perhaps to some extent necessary policy goal. But one should not only refrain from seeing the Soviet Union as the primitive bull. One should also be cautious about crude classifications of East Europe as anti-Soviet, and basically Western oriented.

Large sections of the East European societies have become Soviet-oriented, through conviction, patronage, plain familiarity, or apathy. And it is possible to argue that the long-term economic interests of

Eastern Europe are complementary to those of the Soviet Union rather than to those of the West. The increasing relaxation and tolerance of some East European regimes, and the greater scope for discussion and experimentation which was discernible by the late 1960's, did not necessarily reflect on disarray. Nor did it necessarily reflect negatively on Soviet interests.

One could just as easily contrast the new relaxation with the repression of the immediate post-war period, and conclude that the relaxation reflected instead on a greater degree of basic agreement with Soviet interests. One could argue that the post-war repression was necessary for Soviet control, and reflected Soviet weakness; whereas the late '60's and early '70's relaxation was made possible by a greater East European acceptance of the association with the USSR, and therefore reflected Soviet strength, confidence and sophistication. The point is that most of the developments treated above allow of different interpretations. The conclusion depends on the analyst's initial conceptions and prejudices. Diametrically opposed conclusions can appear equally 'logical'.

NOTES

1. *NATO Letter*, December, 1967, Brussels.
2. See, e.g. K. Grzybowsky, '*The Socialist Commonwealth of Nations*', Yale University Press, 1964, p. 174.
3. See, e.g. Soviet-Czechoslovak Treaty examined in our analysis of '*Soviet Decision-making . . . during and after the Czechoslovak intervention*', NUPI, 1969.
4. A. Korbonski, '*The Warsaw Pact*', International Conciliation (Carnegie), May 1969.
5. Korbonski, *Ibid*, p. 46–7, for Chart; R. Remington, '*The Changing Soviet Perception of the Warsaw Pact*', p. 146–7, MIT Centre for International Studies, Cambridge; '*The Warsaw Pact – Its role in Soviet Bloc Affairs*', Washington, D.C., GPO 1966; 'The Warsaw Pact', *Military Review*, p. 89–95, Fort Leavenworth, July, 1967, for interesting analysis of (then) 'latest WP Conference'.
6. Korbonski, *Ibid*. For an analysis of the organization of the Warsaw Pact with emphasis on the Northern tier – Southern tier complex, see F. Wieners, '*Die Armeen der Ostblockstaaten*' p. 9–32, Truppendienst Taschenbucher, Vol. 2, J. F. Lehmanns Verlag, Munich, 1967 (first published 1965 with title '*Warschauer Pakt Staaten*').
7. Korbonski, *Ibid*.
8. *Tass*, 1 April, 1969. See also The *International Herald Tribune* of 4 March, 1971, for report of Warsaw Pact Defence Ministers' conference in Budapest; Romanian Defence Minister Ion Ionita participated fully.
9. Kazakov's article was in *Neues Deutchland*, 23 February, 1967. The descriptive quote is from the *Research Bulletin*, 4 June, 1969, of Radio Liberty's Central Research Dept., Munich.
10. *CTK*, Prague, 17 March, 1969, and *Izvestia*, 19 March, 1969.
11. See *The Times*, 19 March, 1969, for comments regarding a perceived

(probably incorrectly) Soviet desire for Warsaw Pact troops to be stationed on the Ussuri river.

12. *Rude Pravo*, Prague, 19 March, 1969.
13. See, e.g. report from Prague by Michael Hornsby, *The Times*, 20 March, 1969.
14. *Krasnaya Zvezda*, 15 April, 1969. Garthoff, 'Soviet Military Policy . . . ', *op. cit.*, p. 152, notes that such a dual Soviet-Warsaw Pact PVO command arrangement was first publically referred to in 1964.
15. DDR News Media, 7 and 8 November, 1968.
16. 'Boevoe Bratstvo', *Krasnaya Zvezda*, 27 April, 1970.
17. E.g. Victor Zorza, 'Unified Command for Pact Forces,' *The Irish Times*, 4 February, 1970.
18. Radio Free Europe's *Research Bulletin* of 27 January, 1970. And see the article by Rumanian Defence Minister Col. Gen. Ion Ionita in *Krasnaya Zvezda*, 25 January, 1970.
19. *Krasnaya Zvezda*, 8 May, 1970, – an article by Warsaw Pact Cmdr. Yakubovsky made it quite clear that the Soviet Union would not consider giving up what she deemed legitimate Second World War gains.
20. Kazakov, *op. cit.* NOTE: one might also point to an article by Col. S. Lipitsky in *Voenno Istorichesky Zhurnal*, No. 1, 1969, in which he explicitly draws a parallel between the contemporary situation of 'countries of the socialist community' and the post-revolutionary situation of the Soviet Baltic, Belorussian and Ukrainian republics: eventual unity was then forged through the instrument of military alliance and integration; with regard to the socialist community this venue was all the more necessary to counteract separatism encouraged by pro forma political independence . . . (!).
21. Sokolovsky, *op. cit.*, 2nd edition, Moscow 1963, p. 475.
22. *NATO Letter*, September 1970, *op. cit.*
23. *Pravda*, 23 February, 1970.
24. *Pravda*, 28 May, 1970.
25. *Krasnaya Zvezda*, 30 July, 1970 – lengthy article by Maj. General Professor E. Sulimov and Col. Docent A. Timorin. (Both believed to be political officers). Previous interventions in Czechoslovakia, Hungary and DDR are emphasized to have been both legal and necessary.
26. *Krasnaya Zvezda*, 6 January, 1972. And see footnote 20.
27. As defined in Gromyko's otherwise conciliatory speech to the UN following the intervention in Czechoslovakia. *Pravda*, 4 October, 1968.
28. *Pravda*, 25 September, 1968, and *Pravda*, 26 September, 1968.
29. The Second Congress of the Comintern, *Stenogr. Report*, Moscow, 1920, p. 652.
30. *Pravda*, 11 September, 1968.
31. Sitkovskiy, E. P., Doktor Nauk, 'Marksism-Leninism yedinoe internatsional' noe uchenie rabochevo klassa' in *Filosofskie Nauki*, No. 1, 1970.
32. *Ibid.*
33. *Ibid.*
34. *Kommunist*, No. 5, 1969.
35. *Pravda*, 11 September, 1968.
36. *Pravda*, 7 March, 1970. Art. by Col. S. Lukonin (Chinese policies are the object of the quoted passages).
37. *Ibid.*
38. *Ibid.*
39. This meeting was of some import due to the very widespread rumours at the time that the Soviet Union would force rapid integration on her partners.
40. It provided for more organized consultations between the various planning commissions responsible for product planning, allocation and distribution. NOTE: 'Socialist integration' is defined as 'a process of bringing together and gradually merging the national economies of the several countries into a single system'. See *Pravda*, 13 May, 1970; *Izvestia*, 14 May, 1970; *The Times*, 16 May, 1970.
41. *Rude Pravo*, 5 August, 1971 (interview with L. Strougal).
42. Berghianu, M., in *International Affairs*, Moscow, September, 1968.

43. *Ibid.* See also e.g. *The Times*, 16 May, 1970, *op. cit.*

44. *Pravda*, 7 March, 1970, *op. cit.*, (see above).

45. Jacobsen, C. G., '*Soviet Decision-making During and After the Czechoslovak Crisis*', NUPI, Oslo, 1969.

46. Jacobsen, C. G., '*The Soviet Economic Reforms and Their Effects on Government Procedure*', Glasgow University Dip. Sov. Stud. thesis, 1968.

Selected Bibliography

SOVIET NEWSPAPERS AND PERIODICALS

Aviatsiia i Kosmanovtika
International Affairs (Moscow)
Izvestia
Kommunist
Kommunist Vooruzhiennikh Sil
Krasnaya Zvezda
Mezhdunarodnaya Zhizn
Morskoi Sbornik
Partinaya Zhizn
Politicheskoie Samoobrazovanie
Pravda
Voenno-Istoricheskii Zhurnal
Voennaya Mysl
Voenni Vestnik

SOVIET BOOKS

Azovtsev, N. N., *V. I. Lenin i Sovetskaya Voennaya Nauka*. Izdatelstvo Nauka, Moscow, 1971.

Bagramian, I. Kh., Ivanov, S. P., and others, *Istoria Voin i Voennovo Iskustva*, and *Istoria Voin i Voennovo Iskustva – Albom Skhem*. Voenizdat, Moscow, 1970.

Boevoi put Sovetskovo Voenno-Morskovo Flota. Voenizdat, Moscow, 1969.

Epishev, A. A., *Delo ogromnoi Vashnosti*., Znanie, Moscow, 1965.

Epishev, A. A., *Kommunisti Armi i Flota*, Voenizdat, Moscow, 1971.

Grechko, A. A. (ed)., *Iaderny Vek i Voina*. Izdatelstvo Izvestia, Moscow, 1964.

Grechko, A. A., *Na Strazhe Mira i Stroitelstva Kommunisma*, Voenizdat, Moscow, 1971.

Grudinen, A., *Dialektika i Sovremennoe Voennoe Delo*. Voenizdat, Moscow, 1971.

Iskenderov, A. A., *Natsionalno-Osvoboditelnoe Dvizhenie*. Izdat Mezhdunarodn. Otnoshenie, Moscow, 1970.

Istoria Diplomatia. Vol. III, Izdat. Polit. Lit., Moscow, 1965.

Istoria Vneshnaia Politika SSSR. Vol. 1, Nauka., Moscow, 1966, Vol. 2, Izdat. Nauka., Moscow, 1971.

Ivanov, A., Naumenko, I., and Pavlov, M., *Raketnoladernoi Oruzhie i evo Porazhaioshchee Deistvie*, Nauchno-Populiarnaia Biblioteka, Moscow, 1971.

KPSS o Vooruzhiennikh Silakh Sovetskovo Soiuza. Documents 1917–68, Voenizdat, Moscow, 1969.

Krylov, S. M., *Povushat Bditelnost narodov v otnosheni voennoi opasnosti*, Znanie, Moscow, 1961.

Kuznetsov, N. G., *Nakanune*. Voenizdat, Moscow, 1966.

Mezhdunarodnie Otnosheni Posle Vtoroi Mirovoi Voini. Vol. I., 1962, Vol. II., 1963, Vol. III., 1965. Izdat. Politik. Lit. Moscow.

Nekatorie Voprosi Partino-organizatsionnoi Raboti v Sovetskikh Vooruzhiennikh Silakh, Voenizdat, Moscow, 1963.

Nelin, Jo. G., *Atom i Nato*, Voenizdat, Moscow, 1970.

Okean, Voenizdat, Moscow, 1970.

Petrov, Jo. P., *Stroitelstvo Politorganov Partinikh i Komsomolskikh Organisatsi Armii i Flota*, Voenizdat, Moscow, 1968.

Polkovodtsi i Voenachalniki Velikoi Otechestvennoi, Sbornik, Izdatelstvo TsK-VLKSM, 2nd. ed., Moscow, 1971.

Rybkin, E. I., *Voina i Politika*, Voenizdat, Moscow, 1961.

Savkin, V. E., *Osnovnie Printsipi Operativnovo Iskusstva i Taktiki*, Voenizdat, Moscow, 1972.

Sbornik Osnovnikh Aktov i Dokumentov Verhovnovo Soveta SSSR po Vneshnepoliticheskim Voprosam, 1956–60 g.g.

Sergeev, P. I., and others, *Vooruzhiennie Sili Kapitalisticheskikh Gosudarstv*, Voenizdat, Moscow, 1971.

Sidorenko, A. A., *Nastuplenie*, Voenizdat, Moscow, 1970.

Skidro, M. P., *Narod, Armia, Polkovodets*, Voenizdat, Moscow, 1970.

Sokolovsky, V. D., *Voennaya Strategia*. 2nd. ed., (1963) and 3rd. ed. (1968), Voenizdat, Moscow.

Strokov, A. A., *V. I. Lenin o Voine i Voennom Iskusstve*, Nauka, Moscow, 1971.

Sulimov, E. F., and others, *Spravochnik Offitsera*, Voenizdat, Moscow, 1971.

Sushko, N. Yu. and Kondratkov, T. R., *Metodologicheskiye Problemy Voennoi Teori i Praktiki*, Voenizdat, Moscow, 1967.

Tolnacheva, A. I., *Sovetsko-Amerikanskie Otnoshenie 1956–63*, unpublished MGU Thesis, Moscow, 1966.

Voennaia Psikologia, Voenizdat, Moscow, 1967.

Vneshnaya Politika SSSR na Sovremennom Etape, Moscow, 1964.

Yakubovsky, I. I., *Boevoe Sodruzhestvo*, Voenizdat, Moscow, 1971.

WESTERN NEWSPAPERS AND PERIODICALS

Adelphi Papers (ISS)
Aviation Week and Space Technology
Foreign Affairs
Le Monde
The Military Balance (ISS)
The Military Review (Fort Leavenworth)
The Observer
Revue de Defence Nationale (Paris)
Scientific American
Soldat und Technik (Bundeswehr)
Survey (ISS)
The (London) Times
The New York Times
Bundesinstitut für Ostwissenschaftliche und Internationale Studien publishings
Hudson Research Institute publishings
IDA Research Papers
International Conciliation (Carnegie) papers
Rand Corporation papers
US Naval Institute Proceedings
US Senate and House of Representatives Hearings on Military and Foreign Policy postures and options, present and future – especially such as conducted by the Committee on Armed Services, House of Representatives, and the Committee on Armed Services, US Senate;

    Also Financial Procurement Debates conducted before same – as released by GPO, Washington, D.C.

Annual US Defence Department 'Posture' Statements, released by same, and GPO, Washington, D.C.

WESTERN BOOKS

Chayers, A., and Wiesner, J. B. (eds.), *ABM; An Evaluation of the Decision to Deploy an Anti Ballistic Missile System,* Harper & Row, New York, 1969.

Elliot-Bateman, Michael, (ed.), *The Fourth Dimension of Warfare. Vol. 2. Intelligence/Subversion/Resistance,* Manchester University Press, 1970.

Erickson, John, *The Soviet High Command 1918–41,* St. Martin's Press, New York, 1962.

Garthoff, R. L., *Soviet Military Doctrine,* Rand Corporation, S. M. California, 1953.

Garthoff, R. L., *Soviet Strategy in the Nuclear Age,* Praeger, New York, 1958.

Hohn, Reinhard, *Sozialismus und Heer,* Verlag Gehlen, Bad Hamburg, 2nd. ed., 1961.

Holst, J. J., & Schneider, W., (eds.) *Why ABM? Policy Issues in the Missile Defence Controversy,* Pergamon Press, 1969.

Kolkowicz, Roman *The Soviet Military and the Communist Party,* Princeton University Press, 1967.

Mackintosh, J. M., *Strategy and Tactics of Soviet Foreign Policy,* Oxford University Press, 1962.

O'Ballance, Edgar, *The Red Army,* Faber & Faber, London, 1964.

Scott, Harriet Fast, *Soviet Military Doctrine, Its Continuity 1960–1970,* and *Soviet Military Doctrine, Its Formulation and Dissemination,* Stanford Research Institute, California, 1971, (a later, revised, version is now also available, although not in this author's possession).

Wolfe, T. W., *Soviet Strategy at the Crossroads,* Rand Corporation, 1964.

Index*

* This index is intended to perform the function of a selective guide; for further information the reader is advised to consult the bibliography, and the notes at the end of each chapter.